Terror on the High Seas

Terror on the High Seas

From Piracy to Strategic Challenge

Volume 2

Yonah Alexander and Tyler B. Richardson, editors

Forewords by James Arden Barnett, Jr.,
Robert J. Cox, and Ingar Skaug

PRAEGER SECURITY INTERNATIONAL

An Imprint of ABC-CLIO, LLC

A B C CLIO

Santa Barbara, California • Denver, Colorado • Oxford, England

Library of Congress Cataloging-in-Publication Data

Terror on the high seas : from piracy to strategic challenge / Yonah Alexander and Tyler B. Richardson, eds.
    p. cm.
  Includes index.
  ISBN 978-0-275-99750-2 (hard copy : alk. paper) — ISBN 978-0-275-99751-9 (ebook)
  1. Piracy. 2. Maritime terrorism. 3. Piracy—United States. 4. Maritime terrorism—United States. I. Alexander, Yonah. II. Richardson, Tyler B.
  K5277.T47 2009
  345'.0264—dc22   2009022867

13 12 11 10 09   1 2 3 4 5

This book is also available on the World Wide Web as an eBook.
Visit www.abc-clio.com for details.

ABC-CLIO, LLC
130 Cremona Drive, P.O. Box 1911
Santa Barbara, California 93116-1911

This book is printed on acid-free paper ∞

Manufactured in the United States of America

Contents

U.S. Organizational Structure:
The Role of the Legislature

SELECTED CONGRESSIONAL RESEARCH SERVICE AND GOVERNMENT ACCOUNTABILITY OFFICE REPORTS

MARITIME SECURITY: PROGRESS MADE IN IMPLEMENTING MARITIME TRANSPORTATION SECURITY ACT, BUT CONCERNS REMAIN

Margaret Wrightson
Director, Homeland Security and Justice Issues
Government Accountability Office
Before the Senate Committee on Commerce,
Science, and Transportation
May 17, 2005[*]

Mr. Chairman and Members of the Committee:

I am pleased to be here today to discuss the nation's efforts to improve seaport security. More than 3 years after the terrorist attacks of September 11, 2001, seaport security continues to be a major concern for the nation. For

---

[*]http://www.gao.gov/new.items/d05448t.pdf

example, many seaport areas are inherently vulnerable, given their size, easy accessibility by water and land, large numbers of potential targets, and proximity to urban areas. Also, the large cargo volumes passing through seaports, such as containers destined for further shipment by other modes of transportation such as rail or truck, also represent a potential conduit for terrorists to smuggle weapons of mass destruction or other dangerous materials into the United States. The potential consequences of the risks created by these vulnerabilities are significant as the nation's economy relies on an expeditious flow of goods through seaports. A successful attack on a seaport could result in a dramatic slowdown in the supply system, with consequences in the billions of dollars.

Much has been set in motion to address these risks in the wake of the September 11, 2001, terrorist attacks. Both Congress and the administration have been active, through legislation, presidential directives, and international agreements, in enhancing seaport security. Key agencies, such as the Coast Guard, the Customs Service, and the Transportation Security Administration (TSA), have been reorganized under the new Department of Homeland Security (DHS) and tasked with numerous responsibilities designed to strengthen seaport security. Many of these tasks were required by the Maritime Transportation Security Act of 2002 (MTSA).[1]

My testimony today draws primarily on the work we have done in responding to congressional requests for information and analysis about the nation's homeland security efforts [...] We conducted our work in accordance with generally accepted government auditing standards, and the scope and methodology for this work can be found in the respective products. Over the course of completing this work, we have made a number of recommendations for specific agencies [...] While this body of work does not cover every program or action that has been taken, it does encompass a wide range of these actions. My testimony will (1) provide an overview of the types of actions taken by the federal government and other stakeholders to address seaport security, (2) describe the main challenges encountered in taking these actions, and (3) describe what tools and approaches may be useful in charting a course for future actions to enhance security.

IN SUMMARY

Seaports are vulnerable on many fronts and the actions taken to secure them can be divided into three main categories: reducing vulnerabilities of specific targets within seaports, making the cargo flowing through these seaport gateways more secure, and developing what is called "maritime domain awareness"—a sufficiently informed view of maritime activities by stakeholders involved in security to quickly identify and respond to emergencies, unusual patterns or events, and matters of particular interest. Within each category, several actions have been taken or are under way. For example, assessments of potential targets have been completed at 55 of the nation's most economically and militarily strategic seaports, and more than 9,000 vessels and over 3,000 facilities have developed security plans and have been reviewed by the Coast Guard. Customs inspectors have been placed at some overseas seaports and partnerships struck up with some private sector stakeholders to help ensure that the cargo and containers arriving at U.S. seaports are free of weapons of mass destruction (WMD) or a radiological "dirty bomb." New assets are budgeted and are coming on line, including new Coast Guard boats and cutters and communication systems. Finally, new information-sharing networks and command structures have been created to allow more coordinated responses and increase awareness of activities going on in the maritime domain. Some of these efforts have been completed and others are ongoing; overall, the amount of effort has been considerable.

The efforts we have reviewed over the past three years, many of which were quickly implemented to address pressing security needs, have encountered challenges that could significantly affect their success.

Some of these challenges are likely to be resolved with time, but some reflect greater difficulty and therefore merit more attention. The more complex challenges take three main forms:

- Program design and implementation: Some agencies have failed to design programs and planning components, such as human capital plans and performance measures, that are necessary to successfully implement their programs and ensure they are effective. For example, U.S. Customs and Border Protection (CBP) started implementation of two key container supply chain security initiatives before taking adequate steps to develop plans and strategies to effectively manage critical aspects of the programs such as human capital and achievement of program objectives.
- Coordinating security efforts with stakeholders: Many private sector companies and governmental agencies are involved in seaport security efforts, and in some cases progress has been hampered because of difficulties in communication and coordination between parties. For example, deadlines in the development of an identification card for transportation workers have been missed due in part to a lack of communication and coordination between TSA and DHS.
- Funding security improvements: Economic constraints, such as declining revenues and increased security costs, make it difficult to provide and sustain the funding necessary to continue implementing security measures and activities by maritime stakeholders including the federal government. Consequently, many stakeholders rely heavily on the federal government for assistance, and requests for federal grant funding far outstrip the funding amounts available.

For example, although more than $560 million in grants has been awarded to seaport stakeholders since 2002 under federal grant programs for implementation of security measures and activities, this amount has met only a fraction of the amount requested by these stakeholders.

As actions to enhance homeland security continue, and as it becomes clearer that the price of these actions will be measured in the billions of dollars, it is likely that increasing attention will turn to assessing the progress made in securing seaports and determine where future actions and funds should be allocated to further enhance security. Although there is widespread agreement that actions taken so far have led to a heightened awareness of the need for security and an enhanced ability to identify and respond to many security threats, assessing the degree of progress in making the nation more secure is difficult. Thus far, seaport security actions—and homeland security activities in general—lack performance measures to define what these activities are intended to achieve and measure progress toward these goals. As Congress and the nation continue to evaluate how much security is enough, more attention on defining these goals and measures will likely be needed by stakeholders. Doing so is all the more important because, as groups such as the 9/11 Commission have pointed out, no amount of money can totally insulate seaports from attack by a well-funded and determined enemy. These realities suggest that the future focus in applying resources and efforts also needs to incorporate an approach to identify and manage risk—that is, on assessing critical infrastructure, determining what is most at risk, and applying sound measures designed to make cost-effective use of resources and funding.

BACKGROUND

The vast U.S. maritime system contains more than 300 seaports and 3,700 cargo and passenger terminals. These seaports dot not only our seacoasts but also major lakes and rivers [...] Much of the nation's commercial maritime activities, however, are concentrated in about a dozen major seaports, such as Los Angeles–Long Beach, New York–New Jersey, and Houston.

The nation's seaports are economic engines and a key part of the national defense system. More than 95 percent of the nation's non–North American foreign trade (and 100 percent of certain commodities, such as foreign oil) arrives by ship. Cargo containers, approximately 7 million of which entered the country in 2002, are central to an efficient transportation network because they can be quickly shifted from ships to trains and trucks and back again. Because of these efficiencies, the U.S. and world economies have become increasingly reliant on cargo containers to transport their goods. With regard to national security, the Departments of Defense and Transportation have designated 17 U.S. seaports as strategic because they are necessary for use in the event of a major military deployment. Thirteen of them are commercial seaports.

[Although] the terrorist attacks of September 11, 2001, did not involve seaports, they called attention to ways in which seaports represent an attractive and vulnerable terrorist target. Various studies have pointed out that significant disruptions could result from a seaport-related attack. For example, the Brookings Institution has estimated that costs associated with U.S. seaport closures resulting from a detonated weapon of mass destruction could amount to $1 trillion. The firm of Booz, Allen, and Hamilton studied the potential cost of discovering an undetonated weapon of mass destruction at a U.S. seaport and placed the cost of a 12-day closure of seaports at approximately $58 billion. An actual closure of seaports along the West Coast occurred for 10 days in 2002 due to a labor dispute. According to one estimate, the cost of this closure to the national economy for the first 5 days was estimated at $4.7 billion and increased exponentially after that.[2] Similarly, if one or more of the 17 strategic U.S. seaports (or the ships carrying military supplies) were successfully attacked, not only could massive civilian casualties be sustained and critical infrastructure lost, but the military could also lose precious cargo and time and be forced to rely heavily on already burdened airlift capabilities.

MANY ACTIONS HAVE BEEN TAKEN OR ARE UNDER WAY TO ADDRESS SEAPORT SECURITY

Since September 11, 2001, a number of actions have been taken or are under way to address seaport security by a diverse mix of agencies and seaport stakeholders. Federal agencies, such as the Coast Guard, U.S. Customs and Border Protection (CBP), and TSA, have been tasked with responsibilities and functions intended to make seaports more secure, such as monitoring vessel traffic or inspecting cargo and containers, and procuring new assets such as aircraft and cutters to conduct patrols and respond to threats. In addition to these federal agencies, seaport stakeholders in the private sector and at the state and local levels of government have taken actions to enhance the security of seaports, such as conducting security assessments of infrastructure and vessels operated within the seaports and developing security plans to protect against a terrorist attack. The actions taken by these agencies and stakeholders are primarily aimed at three types of protections: (1) identifying and reducing vulnerabilities of the facilities, infrastructure, and vessels operating in seaports, (2) securing the cargo and commerce flowing through seaports, and (3) developing greater maritime domain awareness through enhanced intelligence, information-sharing capabilities, and assets and technologies.

Identifying and Reducing the Vulnerabilities
of Facilities, Infrastructure, and Vessels

Seaports facilitate the freedom of movement and flow of goods, and in doing so they allow people, cargo, and vessels to transit with relative anonymity. While seaports contain terminals and other facilities where goods bound for import or export are unloaded and loaded, or where people board and disembark cruise ships or ferries, seaports also often contain other infrastructure critical to the nation's economy and defense, such as military installations, chemical factories, power plants, and refineries. The combination of assets, access, and anonymity makes for potentially attractive targets. The facilities and vessels in seaports can be vulnerable on many fronts. For example, facilities where containers are transferred between ships and railroad cars or trucks must be able to screen vehicles entering the facility and routinely check cargo for evidence of tampering. Chemical factories and other installations where hazardous materials are present must be able to control access to areas containing dangerous goods or hazardous substances. Vessels, ranging from oil tankers and freighters to tugboats and passenger ferries, must be able to restrict access to certain areas on board the vessel, such as the bridge or other control stations critical to the vessel's operation.

Given the wide range of potential targets, an effective security response includes identifying targets, assessing risks to them, and taking steps to reduce or mitigate these risks. An essential step in this process is to conduct a security or vulnerability assessment. This assessment, which is needed both for the seaport as a whole and for individual vessels and facilities, identifies vulnerabilities in physical structures, personnel protection systems, processes, and other areas that may lead to a security breach. For example, this assessment might reveal weaknesses in an organization's security systems or unprotected access points such as a facility's perimeter not being sufficiently lighted or gates not being secured or monitored after hours. After the vulnerabilities are identified, measures can be then be identified that will reduce or mitigate the vulnerabilities when installed or implemented.

Most actions to identify and reduce the vulnerabilities within seaports were specifically required by the Maritime Transportation Security Act of 2002 (MTSA). Passage of MTSA was a major step in establishing a security framework for America's seaports. This security framework includes assessment of risks, access controls over personnel and facilities, and development and implementation of security plans, among other activities. [...] [3]

The amount of effort involved in carrying out these actions and implementing these programs has been considerable. For example, after following an aggressive time frame to develop regulations to implement the requirements of MTSA, the Coast Guard reviewed and approved the security plans of the over 3,000 facilities and more than 9,000 vessels that were required to identify their vulnerabilities and take action to reduce them. Six months after July 1, 2004, the date by which the security plans were to be implemented, the Coast Guard reported that it completed on-site inspections of all facilities and thousands of vessels to ensure the plans were being implemented as approved. In addition to its work on the security plans and inspections, the Coast Guard completed security assessments of the nation's 55 most economically and militarily strategic seaports.

Securing the Cargo Flowing through Seaports

[Although] the facilities, vessels, and infrastructure within seaports have vulnerabilities to terrorist attack, the cargoes transiting through seaports also have vulnerabilities that terrorists could exploit.

Containers are of particular concern because they can be filled overseas at so many different locations and are transported through complex logistics networks before reaching U.S. seaports. From the time the container is loaded for shipping to the time the container arrives at a seaport, the containers must go through several steps that involve many different participants and many points of transfer. Each of these steps in the supply chain presents its own vulnerabilities that terrorists could take advantage of to place a WMD into a container for shipment to the United States. A report prepared by the National Defense University's Center for Technology and National Security Policy stated that a container is ideally suited to deliver a WMD or a radiological "dirty bomb." While there have been no known incidents yet of containers being used to transport WMDs, criminals have exploited containers for other illegal purposes, such as smuggling weapons, people, and illicit substances. Such activities demonstrate the vulnerability of the freight transportation industry and suggest opportunities for further exploitation of containers by criminals, including terrorist groups.

In general, the actions taken thus far are aimed at identifying, tracking, and scrutinizing the container cargo shipments moving into the country. Most of these actions are being done by CBP, the DHS agency responsible for protecting the nation's borders and official ports of entry. CBP uses a layered approach that attempts to focus resources on potentially risky cargo containers while allowing other cargo containers to proceed without disrupting commerce. [...] Several of these actions involve a strategy of moving primary reliance for security away from control systems at U.S. seaports of entry and toward improved controls at points of origin and along the way.[4]

The table also shows Operation Safe Commerce, initiated by the private sector and now administered by DHS's Office of Domestic Preparedness, which employs a similar strategy. This action, in pilot-project form that was initially funded by $58 million appropriated by Congress, is intended to help strengthen the security of cargo as it moves along the international supply chain in containers.[5] In late 2004, the second of two initial phases of the project was concluded. This phase involved identifying the security vulnerabilities of 19 separate supply chains and trying out technologies, such as container seals or sensors, and their integration with governmental policies, logistic processes and procedures that could mitigate those vulnerabilities. The project has received additional funding of $17 million that has been targeted to conduct a third phase in which the best technologies and practices identified in the first two phases will be further tested on a high number of containers for their effectiveness and tamper resistance on three separate supply chains. A report on the best practices identified in the first two phases is expected to be issued in June 2005, and completion of the third phase is expected by October 2006.

The other actions taken to enhance the security of cargo and commerce have been substantial. In 2002, CBP quickly rolled out the CSI and C-TPAT programs [...] and enlisted the participation of several countries and companies. By April 2005, CSI was operational at 35 seaports, located in 18 countries. Similarly, C-TPAT membership grew from about 1,700 companies in January 2003 to over 9,000 companies in March 2005. Given the urgency to take steps to protect against terrorism after the September 11, 2001, attacks, some of the actions were taken using an "implement and amend" approach. That is, CBP had to immediately implement the activity with the knowledge it may need to modify the approach later. For example, in August 2002, CBP modified the already developed Automatic Targeting System with new terrorism-related criteria.

DEVELOPING GREATER MARITIME DOMAIN AWARENESS

The third main area of activity to enhance seaport security—maritime domain awareness—is the understanding by stakeholders involved in maritime security of anything associated with the global maritime environment that could adversely affect the security, safety, economy or environment of the United States. This awareness is essential to identify and respond to any unusual patterns or anomalies that could portend a possible terrorist attack. To be effective, maritime domain awareness must be comprehensive and include information on vessels, seaport infrastructures and facilities, shipping lanes and transit corridors, waterways, and anchorages, among other things. It must also identify threats as soon as possible and far enough away from U.S. seaports to eliminate or mitigate the threat. By effectively identifying potential threats, this awareness can be used as a force multiplier to position resources where they are needed most to respond, instead of spreading out limited resources to address all threats, no matter how unlikely they are to occur. In addition, when shared, this awareness has the potential to facilitate the coordination of efforts of local, state, federal, and even international stakeholders in responding to potential threats.

After the attacks of September 11, 2001, the Coast Guard took steps such as increasing the number of security patrols conducted within seaports and waterways that helped contribute to increased maritime domain awareness. Although maritime homeland security duties are not new to the Coast Guard, the number of hours the Coast Guard used resources (such as ships, boats, or aircraft) to carry out seaport, waterway, and coastal security activities during fiscal year 2003 increased by 1,220 percent from their pre–September 11, 2001, level. Relative to the rest of the Coast Guard's responsibilities, this represented an increase from 4 percent of the Coast Guard's total annual resource hours being used for seaport, waterway, and coastal security activities before September 11, 2001, to 34 percent by September 30, 2003. These activities provide an important input to maritime domain awareness as it places Coast Guard personnel out in the seaports where they can observe, report, and respond to suspect activities or vessels. In addition, these patrols provide the Coast Guard with a visible presence out in the seaport that may deter a potential terrorist attack from being carried out.

As the lead federal agency responsible for protecting the U.S. maritime domain, the Coast Guard has spearheaded an interagency approach for establishing maritime domain awareness. Within this approach are several activities and actions intended to collect information and intelligence, analyze the information and intelligence, and disseminate the analyzed information and intelligence to appropriate federal, state, local, or private seaport stakeholders. Some of these actions were required under MTSA, such as the establishment of an Automatic Identification System to track vessels, as well as creation of area maritime security committees of local seaport stakeholders who identify and address risks within their seaport. In addition to these actions, the Department of Defense and DHS formed a Maritime Domain Awareness Senior Steering Group in 2004 to coordinate national efforts to improve maritime domain awareness. Under Homeland Security Presidential Directive 13, issued in December 2004, this steering group is required to develop a national plan for maritime domain awareness by June 2005. According to the head of the Coast Guard's maritime domain awareness program, a draft of this plan is being reviewed before it is submitted to the president. [...]

Although many of the activities to develop maritime domain awareness are still under way, some progress has already been made. One activity in this area that we have recently looked at concerns the process of information sharing between federal and nonfederal seaport stakeholders participating on area maritime security committees.[6] The Coast Guard organized 43 of these committees, covering the nation's 361 seaports. While a primary purpose of the committees is to develop a seaport-wide security plan for their respective seaports, the committees also provide links for communicating threats and security information to seaport stakeholders—links that generally did not exist prior to the creation of the committees. The types of information shared among committee members with security clearances included assessments of vulnerabilities at specific seaport locations, information about potential threats or suspicious activities, and strategies to use in protecting key infrastructure. Our review found that the committees improved information sharing among seaport security stakeholders, including the timeliness, completeness, and usefulness of information shared.

Another aspect of improving maritime domain awareness involves having the assets to communicate and conduct patrols, and in this regard, the Coast Guard has budgeted for and is in the process of receiving substantial new resources. In 1996, the Coast Guard initiated a major recapitalization effort—known as the Integrated Deepwater System—to replace and modernize the agency's aging and deteriorating fleet of aircraft and vessel assets. The focus of the program is not just on new ships and aircraft, but also on newer, more capable assets, with improved and integrated command, control, communications and computers, intelligence, surveillance, and reconnaissance (C4ISR) capabilities. Although the program was started before the attacks of September 11, 2001, the Coast Guard plans to leverage these capabilities of the 20-year, $17 billion program to enhance its maritime domain awareness and seaport security operations such as patrols and response.

CHALLENGES FOR IMPROVING MARITIME SECURITY TAKE THREE MAIN FORMS

Propelled by a strong sense of urgency to secure the seaports, federal agencies, such as the Coast Guard, CBP, and TSA, accomplished a considerable amount in a short time. At the same time, these actions have also shown the strains that often occur when difficult tasks must be done quickly. We have not examined every action that has been started or enhanced regarding maritime security, but our work to date has covered a number of them. It is not surprising that we have found, besides the progress made, a number of missteps, false starts, and inefficiencies. These represent challenges to overcome.

Although some of these challenges will be resolved with time, analysis, and oversight, there are other challenges that bear even more careful watching, because they may prove to be considerably more difficult to overcome. I would like to highlight three of those challenges, providing examples from our recent work. These three challenges involve (1) design and implementing programs, (2) coordinating between different agencies and stakeholder interests, and (3) determining how to pay for these efforts.

Challenges in Program Design and Implementation

I will discuss today two illustrative examples related to challenges in program design and implementation that we have identified from our work. These include the (1) lack of planning and performance measures for program design and (2) lack of experienced personnel for program implementation.

Lack of Planning and Performance Measures for Program Design

One effect of having to design programs quickly is that they may lack such elements as strategic plans and performance measures needed to set program goals and monitor performance. The lack of such tools can create problems that need to be resolved as the program unfolds. For example, we have reviewed CBP's actions to establish a system meant to reliably identify potentially risky cargo containers.

Our work has shown that a need exists for additional efforts in several homeland security activities, including securing cargo, in order to help ensure the effectiveness of the approach.[7] As we noted in a July 2003 report, the former U.S. Customs Service, part of which is now CBP initiated the Container Security Initiative (CSI) in January 2002 in response to security vulnerabilities created by ocean container trade and the concern that terrorists could exploit these vulnerabilities to transport or detonate WMDs in the United States.[8] During the first year, program officials quickly designed and rolled out the initiative, modifying operations over time. The service achieved strong initial participation among the countries that it sought to enroll in the initiative, reaching agreement with 15 governments to place U.S. personnel at 24 seaports, and placing teams in five of these seaports. However, CBP had not taken adequate steps to incorporate human capital planning, develop performance measures, and plan strategically—factors essential to the program's long-term success and accountability. We noted, for example, that:

- More than 1 year into the implementation of the initiative, CBP had not developed a systematic human capital plan to recruit, train, and assign the more than 120 program staff that would be needed for long-term assignments in a wide range of foreign seaports, some of which could require language capabilities and diplomatic skills.
- CBP lacked performance measures for the initiative that demonstrated program achievements and established accountability. For example, the service lacked measures that assessed the impact of collocating U.S. and foreign customs officials in foreign seaports to determine which containers should be targeted for inspection.
- CBP's focus on short-term operational planning in order to quickly implement the program impeded its ability to systematically carry out strategic planning.

We noted that the service did not have a strategic plan for the initiative that describes how it intends to achieve program goals and objectives. As a result, CBP lacked elements of strategic planning that would improve the management of the program and allow CBP to establish accountability for planned expenditures.

As also reported in July 2003, another program that did not take adequate steps to incorporate the human capital planning and performance measures necessary for the program's long-term success and accountability is CBP's Customs-Trade Partnership Against Terrorism (C-TPAT) program. Initiated in November 2001, C-TPAT is an initiative that attempts to improve the security of the international supply chain. It is a cooperative program between CBP and members of the international trade community in which private companies agree to improve the security of their supply chains in return for a reduced likelihood that their containers will be inspected.

During the first year, more than 1,700 companies agreed to participate in the program, and most received the key benefit—a reduced likelihood of inspections for WMDs. However, we noted similar kinds of problems to those in the CSI program. For example, we found that:

- Even as it rolled out new program elements, CBP lacked a human capital plan for increasing the number of C-TPAT staff from 10 to more than 160.
- CBP had not developed performance measures for C-TPAT that would establish accountability and measure program achievements. For example, CBP had no performance measure to assess the impact of C-TPAT on improving supply chain security practices, possibly resulting in benefits being granted to undeserving companies.
- CBP lacked strategic planning in rolling out C-TPAT, failing to communicate how it planned to implement critical program elements designed to verify that companies have security measures in place and follow through with recommended changes.

We are currently reviewing both the CSI and CTPAT programs and will soon be issuing reports to update our earlier evaluation of these programs.

Lack of Experienced Personnel for Program Implementation

One major challenge in program implementation is the lack of experienced personnel, which is to be expected given the rapid increase in newly hired personnel since September 11, 2001. Agencies such as the Coast Guard expect to see large increases in the number of staff over the next few years to help meet new and expanded responsibilities. Consequently, they also face a challenge in absorbing this increase and training them to be fully productive. We pointed out early on that this would be a challenge for the Coast Guard,[9] and subsequent work has shown this to be the case. For example, after a Coast Guard internal review found that readiness of its multimission stations—the shore-based units whose responsibilities include finding and rescuing mariners in danger—had been in decline for an extended period, the Coast Guard began efforts to improve the readiness of the stations.

This effort was complicated by the new homeland security responsibilities the stations assumed after the terrorist attacks of September 11, 2001. In a recent review of staffing and readiness at these multimission stations,[10] we found that the Coast Guard was still in the process of defining new standards for security activities and had yet to translate the impact of security-related mission responsibilities into specific station readiness requirements, such as staffing standards. Consequently, even though station staffing had increased 25 percent since 2001, the Coast Guard was unable to align staffing resources with mission activities, which resulted in a significant number of positions not being filled with qualified personnel and station personnel working significantly longer hours than are allowed under the Coast Guard's work standards.

We also identified personnel or human capital challenges such as lack of experienced personnel related to the Coast Guard's program to oversee implementation of MTSA-required security plans by owners and operators of maritime facilities and vessels. These security plans are performance-based, meaning the Coast Guard has specified the outcomes it is seeking to achieve and has given seaport stakeholders responsibility for identifying and delivering the measures needed to achieve these outcomes. While this approach provides flexibility to owners and operators in designing and implementing their plans, it also places a premium on the skills and experience of inspectors to identify deficiencies and recommend corrective action. Because the Coast Guard had to review and assess for compliance more than 12,000 security plans for facilities and vessels, it had to rely heavily on reservists, which varied greatly in the level of their skills and experience in this area. For example, some reservists had graduate degrees in security management while others had no formal security training or experience.

In June 2004, we recommended that the Coast Guard carefully evaluate its efforts during the initial surge period for inspections.[11] The Coast Guard has adjusted its inspection program to make its compliance assessments more relevant and useful, but it has not yet determined the overall effectiveness of its compliance actions.

Challenges in Coordinating Actions

Coordinating massive new homeland security actions has been an acknowledged challenge since the events of September 11, 2001, and seaport security has been no exception. On the federal side alone, we have for several years designated implementing and transforming the new DHS as a high-risk area.[12] Since the agency's inception in March 2003, DHS leadership has provided a foundation to maintain critical operations while undergoing transformation, and the agency has begun to put systems in place to operate more effectively and efficiently as an agency. In managing its transformation, however, DHS still faces such issues as forming effective partnerships with other governmental and private-sector entities.

We have made numerous recommendations related to information sharing, particularly as it relates to fulfilling federal critical infrastructure protection responsibilities.[13] For example, we have reported on the practices of organizations that successfully share sensitive or time-critical information, including establishing trust relationships, developing information-sharing standards and protocols, establishing secure communications mechanisms, and disseminating sensitive information appropriately. Federal agencies such as DHS and the Coast Guard have concurred with our recommendations that they develop appropriate strategies to address the many potential barriers to information sharing. However, as of January 2005, many federal efforts to do this remain in the planning or early implementation stages especially in the area of homeland security information sharing, including establishing clear goals, objectives, and expectations for the many participants in information-sharing efforts; and consolidating, standardizing, and enhancing federal structures, policies, and capabilities for the analysis and dissemination of information. In this regard, the issue of information-sharing across agency and stakeholder lines has emerged as a significant enough challenge that we have also designated it as a high-risk area. Here are three examples that illustrate the kinds of problems and challenges that remain related to seaport security.

Obtaining Security Clearances

Although coordination of information-sharing at the seaport level appears to have improved, seaports are experiencing challenges with regards to non-federal officials obtaining security clearances. For some time, state and local seaport and law enforcement personnel have reported problems in obtaining federally generated intelligence information about their jurisdictions because they did not have a federal security clearance. However, as of February 2005—over 4 months after the Coast Guard had developed a list of over 350 nonfederal area maritime security committee participants as having a need for a security clearance—only 28 had submitted the necessary paperwork for the background check. Local Coast Guard officials told us they did not clearly understand their responsibility for communicating with state and local officials about the process for obtaining a security clearance. After we expressed our concerns to Coast Guard officials in headquarters in February 2005, officials took action and drafted guidelines clarifying the role that local Coast Guard officials play in the program.

Sharing Information about Security Exercises

In a January 2005 report,[14] we reported that improvement in the coordination of state, local, and federal entities during seaport exercises was needed. While it was still too early to determine how well entities will function in coordinating an effective response to a seaport-related threat or incident, we identified four operational issues that needed to be addressed in order to promote more effective coordination. We found that more than half of the seaport exercises and after-action reports we examined raised communication issues, including problems with information sharing among first responders and across agency lines. We also found that over half of the exercises raised concerns with communication and the resources available, including inadequate facilities or equipment, differing response procedures, and the need for additional training in joint agency response. To a lesser extent, we found concerns with participants' ability to coordinate effectively and know who had the proper authority to raise security levels, board vessels, or detain passengers.

Developing a Transportation Worker Identification Credential

Beyond information-sharing, a host of challenges remain in coordinating across agency lines and in resolving issues that cut across a wide range of stakeholder perspectives. In this regard, there is perhaps no better example in our recent work than the delayed attempts to develop a major component of the security framework envisioned under MTSA—an identification card for maritime workers. The transportation worker identification credential (TWIC) was initially envisioned by TSA before it became part of DHS to be a universally recognized identification card accepted across all modes of the national transportation system, including airports, seaports, and railroad terminals, using biological metrics, such as fingerprints, to ensure individuals with such an identification card had undergone an assessment verifying that they do not pose a terrorism security risk. TSA initially projected that it would test a prototype of such a card system in 2003 and issue the first of the cards in August 2004. After TSA became part of DHS, testing of the prototype was delayed because of the difficulty in obtaining a response from DHS policy officials who also subsequently directed the agency to reexamine additional options for issuing the identification card. In addition to coordinating within DHS, TSA has had to coordinate with over 800 national level transportation-related stakeholders. Several stakeholders at seaports and seaport facilities told us that, while TSA solicited their input on some issues, TSA did not respond to their input or involve them in making decisions regarding eligibility requirements for the card.[15] In particular, some stakeholders said they had not been included in discussions about which felony convictions should disqualify a worker from receiving a card, even though they had expected and requested that DHS and TSA involve them in these decisions. Obtaining stakeholder involvement is important because achieving program goals hinges on the federal government's ability to form effective partnerships among many public and private stakeholders. If such partnerships are not in place—and equally important, if they do not work effectively—TSA may not be able to test and deliver a program that performs as expected. Until TSA and DHS officials agree on a comprehensive project plan to guide the remainder of the project and work together to set and complete deadlines, and TSA can effectively manage its stakeholders' interests, it may not be able to successfully develop, test, and implement the card program. We issued a report on TWIC in December 2004[16] and the Senate Committee on Homeland Security and Governmental Affairs has asked us to review the program again.

Challenges in Providing Funding for Seaport Security Actions and Initiatives

Our reviews indicate that funding is a pressing challenge to putting effective seaport security measures in place and sustaining these measures over time. This is the view of many transportation security experts, industry representatives, and federal, state, and local government officials with whom we have spoken. While some security improvements are inexpensive, most require substantial and continuous funding. For example, a preliminary Coast Guard estimate placed the cost of implementing the International Maritime Organization security code and the security provisions in MTSA at approximately $1.5 billion for the first year and $7.3 billion over the succeeding decade. This estimate should be viewed more as a rough indicator than a precise measure of costs, but it does show that the cost is likely to be substantial.[17]

At the federal level, more than $560 million in grants has been made available to seaports, localities, and other stakeholders since 2002 under the Port Security Grant Program and the Urban Area Security Initiative. The purpose of these programs was to reduce the vulnerability of seaports to potential terrorist attacks by enhancing facility and operation security. The programs funded several projects, including security assessments; physical enhancements, such as gates and fences; surveillance equipment, such as cameras; and the acquisition of security equipment, such as patrol vessels or vehicles.

Awardees have included seaport authorities, local governments, vessel operators, and private companies with facilities in seaport areas. Interest in receiving port security grants has been strong, and [...] applicant requests have far exceeded available funds. We are currently examining the Port Security Grant Program at the request of several Members of Congress, and we are focusing this review on the risk management practices used in comparing and prioritizing applications. Our work is under way, and we expect to issue our report later this year.[18]

Where the money will come from for all of the funding needs is unclear. In our 2002 statement on national preparedness,[19] we highlighted the need to examine the sustainability of increased funding not only for seaport security, but for homeland security efforts in general. The current economic environment makes this a difficult time for private industry and state and local governments to make security investments and sustain increased security costs. According to industry representatives and experts we contacted, most of the transportation industry operates on a very thin profit margin, making it difficult to pay for additional security measures. Budgetary and revenue constraints, coupled with increasing demands on resources, makes it more critical that federal programs be designed carefully to match the priorities and needs of all partners—federal, state, local, and private—and provide the greatest results for the expenditure.

Setting Performance Goals and Measures and Assessing Risk Are Important Next Steps:

The final purpose of my testimony today is to offer observations, based on the work we have done to date, about important next steps for decision makers in charting a course for future actions. The terrorist attacks of September 11, 2001, evoked with stunning clarity the face and intent of enemies very different from those the nation has faced before—terrorists such as al-Qaeda, willing and able to attack us in our territory using tactics designed to take advantage of our relatively open society and individual freedoms. The amount of activity in response has been considerable, and although there have been no serious incidents in the United States in the interim, the threat of terrorism will likely persist well into the twenty-first century. Thus, it is important to continue to make progress in our efforts. Beyond addressing the kinds of challenges discussed above, however, two other matters stand out. One involves developing a better understanding of how much progress has actually been made to secure our seaports; the other involves developing a better strategy to manage risk and prioritize what areas need further progress and how resources can be best allocated.

LACK OF GOALS AND MEASURES MAKES DETERMINING PROGRESS DIFFICULT

Although there is widespread agreement that actions taken so far have led to a heightened awareness of the need for security and an enhanced ability to identify and respond to many security threats, it is difficult to translate these actions into a clear sense of how far we have progressed in making seaports more secure. One reason is that seaport security efforts, like homeland security efforts in general, lack measurable goals, as well as performance measures to measure progress toward those goals. As others such as the Gilmore Commission have stated, a continuing problem for homeland security has been the lack of clear strategic guidance about the definition and objectives of preparedness.[20] For example, the Coast Guard has a set of performance indicators for each of its nonsecurity missions. It regularly reports on how well it is doing in rescuing mariners at sea, interdicting foreign fishing boats attempting to fish the in U.S. exclusive economic zone, or maintaining aids to navigation on the nation's waterways. However, although it has been more than 3 years since the September 11, 2001, attacks, the Coast Guard is still in the process of developing a performance indicator for its seaport security activities that can be used to indicate what progress has been made to secure seaports. Completion of this indicator and careful tracking of it over the long term is essential to help ensure that taxpayer dollars are being spent wisely to make seaports more secure. Similarly, as discussed earlier in describing the actions taken to secure the cargo transiting through seaports in containers, performance measures are needed to determine the progress such actions are making to reduce vulnerabilities of the international supply chain.

A challenge exists in measuring progress in this area, because seaport security, like many aspects of homeland security, relies upon the coordinated actions of many stakeholders and, in many cases, upon "layers" of defenses. In this regard, we have pointed out that systems and service standards—which focus on the performance, design, and overall management of processes and activities—hold great potential to improve coordination across such dimensions and enhance measurement of continued preparedness.[21] While such standards are already being used in many parts of the private sector, creation of performance and results measures for national security in general, and seaport security in particular, remains a work in progress.

RISK MANAGEMENT IS AN ESSENTIAL TOOL FOR FOCUSING EFFORTS EFFECTIVELY

Even with clear goals and effective performance measures, it seems improbable that all risk can be eliminated, or that any security framework can successfully anticipate and thwart every type of potential terrorist threat that highly motivated, well skilled, and adequately funded terrorist groups could think up. This is not to suggest that security efforts do not matter—they clearly do. However, it is important to keep in mind that total security cannot be bought no matter how much is spent on it. We cannot afford to protect everything against all threats—choices must be made about security priorities.

Thus, great care needs to be taken to assign available resources to address the greatest risks, along with selecting those strategies that make the most efficient and effective use of resources.

One approach to help ensure that resources are assigned and appropriate strategies are selected to address the greatest risks is through risk management—that is, defining and reducing risk. A risk management approach is a systematic process for analyzing threats and vulnerabilities, together with the criticality (that is, the relative importance) of the assets involved. This process consists of a series of analytical and managerial steps, basically sequential, that can be used to assess vulnerabilities, determine the criticality (that is, the relative importance) of the assets being considered, determine the threats to the assets, and assess alternatives for reducing the risks. Once these are assessed and identified, actions to improve security and reduce the risks can be chosen from the alternatives for implementation. To be effective, however, this process must be repeated when threats or conditions change to incorporate any new information to adjust and revise the assessments and actions.

Some elements of risk management have been incorporated into seaport security activities. For example, to meet the requirements of MTSA, security plans for seaports, facilities, and vessels have been developed based on assessments that identify their vulnerabilities. In addition, the Coast Guard is using the Port Security Risk Assessment Tool, which is designed to prioritize risk according to a combination of possible threat, consequence, and vulnerability. Under this approach, seaport infrastructure that is determined to be both a critical asset and a likely and vulnerable target would be a high priority for security enhancements or funding. By comparison, infrastructure that is vulnerable to attack but not as critical or infrastructure that is very critical but already well protected would be lower in priority. In a homeland security setting, possible uses of data produced from risk management efforts include informing decisions on where the federal government might spend billions of dollars within and between federal departments, as well as informing decisions on grants awarded to state and local governments.

As the nation moves ahead with seaport security efforts, there are plans to incorporate risk management as part of the nation's larger homeland security strategy. Homeland Security Presidential Directive 7, issued in December 2003, charged DHS with integrating the use of risk management into homeland security activities. The directive called on the Department to develop policies, guidelines, criteria, and metrics for this effort. To meet this requirement, the Coast Guard has taken steps to use risk management in prioritizing the protection of key infrastructure within and between seaports. We are currently in the process of assessing the progress the Coast Guard has made in these efforts. In addition, we are reviewing the extent to which a risk management approach is being used by other DHS agencies, such as the Information Analysis and Infrastructure Protection Directorate, to evaluate the relative risk faced by key infrastructure within seaports and across broad sectors of national activity, such as seaports and aviation, to help ensure funding and resources are allocated to where they are needed most. Our work is still under way and not far enough along to discuss at this time. It is likely, however, that attention to risk management will be a key part of the ongoing dialogue about the nation's homeland security actions in general, and its seaport security actions in particular.

CONCLUDING OBSERVATIONS

Managing the risks associated with securing our nation's seaports involves a careful balance between the benefits of added security and the potential economic impacts of security enhancements. While there is broad support for greater security, the national economy is heavily dependent on keeping goods, trucks, trains, and people flowing quickly through seaports, and bringing commerce to a crawl in order to be completely safe carries its own serious economic consequences. Striking the right balance between increased security and protecting economic vitality is an important and difficult task. Considering this, three things stand out as important from the work we have conducted:

- Seaports are not retreating as a homeland security issue. They are an attractive terrorist target and are likely to remain so, because by their nature they represent a vulnerability that is always open to potential exploitation.
- Seaport security has lived up to its billing as an area in which security measures can be difficult to implement. The range of activity in seaport areas can be extremely wide, as can the range of stakeholders and the fragmentation of responsibility among them. Many of the problems we have identified with individual programs and efforts can likely be overcome with time and effort, but success is not assured. We are already seeing some efforts, such as the TWIC identification card, becoming deeply mired in problems. These activities will thus continue to demand close attention.
- The national dialogue on this issue is likely to focus increasingly in trying to determine what we are getting for our efforts and where we should invest the dollars we have. Therefore, it is critical that federal programs be designed carefully to try to match the priorities and needs of all partners—federal, state, local, and private—and use performance measures to effectively allocate funds and resources. On this point, there is work to do, because agencies such as the Coast Guard currently lack a systematic approach for explaining the relationship between the expenditure of resources and performance results in seaport security, limiting its ability to critically examine its resource needs and prioritize program efforts. Providing answers also requires an ability to carefully assess what the key vulnerabilities are and what should be done to protect them. Only by doing this will we have reasonable assurance that we are doing the best job with the dollars we have.

Mr. Chairman, this concludes my prepared statement. I would be pleased to answer any questions that you or other members of the committee may have.

MARITIME SECURITY: POTENTIAL TERRORIST ATTACKS AND PROTECTION PRIORITIES

John F. Frittelli and Paul W. Parfomak
Analysts in Transportation, Resources, Science, and Industry Division
Congressional Research Service Report for Congress
January 9, 2007*

. . . LIKELIHOOD OF U.S. MARITIME TERRORIST ATTACKS

Clear perspectives on the likelihood of specific types of maritime terrorist attacks are essential for prioritizing the nation's maritime antiterrorism activities. Especially when security policies seek to concentrate resources against a relatively limited number of terrorism scenarios, as appears to be the case for DHS port security grants, the responsible agencies must be confident that these scenarios are credible and do, indeed, pose the greatest threat to the United States. In practice, however, there has been considerable public debate about the likelihood of scenarios frequently identified as having high priority by federal policy makers. As a 2006 RAND study of maritime security concluded "many perceptions of maritime terrorism risks do not align with the reality of threats and vulnerabilities."[22] The following section discusses perceptions and uncertainties pertaining to three prominent maritime attack scenarios, including nuclear or "dirty" bombs smuggled in shipping containers, liquefied natural gas (LNG) tanker attacks, and attacks on passenger ferries.

THE "BOMB IN A BOX" SCENARIO

Type of Bomb

The Bush administration's National Strategy for Maritime Security states that "WMD issues are of the greatest concern since the maritime domain is the likely venue by which WMD will be brought into the United States."[23] One arms control expert believes that, under current maritime security practices,

---

*http://www.fas.org/sgp/crs/homesec/RL33787.pdf

the likelihood of such an attack within the decade "is more likely than not."[24] According to a press report, the operations and emergency management director for the Port of Los Angeles has stated that the probability of a nuclear attack at his port is "not low," and that measures to prevent such an attack are the port's top priority.[25] Although much attention is paid to the threat of nuclear terrorism, there are divergent opinions about the likelihood of a terrorist group such as al-Qaeda constructing or otherwise obtaining a workable nuclear weapon.[26] Expert estimates of the probability of terrorists obtaining a nuclear device have ranged from 50 percent to less than 1 percent.[27] Among other challenges to obtaining such a device, experts believe it unlikely that countries with nuclear weapons or materials would knowingly supply them to a terrorist group.[28] It also may be technically difficult to successfully detonate such a nuclear device. North Korea experienced technical failures in conducting its 2006 nuclear weapons test, and this test took place under highly controlled conditions.[29] Attempting to detonate a nuclear device in a maritime terror attack could pose even greater operational challenges. Consistent with these perspectives, Secretary of Homeland Security Michael Chertoff has stated, "I don't think that in the near term there's a significant likelihood of a traditional nuclear device being detonated" in the United States.[30] Other experts concede that evaluating the likelihood of nuclear terrorism is inherently uncertain, but that such potential attacks warrant attention even if they are unlikely.

The probability of a terrorist attack with an actual nuclear weapon cannot be reliably estimated, and it is surely lower than the probability of virtually any other type of terrorist attack. But the devastation from such an attack would be so overwhelming that, based on expected damages—the probability multiplied by the consequences—this threat must be considered one of the greatest dangers America faces . . .[31]

Terrorist attacks on U.S. ports with radiological dispersion devices ("dirty" bombs) is also considered among the gravest maritime terrorism scenarios.[32] A 2003 simulation of a series of such attacks concluded that they "could cripple global trade and have a devastating impact on the nation's economy."[33] Many terrorism analysts view such a dirty bomb attack as relatively likely. In a 2005 survey, for example, nuclear nonproliferation experts expressed their beliefs (on average) that there was a 25 percent chance of a dirty bomb attack in the United States by 2010 and a 40 percent chance of such an attack by 2015.[34] Studies suggest that the materials required to make a dirty bomb may be widely available and poorly controlled internationally.[35] According to some press reports, U.S. and British intelligence agencies have reportedly concluded that al-Qaeda has succeeded in making such a bomb.[36] Port operators have testified before Congress that they believe "it is just a question of time" before terrorists with dirty bombs successfully attack a U.S. port.[37]

Although many experts consider attacks with dirty bombs among the most likely maritime terrorism scenarios, other experts dispute this conclusion. Scientists have long questioned whether terrorists could actually build a dirty bomb with catastrophic potential since handling the necessary radioactive materials could cause severe burns and would likely expose the builders to lethal doses of radiation.[38] Building and transporting such a bomb safely and to avoid detection would likely require so much shielding that it would be "nearly impossible" to move.[39] Weaker dirty bombs made from less radioactive (and more common) materials would be easier to build and deploy, but would have a much smaller physical impact and would likely cause few human casualties. Consequently, some analysts argue that terrorists will forego dirty bombs, restricting themselves to the use of more conventional explosives.[40] In support of this argument, analysts point to the fact that there have been no U.S. dirty bomb attacks, notwithstanding the supposed ease of perpetrating such attacks.[41] They also note that the 2005 U.S. indictment of alleged "dirty bomber" Jose Padilla, in fact, contained no evidence of, or references to, a dirty bomb plot.[42] Faced with contradictory perspectives on the likelihood of a dirty bomb attack scenario at a U.S. port, analysts and policy makers draw qualified conclusions about such an attack. If a "weak" dirty bomb attack is more likely than a "strong" one, but a weak attack will have limited effects, it is unclear whether such an attack would meet terrorist objectives. On the other hand, the effects on the general public of any dirty bomb attack, even a weak one, may be great enough to motivate potential attackers. As one analyst has stated, notwithstanding the challenges to dirty bombers, "the chances of a dirty bomb being deployed by al-Qaeda cannot be discounted . . . Given the exponential psychological and economic effects of such a weapon, the benefits of deploying one may far outweigh the costs and difficulties entailed in its construction."[43]

Method of Delivery

The potential smuggling and detonation of a nuclear or dirty bomb device in a shipping container at a U.S. port is one of the threats most specifically and frequently mentioned by legislators in the context of maritime security.[44] Shipping containers may be particularly vulnerable to terrorist infiltration compared to other types of cargo for three reasons. First, shipping containers are relatively large. They come in standard sizes from 20 to 53 feet long, although the most common are 40 feet or longer—about the size of a truck semitrailer. Second, the containers on any given ship are packed at the factories or warehouses of many different companies that can be dispersed far and wide from the loading port, making it impossible for government authorities to ensure that only legitimate cargo has been packed. Third, the containers are typically trucked to the port of loading, during which the integrity of the shipments rests entirely on the trustworthiness or due diligence of the truck drivers. A maritime security expert at the Council on Foreign Relations, who is a former commandant of the U.S. Coast Guard, outlines a scenario that most concerns him:

Let me share with you the terrorist scenario that most keeps me awake at night . . . A container of athletic footwear for a name-brand company is loaded at a manufacturing plant in Surabaya, Indonesia. The container doors are shut and a mechanical seal is put into the door pad-eyes. These designer sneakers are destined for retail stores in malls across America. The container and seal numbers are recorded at the factory. A local truck driver, sympathetic to al-Qaeda, picks up the container. On the way to the port, he turns into an alleyway and backs up the truck at a nondescript warehouse where a small team of operatives pry loose one of the door hinges to open the container so that they can gain access to the shipment. Some of the sneakers are removed and in their place, the operatives load a dirty bomb wrapped in lead shielding, and they then refasten the door.

Other analysts assert that if terrorists were to attempt a nuclear or dirty bomb attack in a U.S. port, they would be unlikely to do so using a shipping container because it would put the device beyond a terrorist group's control. These analysts question whether the container shipping system offers the routing or scheduling precision required by terrorists to position the bomb in the right place at the right time. Other observers assert that some types of noncontainerized cargo could also be used for smuggling a bomb.[45] The manager of port security at the Port Authority of New York and New Jersey states that their biggest concern is roll-on/roll-off cargo (ships that carry automobiles, trucks, and other vehicles).[46] Noncontainerized cargo is more plentiful. By tonnage, containers carry only 11 percent of U.S. overseas waterborne trade[47] and container ships account for about one in every three U.S. port calls.[48] Other types of cargo also face less security screening.[49] Relatively low-value cargo might be targeted if terrorists perceive it receives less attention from U.S. Coast Guard and customs officials. For instance, a federal official familiar with New York harbor, pointing to a scrap metal terminal in Jersey City, stated the following to a reporter: "If I wanted to bring an atomic bomb into the port, I'd do it through that scrap operation."[50]

The Government Accountability Office (GAO) investigated the potential for maritime terrorists to use weapons of mass destruction (WMDs) in 2005. In its report, the GAO states that an extensive body of work on this subject by the Federal Bureau of Investigation and academic, think tank, and business organizations concluded that while the likelihood of such use of containers is considered low, the movement of oceangoing containerized cargo is vulnerable to some form of terrorist action. Such action, including attempts to smuggle either fully assembled weapons of mass destruction or their individual components, could lead to widespread death and damage.[51] Liquefied Natural Gas (LNG) Tanker Attacks Potential terrorist attacks on LNG tankers in U.S. waters have been a key concern of policy makers in ports with LNG facilities because such attacks could cause catastrophic fires in port and nearby populated areas. The Coast Guard's FY2006 budget specifically requested funding for "additional boat crews and screening personnel at key LNG hubs."[52] To date, no LNG tanker or land-based LNG facility in the world has been attacked by terrorists. However, similar natural gas and oil assets have been favored terror targets internationally. The attack on the *Limburg,* although an oil tanker, is often cited as an indication of LNG tanker vulnerability.

The Department of Homeland Security (DHS) specifically included LNG tankers among a list of potential terrorist targets in a security alert late in 2003.[53] The DHS also reported that "in early 2001 there was some suspicion of possible associations between stowaways on Algerian flagged LNG tankers arriving in Boston and persons connected with the so-called 'Millennium Plot'" to bomb targets in the United States. While these suspicions could not be proved, DHS stated that "the risks associated with LNG shipments are real, and they can never be entirely eliminated."[54] A 2004 report by Sandia National Laboratories concluded that potential terrorist attacks on LNG tankers could be considered "credible and possible."[55] The Sandia report identified LNG tankers as vulnerable to ramming, preplaced explosives, insider takeover, hijacking, or external terrorist actions (such as a *Limburg*-type, missile, or airplane attack).[56] Former Bush administration counterterrorism advisor Richard Clarke has asserted that terrorists have both the desire and capability to attack LNG shipping with the intention of harming the general population.[57] Although they acknowledge the security information put forth by federal agencies, many experts believe that concern about threats to LNG tankers is overstated.[58] In 2003, the head of one university research consortium remarked, for example, "from all the information we have . . . we don't see LNG as likely or credible terrorist targets."[59] Industry representatives argue that deliberately causing an LNG catastrophe to injure people might be possible in theory, but would be extremely difficult to accomplish. Likewise, the Federal Energy Regulatory Commission (FERC) and other experts believe that LNG facilities are relatively secure compared to other hazardous chemical infrastructures which receives less public attention. In a December 2004 report, the FERC stated that for a new LNG terminal proposal . . . the perceived threat of a terrorist attack may be considered as highly probable to the local population. However, at the national level, potential terrorist targets are plentiful . . . Many of these pose a similar or greater hazard to that of LNG.[60]

The FERC also remarked, however, that "unlike accidental causes, historical experience provides little guidance in estimating the probability of a terrorist attack on an LNG vessel or onshore storage facility."[61] Former Director of Central Intelligence James Woolsey has stated his belief that a terrorist attack on an LNG tanker in U.S. waters would be unlikely because its potential impacts would not be great enough compared to other potential targets.[62] LNG terminal operators, which have conducted proprietary assessments of potential terrorist attacks against LNG tankers, have expressed similar views.[63] In a September 2006 evaluation of a proposed LNG terminal in Long Island Sound, the USCG states that "there are currently no specific, credible threats against" the proposed LNG facility or tankers serving the facility.[64] The evaluation also notes, however, that the threat environment is dynamic and that some threats may be unknown.[65]

PASSENGER FERRY ATTACKS

Congressional policy makers frequently cite passenger ferries as a key maritime security concern. For example, in 2005, one Member of Congress stated that "there is a serious security gap in our ferry systems and we need to ensure that passengers on our nation's waterways are protected."[66] A RAND study in 2006 argued that attacks on passenger ferries in the United States might be highly attractive to terrorists because such attacks are easy to execute, may kill many people, would likely draw significant media attention, and could demonstrate a terrorist group's salience and vibrancy.[67] One U.S. Coast Guard risk analyst reportedly has stated that "in terms of the probability of something happening, the likelihood of it succeeding and the consequences of it occurring, ferries come out at the very high end."[68] Such attacks have occurred overseas. As noted earlier in this report, terrorists linked to al-Qaeda attacked and sank the Philippine vessel *Superferry 14* in 2004.

In a 2006 report, the U.S. Department of Justice (DOJ) identified a ferry bombing as among the most likely types of maritime terror attacks.[69] The DOJ report reached this conclusion based largely on the number of suspicious incidents reported at marine facilities in the Seattle area and at other U.S. ports. However, officials in the Seattle office of the Federal Bureau of Investigation (FBI) reportedly suggested at the time that the DOJ's high ranking of the passenger ferry threat might be due to more aggressive reporting of suspicious incidents in that region than elsewhere in the country.[70] Seattle FBI officials also reportedly stated that they had never been able to tie a specific suspicious incident to a terrorist group or terrorist plan.[71] Thus, while there appears to be a logical case why ferries may be a key type of terrorist target, questions remain about actual terrorist activities related to ferries.

OVERALL LIKELIHOOD OF MARITIME TERRORISM

The prior discussion illustrates the uncertainty surrounding some of the maritime terrorism scenarios of greatest concern to U.S. maritime security officials. Questions about the likelihood of these specific, high priority scenarios beg the larger question of how likely is any maritime terrorism attack against the United States. Some experts suggest that some such attack, in one form or another, is almost inevitable. For example, one senior U.S. military officer has reportedly asserted that "it's just a matter of time until the terrorists try to use a . . . maritime attack against us."[72] Security analysts also point to known terrorist plots to attack U.S. maritime targets, such as those passing the Straits of Gibraltar, as evidence that global terrorist groups continue to plan maritime terrorism activities. Information from captured al-Qaeda member Abd al Rahman al Nashiri reportedly included plans for attacks on a wide range of Western maritime targets, including military vessels, oil tankers, and cruise ships.[73] Other analysts believe future maritime attacks against the United States are relatively unlikely, especially in U.S. waters.

Notwithstanding specific acts of terrorism in the past, such as the *Cole* bombing, they note that fewer than 1 percent of all global terrorist attacks since 1997 have involved maritime targets.[74] Furthermore, international terrorists have attacked no maritime targets in U.S. territory since the anti-Castro attacks in 1976 despite their demonstrated ability to do so overseas.[75] Analysts also argue that U.S. ports and waterways are increasingly well-protected against terrorists due to the ongoing security activities of the U.S. Coast Guard, U.S. Customs and Border Protection (CBP), provisions of the Maritime Transportation Security Act (P.L. 107–295), protections added using DHS port security grants, and other U.S. maritime security measures.[76] Classification issues may also influence differing perceptions of maritime terrorism risk since piracy unrelated to terrorism is common in Southeast Asia and may be conflated with terrorism in maritime security statistics.[77]

A key consideration in assessing the general likelihood of a maritime attack against the United States is the inherent operational difficulty in mounting such attacks, especially compared to land attacks which may alternatively satisfy terrorist objectives. One U.S. naval analyst has identified a number of specific challenges for terrorists in the maritime environment:

- Maritime targets are relatively more scarce than land targets;
- Surveillance at sea offers less cover and concealment than surveillance on land;
- Tides, currents, wind, sea state, visibility, and proximity to land must all be factored into a maritime terror operation;
- Maritime terror operations may require skills that are not quickly or easily acquired such as special training in navigation, coastal piloting, and ship handling;
- Testing weapons and practicing attack techniques, hallmarks of al-Qaeda's typically meticulous preparation, are harder and more difficult to conceal at sea than on land;
- The generally singular nature of maritime targets, the low probability of damage and casualties secondary to the intended target, and the problems associated with filming attacks at sea for terrorist publicity may also reduce the desirability of maritime targets.[78]

Given these challenges, it remains an open question how likely maritime attacks against the United States may be. In terms of the scenario framework in this report, although a successful attack on U.S. maritime targets would likely satisfy certain objectives of known international perpetrators such as al-Qaeda, tactical uncertainties and security deterrents may lead terrorist planners to turn their attention elsewhere. It bears repeating, however, that maritime terror attacks against the U.S. have occurred and there is evidence they have been planned for the future, despite the operational challenges. The same naval analyst cited above calls for continued vigilance: Rather than develop a false sense of security based on the belief that inherent difficulties will limit maritime terrorism . . . caution is warranted in light of al-Qaeda's adaptability, ingenuity, tenacity, and audacity.[79]

Successful development and application of maritime tactics, techniques, and procedures has already occurred within the terrorist community. It appears, therefore, that while maritime terrorist attacks against the United States may be more difficult to execute and, consequently, less likely to occur than other types of attacks, they remain a significant possibility and warrant continued policy attention.

The key challenge in determining the overall likelihood of a terrorist attack on a U.S. port is reducing uncertainty about specific types of attacks and potential attackers. Because historical terrorist activity is not necessarily a reliable predictor of future activity, scenarios derived from attacks like that on the USS *Cole* may not help prepare for actual future attacks. Furthermore, information about the ongoing motivations, capabilities, and plans of terrorist groups is limited and typically not in the public domain. Terrorist intelligence gathered by U.S. and foreign agencies may reduce this uncertainty, but is unlikely to eliminate it. Faced with this uncertainty, decision makers are to some extent forced to rely upon their own best judgment to reach conclusions about the likelihood of maritime terrorist attacks . . .

MARITIME SECURITY: THE SAFE PORT ACT STATUS AND IMPLEMENTATION ONE YEAR LATER

Stephen L. Caldwell
Director, Homeland Security and Justice Issues
Government Accountability Office
Before the House Committee on Homeland Security
Subcommittee on Border, Maritime and Global Counterterrorism
October 20, 2007*

Federal agencies have improved overall port security efforts by establishing committees to share information with local port stakeholders, taking steps to establish interagency operations centers to monitor port activities, conducting operations such as harbor patrols and vessel escorts, writing port-level plans to prevent and respond to terrorist attacks, testing such plans through exercises, and assessing the security at foreign ports. However, these agencies face resource constraints and other challenges trying to meet the SAFE Port Act's requirements to expand these activities. For example, the Coast Guard faces budget constraints in trying to expand its current command centers and include other agencies at the centers.

*http://www.gao.gov/new.items/d08126t.pdf

Similarly, private facilities and federal agencies have taken action to improve security at about 3,000 individual facilities by writing facility-specific security plans, inspecting facilities to determine compliance with their plans, and developing special identification cards for workers to help prevent terrorists from getting access to secure areas. Federal agencies face challenges trying to meet the act's requirements to expand the scope or speed the implementation of such activities. For example, the Transportation Security Administration missed the act's deadline to implement the identification card program at 10 selected ports because of delays in testing equipment and procedures. Federal programs related to the security of cargo containers have also improved as agencies are enhancing systems to identify high-risk cargo, expanding partnerships with other countries to screen containers before they depart for the United States, and working with international organizations to develop a global framework for container security. Federal agencies face challenges implementing container security aspects of the SAFE Port Act and other legislation. For example, Customs and Border Protection must test and implement a new program to scan 100 percent of all incoming containers overseas—a departure from its existing risk-based programs.

Madam Chairwoman and Members of the Subcommittee:

I am pleased to be here today to discuss port and cargo security functions related to provisions of the Security and Accountability for Every Port Act (SAFE Port Act).[80] The nation's 361 seaports are the gateway for more than 80 percent of our foreign trade. Worldwide, some 30 large ports, spread across North America, Asia, and Europe constitute the world's primary, interdependent trading web. Much of this trade—particularly high-value cargo— enters and leaves in cargo containers.

In our post-9/11 environment, however, the potential security weaknesses presented by these economic gateways have become apparent. Sprawling, easily accessible by water and land, often close to urban areas, and containing facilities that represent opportunities for inflicting significant damage as well as for causing economic mayhem, ports present potential terrorist targets. Further, they are potential conduits for weapons prepared elsewhere and concealed in cargo designed to move quickly to many locations beyond the ports themselves.

Since the 9/11 attacks, Congress has established a new port security framework—much of which was set in place by the Maritime Transportation Security Act (MTSA).[81] Enacted in November 2002, MTSA was designed, in part, to help protect the nation's ports and waterways from terrorist attacks by requiring a wide range of security improvements. Among the major requirements included in MTSA were (1) conducting vulnerability assessments for port facilities and vessels; (2) developing security plans to mitigate identified risks for the national maritime system, ports, port facilities, and vessels; (3) developing the Transportation Worker Identification Credential (TWIC), a biometric identification card to help restrict access to secure areas to only authorized personnel; and (4) establishing of a process to assess foreign ports, from which vessels depart on voyages to the United States. The Department of Homeland Security (DHS)—itself a creation of the new security environment brought on by the 9/11 attacks—administers much of this framework, which also attempts to balance security priorities with the need to facilitate legitimate trade.

The SAFE Port Act, which was enacted in October 2006, is one of the latest additions to this port security framework. The act made a number of adjustments to programs within this framework, creating additional programs or lines of effort and altering others. The SAFE Port Act created and codified new programs and initiatives, and amended some of the original provisions of MTSA. The SAFE Port Act included provisions that (1) codified the Container Security Initiative (CSI) and the Customs-Trade Partnership Against Terrorism (C-TPAT), two programs administered by U.S. Customs and Border Protection (CBP) to help reduce threats associated with cargo shipped in containers, as well as established the Domestic Nuclear Detection Office (DNDO), which is responsible for conducting research, development, testing, and evaluation of radiation detection equipment; (2) required interagency operational centers where agencies organize to fit the security needs of the port area at selected ports; (3) set an implementation schedule and fee restrictions for TWIC; (4) required that all containers entering high-volume U.S. ports be scanned for radiation sources by December 31, 2007; and (5) required additional data be made available to CBP for targeting cargo containers for inspection.[82] This statement summarizes our recently completed and ongoing work.

Over the past several years, we have examined and reported on many of the programs in this new port security framework. This statement is designed both to provide an overview of what we have earlier reported about these programs and to describe, with the preliminary information available, what DHS is doing as a result of the SAFE Port Act requirements and the challenges the agency faces in doing so. [...]

This statement is organized into three key areas, as follows:

- Programs related to overall port security, such as those for coordinating among stakeholders, conducting security operations, developing security plans, and conducting exercises to test security procedures
- Programs related specifically to security at individual facilities, such as examining security measures and ensuring that only properly cleared individuals have access to port areas
- Programs related specifically to cargo container security, such as screening containers at ports both here and abroad and forming partnerships with the private sector

This statement is based primarily on a body of work we completed in response to congressional requests and mandates for analysis of maritime, port, and cargo security efforts of the federal government.[83] In some cases, we provide preliminary observations from our ongoing work. Thus, the timeliness of the data that were the basis for our prior reporting varies depending on when our products were issued, and the preliminary observations are subject to change as we complete our work.

We conducted all of our work in accordance with generally accepted government auditing standards. To perform both our completed and ongoing work, we visited several domestic and overseas ports; reviewed agency program documents, port security plans and postexercise reports, and other documents; and interviewed officials from the federal, state, local, private, and international sectors. The officials were from a wide variety of port stakeholders to include Coast Guard, CBP, Transportation Security Administration (TSA), port authorities, terminal operators, vessel operators, foreign governments, and international organizations. While this body of work does not cover all the provisions of the SAFE Port Act, it does cover a wide range of these provisions [...].

We provided a draft of the information in this testimony to DHS. DHS provided technical comments, which we incorporated as appropriate.

CONGRESSIONAL HEARINGS

SEAPORT SECURITY HEARING IN SEATTLE

Senator Patty Murray
July 1, 2002*

(Seattle, WA)—Today U.S. Senator Patty Murray (D-WA) spoke at a Commerce Committee field hearing in Seattle on port security.

Her opening remarks follow:
This is one of several hearings being held in port communities around the nation. These hearings will help us in the Senate respond to the new security challenges facing our ports in the wake of September 11.

Our solutions to these challenges must be comprehensive. But they must also be flexible enough to reflect the unique elements of each port—including those here in the Pacific Northwest.

No survey of our nation's port systems would be complete without a look at Washington State. We provide a unique perspective on challenges and solutions.

To help us do that, we've assembled representatives from the domestic port community, government, foreign seaports, technology companies, and organized labor to share their ideas on improving security.

It's going to take all of us working together to implement good solutions so I want to thank all of the witnesses for being here today.

*http://murray.senate.gov/news.cfm?id=189093

I want to extend a special welcome to one of our witnesses, Mr. Robert Yap, the executive vice president of the PSA Corporation, which handles the Port of Singapore and others international ports. He is accompanied today by Mr. Vincent Lim, Deputy President of PSA. Welcome, Mr. Lim. Their perspective from a foreign port will help us understand how various proposals would affect our ability to trade with other countries. As we improve our security, we don't want to penalize the foreign shippers who use our ports, or we'll pay the price in lost jobs and commerce.

Mr. Chairman, as you know, Washington State is in a unique position to help shape our nation's seaport security work. Washington is the most trade dependant state in the nation, and our seaports are the lifeblood of our economy.

The ports of Tacoma and Seattle together form the third-largest load center for containerized cargo in the United States—1.8 million containers pass through this region each year. That cargo generates billions of dollars of goods each day and supports tens of thousands of good-paying, family-wage jobs.

The Puget Sound also has marine security challenges that other regions do not.

- We share a land and sea border with Canada.
- We have several important defense installations that share our waterfront.
- And we have the largest passenger ferry system in the country.

In the Northwest, we must balance all of these security needs with the continuing need to keep cargo moving efficiently. I want to outline the challenge before us, talk about the steps we've taken so far, and finally lay out some principles for a national solution.

THE CHALLENGE

For decades, we've built our port infrastructure and procedures around economic efficiency, and we've done a good job. Many of the folks in this room have helped make our port system efficient and that's helped our economy and our community.

But since September 11, we now need to add a new element to the equation—security.

We've got to realign our port system around efficiency and security. We're really starting from scratch. There are few standards for handling or inspecting foreign cargo as it enters our ports. Often, we don't know where a container has come from or what's inside.

There are also many players involved in moving goods to and from our ports including buyers, sellers, banks, inland carriers, foreign seaports, carriers, governments, and consolidators. The wide range of participants in itself adds to the security challenge.

Because we're starting from scratch and involving so many players, our response must be prompt and it must be comprehensive. We can't wait 10 years for one group or agency to develop a plan. I hope today's hearing will help us meet these new challenges together.

Whatever we do, we must be mindful that it does not slow down the progress we have made in expanding the productivity and efficiency of our ports.

The United States receives some $750 billion worth of cargo at 360 seaports every year. That's roughly one-fifth the U.S. economy. We don't want to gamble with such an important part of our economy.

PROGRESS SO FAR

In Congress, we've been working on seaport security for several months, and I want to so briefly summarize what we've accomplished.

First, the Puget Sound will get its own Marine Safety and Security Team because of funding I secured in last year's Defense Supplemental Appropriations Bill.

We will receive one of the first of four teams in the nation trained to operate fast response boats that can intercept ships carrying suspicious cargo well before they reach the port or even the coast. I'm pleased to report that the commissioning ceremony is this Wednesday.

I also included $93.3 million in the Defense bill for port security grants. This money will help ports pay for security assessments, enhance facilities and operations, and create better security partnerships. These grants were released on June 17. They provide $5.7 million for seaports and maritime security activities in Washington State including $653,000 to assist security efforts on the Columbia River.

In addition, I've used my position as chairman of the Senate Transportation Subcommittee to review our government's security efforts.

I've held hearings to examine the proposed budgets for the Coast Guard and for the new Transportation Security Agency. In May, I held a hearing on cargo security in Washington DC. In April, I held an Appropriations Subcommittee field hearing on this topic in this very chamber. I also attended a set of full Senate Appropriations Committee hearings on homeland security where seaport security was discussed.

Because we've had an overwhelming number of applications for the original funding, I included an additional $200 million in this year's Senate Supplemental Appropriations bill for seaport security grants.

I also included $28 million for an initiative called "Operation Safe Commerce" in the Supplemental. This is an initiative at the nation's three largest container ports—which includes the Ports of Seattle/Tacoma—to test and deploy a program that applies a system-wide approach to seaport security. The initiative calls for all stakeholders to develop international standards from the point of origin to the final destination. These standards would provide advanced information about cargo and ways to monitor the cargo during transit.

The Supplemental includes $59 million for the U.S. Customs Service Container Security Initiative, which has similar goals to "Operation Safe Commerce."

Finally, let's not forget that this Committee passed the Port and Maritime Security Act in December of last year. That legislation would

- Improve cooperation among all the stakeholders
- Force ports to evaluate their security needs
- Better secure port facilities
- Require information about cargo shipments be evaluated before they're granted entry into a U.S. port
- Improve reporting of cargo and crew
- Authorize grants to ports to help comply with these new mandates

That bill is now in conference with the House.

PRINCIPLES

After looking at the challenge and our work so far, I'd like to close by laying out a few principles for policy solutions.

First, our solution must involve all the stakeholders in the shipment of goods, both private and public, foreign and domestic. By developing a plan together, we can establish the trust and cooperation we'll need to carry it out. The nature of container traffic makes it difficult to secure the trade route. Foreign manufactures, ports of origin, shippers, destination port authorities, and organized labor are all critical elements in the shipping chain. They are our best allies to securing the trade lanes. Without cooperation among all of these players, any system we create will be vulnerable.

Second, we must create international standards, where none exist today. Those standards must do two things. They must provide reliable information on cargo to everyone in the supply chain. That way officials at home and abroad can identify suspicious cargo and quickly determine if it poses a security risk. These standards must also ensure good communication between all the players in the system.

Third, the costs of these improvements must be shared so that no single entity in the system is burdened with ensuring the security of the system as a whole.

Because most of the players are private businesses—concerned with the bottom line—our approach should provide economic incentives to encourage everyone to work within the system.

It must include a way for safe, reliable players to have better access to our markets and to remain active even if an incident should occur. A complete shutdown in the cargo container business could have a severe impact on our economy—a much larger impact than the one we saw when the aviation industry was grounded immediately after September 11. I think most of the private entities who are involved in transshipment of commercial goods would pay a premium for such an incentive.

Fourth, our new system should not disadvantage American ports in this highly competitive environment.

So as I see it, port security plans need to involve all stakeholders, must create international standards for information and communication, must spread the costs around, and must not disadvantage American ports. I recognize that's a tall order, but working together I think we can meet those principles.

One thing that would help would be more interest and support from the current administration. Customs, the INS, and the Coast Guard are all doing a great job of trying to address the vulnerability of our seaport, but this initiative needs more support from the very top.

So far, the Transportation Security Administration has only doled out responsibilities. It hasn't yet developed the comprehensive approach that is needed to properly secure our trade routes.

In fact, the additional $200 million in the pending Supplemental for seaport security grants, and the money in the Supplemental for "Operation Safe Commerce" and for the Customs' "Container Security Initiative" are not supported by the president.

The president has said he will veto any appropriations bill that is above what he requested. So I hope we'll have a more cooperative approach from the White House and the TSA to help us and our ports make these needed improvements. It's clear we have some very critical issues to discuss today. So I again thank all of the witnesses and everyone here today.

DEPARTMENT OF HOMELAND SECURITY LAW ENFORCEMENT EFFORTS AT U.S. PORTS OF ENTRY

Representatives Howard Coble, North Carolina, and Robert C. Scott, Virginia
Before the House Committee
on the Judiciary, Subcommittee on Crime, Terrorism,
and Homeland Security
March 15, 2005*

The Subcommittee met, pursuant to notice, at 3:02 P.M., in Room 2141, Rayburn House Office Building, Hon. Howard Coble (Chair of the Subcommittee) presiding.

Mr. Coble: Good afternoon, ladies and gentlemen. The Subcommittee will come to order. Today, the Committee on the Judiciary, Subcommittee on Crime, Terrorism, and Homeland Security, convenes a very important

---

* http://bulk.resource.org/gpo.gov/hearings/109h/20016.pdf

oversight hearing of the Department of Homeland Security to examine the security of the nation's seaports and the cargo entering these ports.

I have long contended that protecting our nation's seaports is a vital aspect of the overall war on terror. Press reports have indicated there's a lack of cargo inspections taking place at our ports of entry. This Subcommittee is concerned about these reports and looks forward to hearing the Department's response to these accounts and the plans to assure adequate inspections to protect our ports and the cargo entering the United States are taking place. Today's hearing will focus on the efforts of three vital entities charged with protecting our nation's seaports from hostile threats.

First, we will hear from the two primary agencies within the Department of Homeland Security charged with protecting our ports—that is, the United States Coast Guard and the United States Customs and Border Protection. The United States Coast Guard is the nation's leading maritime law enforcement agency and has broad multifaceted jurisdictional authority. As part of Operation Noble Eagle, the Coast Guard is at a heightened state of alert, protecting more than 361 ports and 95,000 miles of coastline, which is America's longest border. The Coast Guard utilizes both Maritime Safety and Security Teams as well as Port Security Units to protect our seaports. Maritime Safety and Security Teams were created in direct response to the terrorist attacks on September 11, 2001, and are a part of the Department of Homeland Security's layered strategy directed at protecting our seaports and waterways. MSSTs provide waterborne and a modest level of shoreside antiterrorism force protection for strategic shipping, high-interest vessels, and critical infrastructure. MSSTs are a quick response force capable of rapid nationwide deployment via air, ground, or sea transportation in response to changing threat conditions and evolving maritime homeland security mission requirements. The Coast Guard Port Security Units, the PSUs, are Coast Guard units staffed primarily with selected Reservists. They provide waterborne and limited land-based protection for shipping and critical port facilities, both within the continental United States and in other theaters.

We will also hear from Customs and Border Protection. The CBP antiterrorism mission is not limited to the physical examination of cargo when it arrives in United States ports. The CBP, or the Customs and Border Protection, is also using intelligence from a number of sources to identify high-risk shipments in order to concentrate its inspection resources on them. For example, under bilateral agreements as part of the Container Security Initiative, CBP inspectors work in nearly 20 foreign ports to help ensure the security of U.S.-bound cargo before it disembarks.

Additionally, in November of 2001, the CBP established the National Targeting Center to serve as the national clearinghouse for targeting imported cargo for inspection. Among other tasks, the NTC interacts with law enforcement and the intelligence community to disseminate intelligence alerts to the ports. NTC, furthermore assists, in conducting research on incoming cargo, attempts to improve the targeting of cargo, and manages a National Targeting Training Program for CBP targeters.

Next, we will hear testimony from a local port authority, the Virginia Port Authority. The VPA has led the nation in radiological testing at its seaports and has successfully employed radiological monitoring equipment since December of 2002. In just this past year, in cooperation with Customs and Border Protection, VPA deployed some of its equipment to national security events, including the presidential inauguration.

Finally, we will hear testimony from a representative from the International Cargo Security Council. The International Cargo Security Council is a professional association of cargo transportation and security professionals from the entire spectrum of cargo security. One of ICSC's goals is to improve cargo transportation security through voluntary Government/industry efforts. In order to further this effort, ICSC is a leading proponent of encouraging industry to partake in CBP's Customs-Trade Partnership Against Terrorism. C-TPAT is a joint Government/business partnership where companies agree to improve the security in their supply chain in return for fast-lane border crossings and other important incentives. It is important to recognize that cargo and port security require the multilayered approach in order to deter and detect all vulnerabilities and hostile cargo. I am pleased that we have this representation here before us today and I look forward to their testimony, and I apologize to all of you. I normally don't give an opening statement this lengthy, but I think the subject matter at hand requires some detail.

And prior to introducing our distinguished witnesses, I am pleased to recognize the distinguished gentleman from Virginia, the ranking member of this subcommittee, Mr. Bobby Scott.

Mr. Scott: Thank you, Mr. Chairman. I'm pleased to join you in this hearing on law enforcement efforts at our ports. The development of the Department of Homeland Security in the wake of the 9/11 tragedies brought about a shift of several law enforcement agencies from one Department to another with changes and reorganizations of their responsibilities in some cases. There has been a significant change in responsibilities of the federal law enforcement entities to communicate, coordinate, and cooperate with state and local law enforcement entities. As a result, some confusion exists in the public and Congress and among the various federal and state agencies as to where the oversight responsibilities for these operations reside. I am of the opinion that we should seek to clarify any such confusion by first asserting our jurisdiction over all federal law enforcement entities and then working with those entities to insist their coordination and cooperation with each other and with state and local law enforcement entities. So I'm pleased to join you in this first of a series of hearings that we'll be conducting in this regard and commend you for your foresight and leadership in this matter. I'm particularly pleased to have Jeff Keever, the deputy director of our Virginia Port Authority, as one of our witnesses today. Our ports are a vital part of the nation's economy, handling over 2 billion tons of freight each year, and the Port of Virginia is the seventh-largest U.S. port in terms of general tonnage handled annually and the second largest on the East Coast.

Operating alongside the nation's largest naval base, assisting missions of the Defense Logistics Agency and the U.S. Transportation Command, security has always been a big job for the Port of Virginia. Secure, smooth, and efficient operations not only are critical to the deployment of our troops around the globe but also are why the port has maintained a robust annual growth rate of more than 9 percent over the past few years. As part of its focus on security, the Port of Virginia checks 100 percent of the containers leaving the port for radiation detection and monitoring equipment before they leave the port on trucks. And as a result of its successful cooperation with the U.S. Customs agencies, there has not been a theft at the port for about 8 years. That's quite a record in security when you consider that estimates of thefts from other ports across the U.S. range as high as $30 billion annually.

Yet despite the fact that our ports have risen to the challenges, their ability to continue to meet them in a world of changing threats and circumstances will depend in large measure on our assistance and support. I'm concerned, Mr. Chairman, that we have not been as diligent in supporting our seaports as we have with our airports and our other border crossings. It appears that we have left much of the responsibility to the ports themselves compared to what we have done to assist our airport and border crossing operations.

I expect that we'll hear about details of what we can do from our witnesses, so I look forward to their testimony and to working with you, Mr. Chairman, in clarifying our oversight responsibilities for the various law enforcement entities and strengthening our ports so that they can do their vital job in securing and sufficiently moving cargo and people. Again, I appreciate your leadership in this manner.

LEGISLATION

PROTECTING AMERICA'S PORTS, MARITIME TRANSPORTATION SECURITY ACT OF 2002
United States Department of Homeland Security,
Office of the Press Secretary
July 2003*

Contents
I. Press Release: Maritime Security Regulations
II. Fact Sheet: Implementation of the Maritime
            Transportation Security Act of 2002
III. Fact Sheet: Summarized Regulations

*http://users.mo-net.com/district8wr/public/MTSA_Port_Presskit.pdf

I. PRESS RELEASE: MARITIME SECURITY REGULATIONS

U.S. DEPARTMENT OF HOMELAND SECURITY
Office of the Press Secretary
FOR IMMEDIATE RELEASE July 1, 2003
Department of Homeland Security issues maritime security regulations

Rules mandate security improvements in the nation's seaports

WASHINGTON DC—The U.S. Department of Homeland Security announced the publication of security regulations today requiring sectors of the maritime industry to implement measures designed to protect America's ports and waterways from a terrorist attack.

"With 95 percent of our nation's international cargo carried by ship, port security is critical to ensuring our Nation's homeland and economic security," Secretary of Homeland Security Tom Ridge said. "The port security measures we are putting in place, both here at home and abroad, are about expanding our capabilities—strengthening a vitally important system with additional layers of defense.

"This effort is part of a broad international effort to increase global shipping security and one of many steps we are taking to better protect our ports and the ships traveling in our waters." The result of intense international and domestic efforts that began in November 2001, these regulations significantly strengthen the security of our ports by requiring preventive security measures and plans to deter threats and provide a framework for response in the event of an attack.

The regulations build on a comprehensive port security strategy and range of enhancements directed by the president following September 11, 2001, and implement significant portions of the Maritime Transportation Security Act of 2002 (MTSA). By requiring completion of security assessments, development of security plans, and implementation of security measures and procedures, these regulations will reduce the risk and mitigate the exposure of our ports and waterways to terrorist activity.

Developed using risk-based methodology, the security regulations focus on those sectors of maritime industry that have a higher risk of involvement in a transportation security incident, including various tank vessels, barges, large passenger vessels, cargo vessels, towing vessels, offshore oil and gas platforms, and port facilities that handle certain kinds of dangerous cargo or service the vessels listed above. An estimated 10,000 vessels, 5,000 facilities, and 40 outer continental shelf facilities will be directly affected.

The regulations require security measures that have three scalable security levels. Depending on security needs, measures may include passenger, vehicle and baggage screening procedures; security patrols; establishing restricted areas; personnel identification procedures; access control measures; and/or installation of surveillance equipment.

To promote innovation and flexibility, the Department of Homeland Security is also encouraging the private sector to develop acceptable alternatives to accommodate specific security measures. Alternatives that afford a level of security equal to the original regulation may be presented by individual industry entities.

The regulations published today amend other sections of the Code of Federal Regulations to implement Automatic Identification System (AIS) requirements for certain vessels, as required by MTSA. AIS is a system of equipment and technologies that automatically sends detailed ship information to other ships and shore-based agencies. Installing AIS equipment on certain vessels traveling in our waters will allow comprehensive, virtually instantaneous vessel tracking and monitoring, increasing security and safety in our shipping channels, and our awareness of maritime activity.

The regulations were developed through interagency teamwork within the Department of Homeland Security (the Coast Guard, Transportation Security Administration, and the Bureau of Customs and Border Protection) and with the Department of Transportation's Maritime Administration.

The interim final rules are effective as of July 1, 2003. They will be replaced by final rules by October 25, 2003. The Coast Guard is accepting written comments on the regulations for 30-days, and will hold a public meeting to discuss all of the maritime security interim final rules and the AIS interim rule on July 23, 2003, in Washington DC at the Grand Hyatt Hotel on 1000 H Street NW.

The regulations and details on submitting comments are published in a series of Federal Register notices that include a request for comment on the further implementation of the AIS, as required by MTSA. The Federal Register Docket can be viewed online at http://dms.dot.gov.

The docket numbers are as follows.

General USCG-2003-14792
Ports USCG-2003-14733
Vessels USCG-2003-14749
Facilities USCG-2003-14732
Outer continental shelf facilities USCG-2003-14745
AIS USCG-2003-14757
AIS request for comments USCG-2003-14878

II. FACT SHEET: IMPLEMENTATION OF THE MARITIME TRANSPORTATION SECURITY ACT OF 2002

U. S. DEPARTMENT OF HOMELAND SECURITY
Office of the Press Secretary
July 2003—Fact Sheet

Implementation of the Maritime Transportation Security Act

The Maritime Transportation Security Act of 2002 (MTSA), signed on November 25, 2002, by President Bush, is a landmark piece of legislation that is designed to protect the nation's ports and waterways from a terrorist attack. While the publication of new regulations on July 1 marks a significant milestone in the implementation of MTSA, the Department of Homeland Security has been taking major steps to implement the entire act. Below are the major components of the MTSA and the actions we have undertaken.

Threat and Security Assessments

Port Threat and Vulnerability Assessments

Preliminary assessments have been completed and we are now conducting comprehensive assessments at 55 critical ports that will provide local threat profiles and evaluate all aspects of security surrounding each port.

Vessel and Facility Vulnerability Assessments

Security plans are required on over 10,000 vessels and 5,000 facilities in the new regulations.

The regulations require the individual vessel owner to conduct a self-assessment and develop a security plan. The Transportation Security Administration, in conjunction with the Coast Guard and Information Analysis and Infrastructure Protection directorate, is developing an assessment tool that may be used by ports, vessels, and facilities that are required to conduct these self-assessments.

Foreign Port Assessments

Shipping is a global system. The security of the ports in other nations is important to the security of our ports. We will deploy verification and audit teams to ensure that 2,500 foreign ports have effective security programs.

Security Plans and Advisory Committees

National Maritime Security Plan and Advisory Committee

Another element of our layered maritime security strategy is the National Maritime Transportation Security Plan, an interagency initiative to build an overarching national strategy for protecting America's ports. The National Maritime Security Advisory Committee will advise the Secretary on this national strategy.

Area Maritime Transportation Security Plans and Committees

Adding yet another layer to our security strategy are Area Maritime Transportation Security Plans that will detail the response and preventative security policies. In addition, port security committees have already been informally established around the country and the new regulations establish Area Maritime Security Committees that will address the complex and diverse security needs of each of our 361 ports. In addition, the International Maritime Organization now requires all ships and port facilities to have security plans—making this a worldwide standard.

Vessel and Facility Security Plans

The new regulations require the owners and/or operators of over 10,000 vessels and 5,000 facilities to develop and implement security plans that may include passenger, vehicle and baggage screening procedures; security patrols; establishing restricted areas; personnel identification procedures; access control measures; and/or installation of surveillance equipment.

Security Incident Response Plans

The Coast Guard and other agencies have long had a suite of contingency and response plans for domestic incidents and terrorist activities. In addition, the new regulations require that key portions of industry address how they would respond to an incident in security plans that they must develop and submit to the Coast Guard for approval. Finally, we are coordinating security plans with other plans that already exist for other emergencies, such as oil spills and natural disasters.

Other Initiatives and Programs

Transportation Security Cards

The Transportation Security Administration is working on developing the Transportation Worker Identification Credential (TWIC). Over time, the TWIC will be used as a credential for transportation workers from all modes who have undergone, and passed, required background checks. TWIC will introduce a common credential, one that positively ties the person to the credential to the background check, which can be used in conjunction with access control to critical components of the nation's transportation infrastructure.

Maritime Safety and Security Teams

Maritime Safety and Security Teams are a Coast Guard rapid response force capable of nationwide deployment via air, ground, or sea transportation to meet emerging threats and were created in direct response to the terrorist attacks on September 11, 2001. Maritime Safety and Security Teams are already deployed to Seattle; Chesapeake, Virginia; Los Angeles/Long Beach; and Houston/ Galveston. More teams will be deployed by the end of this year to St. Mary's, Georgia, and the Port of New York/New Jersey. President Bush has included funds for six additional teams in his fiscal year 2004 budget request to Congress.

Grants

We made available $170 million in port security grants in June 2003 to 387 ports and facilities. Later this year we will make available an additional $105 million. This is on top of $92 million awarded by the Transportation Security Administration in 2002. In addition, the Office for Domestic Preparedness awarded another $75 million to 13 critical national seaports.

Maritime Intelligence

Using a variety of current and future operations, including the National Maritime Intelligence Center, and local and regional intelligence centers, we are focusing on gathering, analyzing and disseminating information. The president's fiscal year 2004 budget request to Congress includes $34 million to increase our intelligence capabilities.

Automatic Identification Systems

Automatic Identification Systems (AIS) immediately sends detailed ship information to other ships and shore-based agencies. The installation of AIS on certain vessels traveling in our waters, as required by the new regulations, will allow comprehensive, virtually instantaneous vessel tracking and monitoring, increasing safety and security in our shipping channels. This is also an international initiative.

Secure Systems of Transportation

Programs such as Operation Safe Commerce, which is led by TSA and the Bureau of Customs and Border Protection (CBP), and CBP's Customs-Trade Partnership Against Terrorism will help identify ways to better secure cargo containers and add additional layers of security throughout the entire sea transportation system.

International Seafarer Identification

Recently adopted international agreements provide for a program to improve the security of seafarers documents through the use of a biometric indicator, enhanced tamper resistant features, and the establishment of national databases, all of which will create uniform and verifiable credentials for the mariners around the world.

Extension of Seaward Jurisdiction

MTSA extended certain Coast Guard authorities out to 12 nautical miles from the U.S. coast. This measure is part of our strategy to push our borders out—to gain information about what is coming in and deal with it as far away from our shores as possible and have the authority to exercise protective actions and measures.

Deepwater Ports

This provision added natural gas facilities to the Coast Guard's previous authority to regulate other kinds of deepwater ports. We expect to receive two to three applications per year. These facilities will allow for the unloading of natural gas offshore, and will help increase our ability to import natural gas.

Sea Marshals

Since shortly after September 11, 2001, the Coast Guard has been placing armed personnel on key vessels as they transit in and out of port to keep those vessels from being used by terrorists as weapons. Sea marshals ensure positive control, 24 hours a day, seven days a week of over 21,000 vessels arrivals, departures and interport transits in the 55 most critical ports. The president has included funding for 53 sea marshals in his fiscal year 2004 budget request to Congress.

Maritime Security Professional Training

The publication of these regulations is the beginning of the work begun by the Maritime Administration at the Department of Transportation, in cooperation with the Coast Guard and the Transportation Security Administration, to establish standards for training. We are continuing the cooperative effort of these agencies and the international community to fully leverage existing security training expertise.

III. FACT SHEET: SUMMARIZED REGULATIONS

U. S. DEPARTMENT OF HOMELAND SECURITY
Office of the Press Secretary
July 2003—Summarized Regulations

New Maritime Security Regulations

Making Our Waters Safer

The Maritime Transportation Security Act of 2002 (MTSA), the new security amendments to the International Convention for the Safety of Life at Sea 1974 (SOLAS), and its complementary International Ship and Port Facility Security Code (ISPS) strengthen and add additional protective layers of defense to our nation's port security.

- MTSA: Designed to protect the nation's ports and waterways from a terrorist attack. Landmark legislation that requires area maritime security committees, security plans for facilities and vessels that may be involved in a transportation security incident
- ISPS: First multilateral ship and port security standard ever created. Implementation scheduled for 2004; requires all nations to develop port and ship security plans.

Regulations specify requirements for:

- Security assessments, development of security plans, implementation of measures to address access control, security monitoring, and physical, passenger, personnel, baggage and cargo security.
- Annual exercises and/or drills
- Designation of security personnel for each vessel or facility
- Installation of Automatic Identification System (AIS), equipment that automatically sends detailed ship information to other ships and shore-based agencies

Who the Regulations Will Apply To

The regulations focus on those entities that may be involved in a transportation security incident, including various tank vessels, barges, large passenger vessels, cargo vessels, towing vessels, offshore oil and gas platforms, and port facilities that handle certain kinds of dangerous cargo or service the vessels listed above.

When

July 1, 2003: Temporary Interim Rules published; effective date of regulations
July 23, 2003: Public meeting in Washington DC
July 31, 2003: Deadline for submission of written comments
October 2003: Projected publication of Final Rule
November 2003: Effective date of Final Rules (30 days from publication)
Dec. 31, 2003: Deadline for submission of security plans
July 1, 2004: International and domestic deadline for implementation of MTSA
                regulations & ISPS requirements

Where

Ports of all sizes throughout the country and the world.

Regulatory Highlights

The new MTSA security regulations cover vessels and facilities operating on or adjacent to waters subject to the jurisdiction of the United States and are split into six separate parts. Following a general section that discusses general requirements and definitions, each of the sections focuses on a specific segment of the marine industry: ports, vessels, facilities, and outer continental shelf facilities. A final regulation addresses the installation of Automatic Identification Systems (AIS). These regulations are part of the new Subchapter H of Title 33 of the Code of Federal Regulations (CFR), except for AIS, which amends several sections of the CFR. The regulations have common elements, including the following:

Security Officers and Training for All Personnel

Requires the designation of an individual who will be responsible for the vessel or facility security program, outlines the qualifications for security officers, and requires all personnel to have training so that they are ready and able to implement the security plan.

Security Assessments and Plans

Requires owners and operators to assess the vulnerabilities, and develop plans that may include passenger, vehicle and baggage screening procedures; security patrols; establishing restricted areas; personnel identification procedures; access control measures; and/or installation of surveillance equipment.

General—Parts 101 & 102

Alternative Security Programs/Equivalencies

Provides flexibility and encourages innovation by allowing industry to submit, for Coast Guard approval, alternative security programs that provide an equal level of security as required in the regulations.

Maritime Security Directives

- Gives the Coast Guard the authority to issue supplemental directives that require the implementation of specific security measures within the context of security plans, allowing the government to communicate sensitive security information to industry
- Increased threat = increased security
- Establishes three levels of security, which align with an international system, and correspond to the Homeland Security Advisory System. These levels allow industry to increase and decrease security measures based on threat conditions, providing reasonable and effective security.

Communication of Maritime Security Information

Requires the Coast Guard to communicate information on threats to the appropriate members of maritime industry and other authorities in the port.

Ports—Part 103

Federal Maritime Security Coordinators

Designates the Coast Guard Captains of the Port as Federal Maritime Security Coordinators, giving them the authority to oversee and direct the necessary activities of increasing security of our ports.

Area Maritime Security Committees (AMS)

Establishes Area Maritime Security Committees, made up of members of other federal, state and local agencies, industry and others, to assess the specific vulnerabilities in each of our 361 ports and develop plans for very complex and diverse security requirements within the port areas.

Risk Assessments and Security Plans

Requires the AMS Committees to conduct risk assessments, building on preliminary assessments already conducted in 47 key ports, which examine the threats, consequences, and vulnerabilities of the port. Details the elements of Area Maritime Security Plans, including requiring an annual exercise.

Vessels—Part 104

Examples of vessels most directly impacted by the new regulations:

- Small cruise ship traveling from Chicago to Montreal
- SOLAS-certified cargo ship carrying grain traveling from Jacksonville to New York
- Container vessel carrying cargo from New Orleans to San Juan
- Container vessel carrying cargo from Hong Kong to Los Angeles
- Barge carrying auto part containers traveling from Seattle to Vancouver
- Cruise ship on a Caribbean voyage
- Dinner boat on the Chesapeake Bay carrying more than 150 people
- Gaming boat on the Mississippi
- Ferries operating in Puget Sound, Washington
- Barge carrying home heating oil on the Hudson River
- Tanker carrying liquefied natural gas
- Supply vessel heading to an offshore oil rig
- Towing vessel pushing an oil barge on the Mississippi River

Facilities—Part 105

Examples of maritime facilities most directly impacted by the new regulations:

- Facility that handles dangerous cargo, including oil, chemicals, and explosives
- Facility that services vessels that carry more than 150 passengers
- Facility that receives vessels on international voyages, including vessels solely navigating the Great Lakes.

Outer Continental Shelf Facilities—Part 106

Examples of offshore oil & gas platforms most directly impacted by the new regulations:

- Oil rig that produces more than 100,000 barrels of oil per day
- Platform that produces more than 200 million cubic feet of natural gas per day
- Platform that is consistently manned by more than 150 people

Automatic Identification Systems

The regulations require the installation of Automatic Identification System (AIS) on certain vessels. AIS equipment is a system that automatically sends detailed ship information to other ships and shore-based agencies. Installing AIS equipment on certain vessels traveling in our waters will allow comprehensive, virtually instantaneous vessel tracking and monitoring, increasing security and safety in our shipping channels.

Examples of vessels required to install an Automatic Identification System:

- Ships on an international voyage
- Large passenger vessels
- Other commercial vessels operating in a Vessel Traffic System

PRESIDENTIAL STATEMENT ON THE PORT SECURITY IMPROVEMENT ACT OF 2006

President George W. Bush
The White House, Office of the Press Secretary
September 14, 2006*

Today, the Senate passed legislation to strengthen my administration's efforts to secure our ports and detect dangers before they reach America's shores.

By furthering our coordination with responsible countries throughout the world, the Port Security Improvement Act of 2006 will help secure the global supply chain and help ensure the smooth flow of commerce into and out of the United States. I am pleased this bill codifies several administration efforts that have already substantially improved security at our ports, including the Container Security Initiative, which identifies and inspects cargo at foreign ports before they are placed on vessels destined for the United States, and the Customs-Trade Partnership Against Terrorism, which helps our international trading partners secure their supply chains before shipping goods into our country.

I look forward to the House and Senate resolving their differences in Conference and sending this legislation to me for my signature.

---

*http://www.whitehouse.gov/news/releases/2006/09/20060914-9.html

Notes

1. Pub. L. No. 107–295, 116 Stat. 2064 (2002).

2. Zeigert, Amy, et al. "Port Security: Improving Emergency Response Capabilities at the Ports of Los Angeles and Long Beach." *California Policy Options 2005*. University of California Los Angeles, School of Public Affairs (Los Angeles, Calif. 2005).

3. None of the listings in this testimony is meant to be exhaustive of all the efforts under way. The Coast Guard has a range of activities under way for reducing seaport vulnerabilities that extends beyond the actions shown here. Such activities include, among others the use of armed boarding officers, formerly known as sea marshals, who board high-interest vessels arriving or departing U.S. seaports and stand guard in critical areas of the vessels; the establishment of Maritime Safety and Security Teams (MSST) to provide antiterrorism protection for strategic shipping, high-interest vessels, and critical infrastructure; and the underwater port security system, which uses trained divers and robotic cameras to check ship hulls and piers and an underwater intruder detection system. We have not evaluated the effectiveness of these activities.

4. Another program to help secure the overseas supply chain process is the Coast Guard's International Port Security Program. In response to being required under MTSA to assess antiterrorism measures maintained at foreign seaports, the Coast Guard established this program in April 2004 to protect the global shipping industry by helping foreign nations evaluate security measures in their seaports. Through bilateral or multilateral discussions, the Coast Guard and the host nations review the implementation of security measures against established security standards, such as the International Maritime Organization's ISPS Code. To conduct the program, the Coast Guard has assigned officials to three regions (Asia-Pacific, Europe/Africa/Middle East, and Central/South America) to facilitate the discussions. In addition, a Coast Guard team has been established to conduct country/port visits, discuss security measures implemented, and develop best practices between countries. Each year the Coast Guard seeks to visit approximately 45 countries that conduct maritime trade with the United States.

5. The nation's three largest container port regions (Los Angeles/Long Beach, New York/New Jersey, and Seattle/Tacoma) are involved in the Operation Safe Commerce pilot project.

6. GAO, *Maritime Security: New Structures Have Improved Information Sharing, but Security Clearance Processing Requires Further Attention*, GAO-05-394 (Washington DC: April 15, 2005).

7. GAO, Container Security: Expansion of Key Customs Programs Will Require Greater Attention to Critical Success Factors, GAO-03-770 (Washington DC: July 2003); and GAO, Homeland Security: Summary of Challenges Faced in Targeting Oceangoing Cargo Containers for Inspection, GAO-04-557T (Washington DC: March 2004). In addition, we have additional work under way regarding the Container Security Initiative program and expect to issue our report in May.

8. GAO, *Container Security: Expansion of Key Customs Programs Will Require Greater Attention to Critical Success Factors*, GAO-03-770 (Washington, D.C: July 2003).

9. GAO, Homeland Security: Challenges Facing the Coast Guard as It Transitions to the New Department, GAO-03-467T (Washington DC: February 2003).

10. GAO, Coast Guard: Station Readiness Improving, but Resource Challenges and Management Concerns Remain, GAO-05-161 (Washington DC: Jan. 31, 2005).

11. GAO, *Maritime Security: Substantial Work Remains to Translate New Planning Requirements into Effective Port Security,* GAO-04-838 (Washington DC: June 30, 2004).

12. GAO, *High-Risk Series: An Update,* GAO-05-207 (Washington DC: Jan. 2005).

13. GAO, Homeland Security: Information Sharing Responsibilities, Challenges, and Key Management Issues, GAO-03-1165T (Washington DC: Sept. 17, 2003); and Homeland Security: Information-Sharing Responsibilities, Challenges, and Key Management Issues, GAO-03-715T (Washington DC: May 8, 2003).

14. GAO, Homeland Security: Process for Reporting Lessons Learned from Seaport Exercises Needs Further Attention, GAO-05-170 (Washington DC: January 2005).

15. Of the facilities testing TSA's prototype, we visited ports and facilities in the Delaware River Region, including Wilmington Port Authority, the Philadelphia Maritime Exchange, and the South Jersey Port. We also visited ports and facilities on the West Coast, including those in the Port of Seattle, Port of Los Angeles, and Port of Long Beach as well as ports and facilities in Florida, including Port Everglades and the Port of Jacksonville.

16. GAO, Port Security: Better Planning Needed to Develop and Operate Maritime Worker Identification Card Program, GAO-05-106 (Washington DC: December 2004).

17. GAO, *Maritime Security: Substantial Work Remains to Translate New Planning* Requirements into Effective Port Security, GAO-04-838 (Washington DC: June 2004).

18. DHS has proposed consolidating homeland grant programs into a single program. Known as the Targeted Infrastructure Protection Program (TIPP), the program would lump together grant funding for transit, port security and other critical infrastructure, and eliminate specific grant programs for port, rail, truck, intercity bus, and nongovernmental organizations security. In its fiscal year 2006 budget request, the administration proposed $600 million for TIPP, a $260-million increase in overall funding from fiscal year 2005 for the specific transportation security grant programs. In fiscal year 2005, funding for port, rail, truck, intercity bus, and nongovernmental organizations security totaled $340 million.

19. GAO, *National Preparedness: Integration of Federal, State, Local, and Private Sector Efforts Is Critical to an Effective National Strategy for Homeland Security*, GAO-02-621T (Washington DC: April 2002).

20. The Advisory Panel to Assess Domestic Response Capabilities for Terrorism Involving Weapons of Mass Destruction, *V. Forging America's New Normalcy* (Arlington, VA: Dec. 15, 2003).

21. GAO, Homeland Security: Observations on the National Strategies Related to Terrorism, GAO-04-1075T (Washington DC: Sept. 22, 2004).

22. Greenberg, Michael D., Chalk, Pete, Willis, Henry H., Khilko, Ivan. and Ortiz, David S.; *Maritime Terrorism: Risk and Liability.* RAND Center for Terrorism Risk Management Policy. 2006. p. xxi.

23. Executive Office of the President. *The National Strategy for Maritime Security.* September 20, 2005. p. 4.

24 Allison, Graham. Remarks on "CNN Presents: Nuclear Terror." *CNN Presents.* Broadcast transcript. Sept. 12, 2004. [http://transcripts.cnn.com/TRANSCRIPTS/0409/12/cp.00.html].

25. Gorman, Siobhan and Sydney J. Freedberg, Jr. "Early Warning." *The National Journal.* June 11, 2005.

26. For further analysis on this topic, see CRS Report RS21293, *Terrorist Nuclear Attacks on Seaports: Threat and Response*, by Jonathan Medalia.

27. Hegland, Corine, and Webb, Greg. "The Threat," *National Journal*. April 15, 2005. [http://nationaljournal.com/members/news/2005/04/0415nj1.htm]; Senator Richard G. Lugar. "The Lugar Survey on Proliferation Threats and Responses." June 2005. p. 6. [http://lugar.senate.gov/reports/NPSurvey.pdf].

28 Bunn, Matthew and Weir, Anthony. *Securing the Bomb 2006*. John F. Kennedy School of Government Harvard University. Commissioned by the Nuclear Threat Initiative. July 2006. p. 29.

29. Collins, Graham P. "Kim's Big Fizzle: The Physics Behind A Nuclear Dud." *Scientific American*. Jan. 2007.

30. Department of Homeland Security (DHS). Remarks by Secretary of Homeland Security Michael Chertoff at George Mason University. Fairfax, VA. April 26, 2006.

31. de Rugy, Veronique. "Is Port Security Spending Making Us Safer?" American Enterprise Institute. Working Paper #115. Sept. 7, 2005. p. 8.

32. For further information on dirty bombs, see CRS Report RS21528, *Terrorist 'Dirty Bombs': A Brief Primer*, by Jonathan Medalia.

33. Ibid. Booz Allen Hamilton. 2003. p. 1.

34. Senator Richard G. Lugar. "The Lugar Survey on Proliferation Threats and Responses." June 2005. p. 6. [http://lugar.senate.gov/reports/NPSurvey.pdf].

35. Government Accountability Office (GAO). *Nuclear Nonproliferation: U.S. and International Assistance Efforts to Control Sealed Radioactive Sources Need Strengthening*. GAO-03-638. May 16, 2003. p. 65.

36. Mayer, Josh. "Al Qaeda Feared to Have Dirty Bombs." *Los Angeles Times*. Feb. 8, 2003. p. 1.

37. Gilbert, Gary. Senior V.P., Hutchison Port Holdings. Statement before the Senate Homeland Security and Governmental Affairs Committee, Permanent Investigations Subcommittee. March 30, 2006.

38. Singer, S. Fred., Hoover Institution, Stanford Univ. "Nuclear Terrorism: Facts and Fantasies." *Washington Times*. (Commentary). April 5, 2002.

39. *"Dirty Bomb" Fact Sheet*. Center for International Security and Cooperation, Stanford University. Oct. 2006. [http://iis-db.stanford.edu/pubs/20769/dirty_bomb_facts.pdf].

40. Burgess, Mark. "Pascal's New Wager: The Dirty Bomb Threat Heightens." Center for Defense Information. Washington. Feb. 4, 2003. [http://www.cdi.org/terrorism/dirty-bomb.cfm].

41. Sterngold, James. "Assessing the Risk of Nuclear Terrorism" *San Francisco Chronicle*. April 18, 2004.; Dotinga, Randy. "After the Beep, Exit the Premises." *Wired News*. May 6, 2004. [http://www.wired.com/news/technology/1,63328-0.html].

42. Taylor, Guy. "Padilla Case Mum on 'Dirty Bomb'." *Washington Times*. Nov. 24, 2005. p. A03.

43. Burgess, Mark. Feb. 4, 2003.

44. See, for example, Hon. Edward J. Markey. "Rep. Markey Urges Scanning for Nuclear Devices in Container Ships Before They Arrive at U.S. Ports." Press release. Sept. 28, 2006; Office of Senator Patty Murray. "Cargo Security: Floor Remarks by Senator Patty Murray Introducing the GreenLane Bill for Senate Consideration." Press release. Sept. 7, 2006.

45. For an analysis of smuggling a nuclear weapon in an oil tanker, see CRS Report RS21997, *Port and Maritime Security: Potential for Terrorist Nuclear Attack Using Oil Tankers*, by Jonathan Medalia.

46. Ibid.

47. U.S. Department of Transportation (DOT). *An Assessment of the U.S. Marine Transportation System.* Report to Congress. Sept. 1999.

48. U.S. Maritime Administration (MARAD). *Vessel Calls at U.S. and World Ports 2005.* April 2006. p. 1.

49. Stables, Eleanor. "For Better Cargo Security, Government Needs to Think 'Outside the Box,' Experts Say." *CQ Homeland Security.* Oct. 1, 2006.

50. Finnegan, William. "Watching the Waterfront." *The New Yorker.* June 19, 2006. p. 63.

51. Government Accountability Office (GAO). *Cargo Security: Partnership Program Grants Importers Reduced Scrutiny With Limited Assurance of Improved Security.* GAO-05-404. March, 2005. p. 7.

52. Dept. of Homeland Security (DHS). *Budget-in-Brief, Fiscal Year 2006.* [https://www.dhs.gov/xlibrary/assets/Budget_BIB-FY2006.pdf].

53. Office of Congressman Edward J. Markey. Personal communication with staff. Jan. 5, 2004.

54. Turner, Pamela J., Assistant Secretary for Legislative Affairs, Department of Homeland Security (DHS). Letter to U.S. Representative Edward Markey. April 15, 2004. p. 1.

55. Sandia National Laboratories (SNL). *Guidance on Risk Analysis and Safety Implications of a Large Liquefied Natural Gas (LNG) Spill Over Water.* SAND2004-6258. Albuquerque, NM. Dec. 2004. pp. 49–50.

56. SNL. Dec. 2004. pp. 61–62.

57. Clarke, Richard A., et al. *LNG Facilities in Urban Areas.* Good Harbor Consulting, LLC. Prepared for the Rhode Island Office of Attorney General. GHC-RI-0505A. May 2005.

58. McLaughlin, J. "LNG is Nowhere Near as Dangerous as People Are Making it Out to Be." *Lloyd's List.* Feb. 8, 2005. p5.

59. Behr, Peter. "Higher Gas Price Sets Stage for LNG." *Washington Post.* July 5, 2003. p. D10.

60. Federal Energy Regulatory Commission (FERC). *Vista del Sol LNG Terminal Project, Draft Environmental Impact Statement.* FERC/EIS-0176D. Dec. 2004. p. 4–162.

61. FERC. FERC/EIS-0176D. Dec. 2004. p4–162. Notwithstanding this assertion, in its subsequent draft review of the Long Beach LNG terminal proposal, the FERC states that "the historical probability of a successful terrorist event would be less than seven chances in a million per year . . ." See FERC. Oct. 7, 2005. p. ES-14.

62. Woolsey, James. Remarks before the National Commission on Energy LNG Forum, Washington DC, June 21, 2006.

63. Grant, Richard, President, Distrigas. Testimony before the Senate Committee on Energy and Natural Resources, Subcommittee on Energy hearing on "The Future of Liquefied Natural Gas: Siting and Safety." Feb. 15, 2005.

64. U.S. Coast Guard. *U.S. Coast Guard Captain of the Port Long Island Sound Waterways Suitability Report for the Proposed Broadwater Liquefied Natural Gas Facility.* Sept. 21, 2006. p. 146.

65. Ibid.

66. Congressman Frank Pallone, Jr. "Pallone Calls for Increased Funding for Ferry Security." Press release. July 15, 2005.

67. Greenberg, M.D. et al. 2006. p. 95.

68. Lipton, Eric. "Trying to Keep the Nation's Ferries Safe from Terrorists." New York Times. March 19, 2005.

69. U.S. Dept. of Justice, Office of the Inspector General. *The Federal Bureau of Investigation's Efforts to Protect the Nation's Seaports.* Audit Report 06-26. March 2006. p. 52.

70. Shukovsky, Paul and Barber, Mike. "Ferries a Top Terror Target, FBI Cautions." *Seattle Post-Intelligencer.* April 21, 2006. p. A1.

71. Ibid.

72. Gen. Ralph Eberhart, U.S. Northern Command, as quoted in "Militants Eyeing Seaborne Attack, U.S. General Says." Reuters. Aug. 25, 2004.

73. Köknar, Ali M. "Maritime Terrorism: a New Challenge for NATO." *Energy Security.* Institute for the Analysis of Global Security (IAGS). Jan. 24, 2005.

74. National Memorial Institute for the Prevention of Terrorism (MIPT). Terrorist incident reports. July 20, 2006. [http://www.tkb.org/IncidentTargetModule.jsp].

75. MIPT. July 20, 2006.

76. For further discussion, see CRS Report RL31733, *Port and Maritime Security: Background and Issues for Congress,* by John F. Frittelli.

77. Valencia, Mark J. and Young, Adam J. "Conflation of Piracy and Terrorism in Southeast Asia: Rectitude and Utility." *Contemporary Southeast Asia.* Vol. 25. No. 2. Aug. 2003. pp. 269–283.

78. Captain James Pelkofski, U.S. Navy. "Before the Storm: al Qaeda's Coming Maritime Campaign." *Proceedings.* U.S. Naval Institute. Vol. 132. No. 12. Dec. 2005. [http://www.usni.org/proceedings/Articles05/Pro12Pelkofski.html].

79. Ibid.

80. Pub. L. No. 109–347, 120 Stat. 1884 (2006).

81. Pub. L. No. 109–347, 120 Stat. 1884 (2006).

82. The Implementing Recommendations of the 9/11 Commission Act of 2007 amended a SAFE Port Act provision on scanning all United States-bound containers at foreign ports. See Pub. L. No. 110–53, §1701(a), 121 Stat. 266, 489–90. This amendment is discussed later in this testimony.

83. A list of related GAO products may be found at the end of this testimony.

8

International Perspectives:
Regional and Global

REGIONAL PERSPECTIVES

Southeast Asia

ARF STATEMENT ON COOPERATION AGAINST PIRACY AND
OTHER THREATS TO SECURITY
Association of Southeast Asian Nations Regional Forum
June 17, 2003*

The chairman of the ASEAN Regional Forum (ARF), on behalf of the participating states and organization, issues the following statement:

1. Recognizing that:
    a. Piracy and armed robbery against ships and the potential for terrorist
        attacks on vulnerable sea shipping threaten the growth of the Asia-
        Pacific region and disrupt the stability of global commerce, particularly
        as these have become tools of transnational organized crime;

---

*http://www.aseansec.org/14837.htm

b. ARF countries represent approximately 80 percent of the world's GDP and trade, and even more of maritime or container shipping trade;

c. Maritime security is an indispensable and fundamental condition for the welfare and economic security of the ARF region. Ensuring this security is in the direct interest of all countries, and in particular the ARF countries;

d. Most maritime armed robberies in the Asia-Pacific region tend to occur in the coastal and archipelagic waters. Trends over the last few years indicate that piracy and armed robbery against ships continue to threaten to be a significant problem in the Asia-Pacific region;

e. To deal with this increasingly violent international crime, it is necessary to step up broad-based regional cooperative efforts to combat transnational organized crime, including through cooperation and coordination among all institutions concerned, such as naval units, coastal patrol and law enforcement agencies, shipping companies, crews, and port authorities;

f. Such efforts must be based on relevant international law, including the 1982 Law of the Sea Convention;

g. It is important that there be national and regional cooperation to ensure that maritime criminals and pirates do not evade prosecution;

h. Effective responses to maritime crime require regional maritime security strategies and multilateral cooperation in their implementation;

i. National, regional, and international efforts to combat terrorism also enhance the ability to combat transnational organized crime and armed robberies against ships.

2. The Participants of ARF endeavor to achieve effective implementation of the relevant international instruments and recommendations/guidelines for the suppression of piracy and armed robbery against ships, including the United Nations Convention on the Law of the Sea, the Convention for the Suppression of Unlawful Acts against the Safety of Maritime Navigation (1988) and its Protocol for the Suppression of Unlawful Acts against the Safety of Fixed Platforms Located on the Continental Shelf; and the International Maritime Organization's recommendations and guidelines for preventing and suppressing piracy and armed robbery against ships at sea; the International Convention for the Safety of Life at Sea (1974), particularly the new Chapter XI-2 and the International Ship and Port Facilities Security (ISPS Code); and to enhance their coordination and cooperation to that end. The members of ARF express their commitment to become parties to the Convention for the Suppression of Unlawful Acts Against the Safety of Maritime Navigation, 1988 and its Protocol for the Suppression of Unlawful Acts Against the Safety of Fixed Platforms Located on the Continental Shelves as soon as possible, if they have not yet done so.

3. The ARF Participants will work together to protect ships engaged in international voyages by:

a. Enhancing cooperation on fighting piracy and armed robbery in the region between ARF participants' shipping and organizations such as the

International Maritime Organization (IMO) and the Piracy Reporting Center of the International Maritime Bureau (IMB);

b. Early implementation of the comprehensive amendment to the International Convention for the Safety of Life at Sea, 1974, and the new ISPS Code adopted by the Diplomatic Conference on Maritime Security in December 2002; as called for in Conference Resolution 6.

c. Affirming their responsibilities to prosecute, in accordance with relevant domestic laws, perpetrators of acts of piracy and armed robbery against ships.

d. Endorsing the development by the International Maritime Organization of the following instruments and recommendations/guidance for use in preventing and suppressing piracy and armed robbery against ships:

- Recommendations to governments for preventing and suppressing piracy and armed robbery against ships, MSC/Circ. 622/Rev. I, June 16, 1999;
- Guidance to shipowners and ship operators, shipmasters and crews on preventing and suppressing acts of piracy and armed robbery against ships, MSC/Circ. 623/Rev. 3, May 29, 2002; Directives for Maritime Rescue Coordination Centers (MRCCs), MSC/Circ. 967, June 6, 2000;
- Interim Procedures for MRCCs on Receipt of Distress Alerts, MSC/Circ. 959, June 20, 2000;
- Resolution A. 922 (22)—Code of Practice for the investigation of the crimes of piracy and armed robberies against ships;
- Resolution A. 923 (22)—"Phantom" ships and registration process; and
- Convention for the Suppression of Unlawful Acts Against the Safety of Maritime Navigation, 1988 and its Protocol for the Suppression of Unlawful Acts Against the Safety of Fixed Platforms Located on the Continental Shelf.

4. The ARF participants commit to undertake the following actions:

a. Encourage bilateral and multilateral maritime cooperation among ARF members to combat piracy, including at the present increased personnel contact among personnel, information exchanges and antipiracy exercises on the basis of respecting territorial integrity, sovereignty, sovereign rights and jurisdiction and in accordance with the principles of voluntary participation and agreement in line with the respective applicable international conventions.

b. Encourage ARF consideration and future discussion of new IMB proposals (10/23/02) on prescribed traffic lanes for large supertankers with coastguard or naval escort whenever and wherever possible on the high sea upon the consent of all ARF countries concerned. If considered feasible, forward to IMO for adoption as appropriate.

c. Provide, where and when possible, technical assistance and capacity-building infrastructure to countries that need help in developing necessary laws, extending training, and where and when possible, providing equipment.

d.   Enhance ARF participants' ability to share information domestically and internationally as a vital component in the fight against maritime piracy and armed robberies.

e.   Institute regional ARF cooperation and training in antipiracy and security. Cooperate with the world maritime university (under the IMO) as regards education and training of personal engaged in antipiracy and security.

f.   Encourage greater ARF member states' transport industries and shipping community to report incidents to the relevant coastal states and to ships' flag administration for follow up action by the proper authorities as prescribed in MSC/Circ. 623. In addition to the IMO, ships may also report to secondary reporting centers such as the International Maritime Bureau's Piracy Reporting Center in Kuala Lumpur.

g.   Encourage the ARF Chair to explore with the ASEAN Secretariat or an ARF participant whether it would be willing to coordinate logging of requests for assistance by ARF participants in implementing the provisions of the Convention for the Suppression of Unlawful Acts Against the Safety of Maritime Navigation, 1988 and its Protocol for the Suppression of Unlawful Acts Against the Safety of Fixed Platforms on the Continental Shelf and other relevant instruments.

h.   Review progress on efforts to combat maritime piracy and armed robberies against ships at the 11th ARF Ministerial meeting in 2004, and share their experiences with member states of the IMO.

i.   Endorse the ongoing efforts to establish a legal framework for regional cooperation to combat piracy and armed robberies against ships.

j.   Welcome the discussion in the IMO on various issues relating to the delivery of criminals who have committed crimes on a ship on the high sea or on the exclusive economic zone to the authorities of port state by the master of the ship, and hope to reach a conclusion as soon as possible (IMO document "LEG 85/10").

k.   Nothing in this statement, nor any act or activity carried out in pursuant to this statement, should prejudice the position of ARF countries with regard to any unsettled dispute concerning sovereignty or other rights over territory.

APEC AND MARITIME SECURITY MEASURES

Ambassador Makarim Wibisono
Chairman of the APEC Counterterrorism Task Force
Presented to the APEC High-Level Conference
on Maritime Security
Manila, Philippines
September 8–9, 2003

International terrorism has made the world a far more dangerous place than when the Asia Pacific Economic Cooperation (APEC) was born in 1989. And the need to secure our region's economy and trade from terrorism has become an important and major focus of the APEC agenda. At the meeting of APEC leaders in Shanghai in 2001, counterterrorism efforts were placed firmly on the APEC agenda.

The simple reason for this is that terrorism is one of the most destructive threats to the APEC goals of free trade and investment in the Asia-Pacific region. Terrorism not only destroys lives and property, but undermines market confidence, inflates the cost of trade and reduces market activity.

At the same time, more stringent security measures have the potential to increase the cost of trading goods and services, and slow the movement of passengers across borders. Therefore, failure to act would have severe repercussions and puts APEC's economies at risk.

Following the tragic events of September 11, 2001, the International Maritime Organization (IMO) has developed new measures relating to the security of ships and port facilities. In December 2002, the Diplomatic Conference on Maritime Security adopted new provisions for the 1974 International Convention of Safety of Life at Sea. The International Ship and Port Facility Security Code (ISPS Code) provides us measures and procedures to prevent acts of terrorism that threaten the security of passengers and crews and the safety of ships.

Implementing new counterterrorism measures will require a substantial investment in new infrastructure. In the case of shipping, the Organization of Economic Cooperation and Development (OECD) calculates that the cost to implement the IMO package of security measures contained in the Safety of Life At Sea (SOLAS) Convention and the ISPS Code to be over US$2 billion. The APEC economies believe that these costs should be viewed as an investment that will reduce the risk premiums and ensure continued economic growth.

APEC's comprehensive strategy to protect our region from terrorism was unveiled by APEC leaders in Los Cabos, Mexico, last October when they issued their statement on fighting terrorism and promoting growth. APEC's counterterrorism strategy includes the Secure Trade in the APEC Region (STAR) Initiative; preventing the flow of funds to terrorists; protecting critical infrastructure; and working in partnership with the private sector to implement these measures.

APEC represents about 60 percent of the world's GDP and half of its trade. Most of the world's largest seaports and busiest airports are located in APEC economies. The threat of terrorism not only reduces trade flow, but if terrorists were to successfully cause a shutdown of major ports, this would severely affect the economies of the region.

To protect our trade, APEC leaders have committed their economies to implement the Standard Terminal Arrival Route (STAR) Initiative to strengthen security against terrorist threats while simultaneously boosting trade efficiency. The program involves protecting cargo, ships, aviation, and people crossing borders.

APEC recognizes that considerable investment will be needed to fully implement the system. However, by reducing the economic costs of terrorism while facilitating the more efficient movement of goods and people across borders, such an investment is expected to result in significant economic returns.

APEC economies are also working to protect cargo by implementing a Container Security Regime. This initiative ensures the in-transit integrity of containers and provides electronic information on a container's contents to customs, port, and shipping officials as early as possible in the supply chain.

By the year 2005, the APEC economies have also agreed to implement common standards for an electronic customs reporting system developed by the World Customs Organization (WCO), which will provide the data necessary to target high-risk shipments for inspection and facilitate trade. APEC is pursuing a number of programs, including training, to simplify and harmonize customs procedures so as to improve the accuracy, certainty, uniformity, and transparency of customs procedures.

APEC is also helping to build the systemic risk management capacity necessary to allow customs administrations to target resources where they are most needed. The main way that the STAR Initiative is anticipated to protect ships engaged in international voyages is through the promotion of ship and port security plans by July 2004. This will be followed by the installation of automatic identification systems on certain ships by December 2004.

The fight against pirates in the region is also being enhanced with increased cooperation between APEC fora and organizations such as the International Maritime Bureau's Piracy Reporting Center. It is also developing standards for detection equipment and other security technology. The Accreditation of Seafarer Manning Agencies in the APEC Region Project aims to develop a system for accrediting manning agents who provide employees to maritime companies in the Asia-Pacific region.

The Transport Working Group is also undertaking projects to assess the benefits of new technologies as they relate to the transportation industry. The working group agreed to a Pathfinder Initiative on the Global Navigational Satellite Systems. This will significantly enhance the safety of international shipping. Another project involves applying track and trace technologies to the logistics chain. These measures not only improve the visibility, quality, and reliability of delivery of products to export markets but also enhance the security of the supply chain.

The use of Intelligent Transportation Systems (ITS) will also enhance the end-to-end supply chain security and increase the efficiency of trade. These systems involve the use of smart container technologies such as electronic cargo seals and sensors, increased efficiency in inspecting seals and the use of electronic cargo manifests.

Some of the other components of APEC's comprehensive counterterrorism strategy are measures to deny terrorists access to the world's financial system, while at the same time, using the money trail to locate and apprehend terrorists. Last October, APEC leaders agreed to ratify the International Convention for the Suppression of the Financing of Terrorism no later than October 2003, and to implement, as soon as possible, the measures called for in UN Security Council Resolutions 1373 and 1390.

These measures include the blocking of terrorist assets and making the financing of terrorism a criminal offense, promoting better monitoring of alternative remittance systems and to enhance information sharing and law enforcement activities.

Given the importance of cyber security to international trade, APEC leaders are also committed to protect the Internet from cyber criminals. By the end of this year, APEC members will endeavor to enact a comprehensive set of laws relating to cyber security and cyber crime.

These will be consistent with the provisions of international legal instruments, such as the United Nations General Assembly Resolution 55/63 (2000) and the Convention on Cyber-crime (2001). APEC has also undertaken a number of projects to protect the stable supply of energy required for economic growth in our region. One of these projects was a sea-lane disruption simulation exercise conducted by the Asia Pacific Energy Research Center last April.

This exercise highlighted the inadequacy of navigational aids in the straits of Sunda and Lombok in the event that a shipping incident blocked the Strait of Malacca. Work is also underway to create a real-time, emergency information-sharing network. The Energy Working Group will conduct a half-day workshop on oil supply emergency response arrangements to assist member economies to develop and implement energy emergency preparedness plans.

To facilitate the exchange of information between APEC member economies, in February 2003, APEC senior officials endorsed the completion of the Counter-Terrorism Action Plans (CTAP) by all member economies.

The CTAP lists specific objectives and expected outputs by each economy to secure cargo, protect people in transit, secure ships engaged in international voyages, secure international aviation, halt the financing of terrorism, enhance cyber security, secure energy supplies, and protect the health of our communities.

Relevant APEC fora, including the Transport Working Group, are now looking at the CTAP to determine specific regional gaps in counterterrorism capacity relevant to their fields. It is proposed that next year, the completed CTAP and data provided by the APEC fora will form the basis of a rigorous qualitative cross-analysis by Asia-Pacific security experts.

This analysis would seek to identify linkages between the various CTAP objectives and regional needs to promote effective regional and multidisciplinary/ multiagency approaches to shared challenges.

To oversee the implementation of these Action Plans, this February, APEC Senior Officials established a Counter-Terrorism Task Force. The aim of this high-level group is to coordinate the fight against terrorism; facilitate cooperation between APEC working groups and committees on counterterrorism issues; and coordinate regional and bilateral capacity building and technical assistance programs, including consultations with international financial institutions.

APEC recognizes that terrorists know no boundaries, and that members must work with other regional and international bodies to protect our maritime environment from terrorism. One of the key roles of the Counter-Terrorism Task Force is to cooperate with other international organizations such as the International Maritime Organization (IMO), the World Customs Organization (WCO), and the International Civil Aviation Organization.

Building the Asia Pacific into a region that is more secure and more efficient is a significant undertaking. To achieve this goal will require enhanced cooperation, new procedures, and the greater use of advanced technology. Capacity building, in particular the need to strengthen the institutional capacity of governments, is essential to the success of protecting the economy of the Asia Pacific. APEC's programs to secure efficient trade start with the identification of capacity building needs.

These needs will be coordinated internally within APEC and with other international organizations to match each target economy's unique situation. APEC members also consider that a partnership between the public and the private sectors is essential in the fight against terrorism. Private sector representatives, therefore, should be encouraged to work in partnership with APEC economies to implement necessary measures to secure trade.

The member economies are investing great efforts in undertaking reforms to protect our growing prosperity, and where possible, to use these reforms not only to protect, but also to enhance trade efficiency. As we have discovered through the APEC process, investment in security can result in significant economic efficiency gains, not only by reducing the economic costs of terrorism, but also by facilitating the movement of goods and people.

The APEC Counter-Terrorism Action Plan, APEC Counter-Terrorism Task Force, the Secure Trade in the APEC Region (STAR) Initiative and numerous programs that support these efforts are at the heart of our efforts to promote trade, to expand business opportunities and to create jobs in our region.

Further initiatives are being developed to build on the progress achieved to date and to ensure that the region's maritime environment is protected. However, the goal set by APEC leaders of ensuring secure trade in the Asia Pacific will be realized only if we work closely together.

REGIONAL COOPERATION AGREEMENT ON COMBATING PIRACY AND ARMED ROBBERY AGAINST SHIPS IN ASIA
ReCAAP Agreement, Tokyo, Japan
November 11, 2004*

The Contracting Parties to this Agreement,

Concerned about the increasing number of incidents of piracy and armed robbery against ships in Asia,

Mindful of the complex nature of the problem of piracy and armed robbery against ships,

Recognizing the importance of safety of ships, including their crew, exercising the right of navigation provided for in the United Nations Convention on the Law of the Sea of December 10, 1982, hereinafter referred to as "the UNCLOS,"

Reaffirming the duty of States to cooperate in the prevention and suppression of piracy under the UNCLOS,

Recalling "Tokyo Appeal" of March 2000, "Asia Anti-Piracy Challenges 2000" of April 2000 and "Tokyo Model Action Plan" of April 2000,

Noting the relevant resolutions adopted by the United Nations General Assembly and the relevant resolutions and recommendations adopted by the International Maritime Organization,

Conscious of the importance of international cooperation as well as the urgent need for greater regional cooperation and coordination of all States affected within Asia, to prevent and suppress piracy and armed robbery against ships effectively,

Convinced that information sharing and capacity building among the Contracting Parties will significantly contribute towards the prevention and suppression of piracy and armed robbery against ships in Asia,

Affirming that, to ensure greater effectiveness of this Agreement, it is indispensable for each Contracting Party to strengthen its measures aimed at preventing and suppressing piracy and armed robbery against ships,

Determined to promote further regional cooperation and to enhance the effectiveness of such cooperation,

Have agreed as follows:

PART I: INTRODUCTION

Article 1: Definitions

1. For the purposes of this Agreement, "piracy" means any of the following acts:
    (a) any illegal act of violence or detention, or any act of depredation, committed for private ends by the crew or the passengers of a private ship or a private aircraft, and directed:

---

*http://www.mofa.go.jp/mofaj/gaiko/kaiyo/pdfs/kyotei_s.pdf

      (i) on the high seas, against another ship, or against persons or property on board such ship;

     (ii) against a ship, persons or property in a place outside the jurisdiction of any State;

    (b) any act of voluntary participation in the operation of a ship or of an aircraft with knowledge of facts making it a pirate ship or aircraft;

    (c) any act of inciting or of intentionally facilitating an act described in subparagraph (a) or (b).

2.   For the purposes of this Agreement, "armed robbery against ships" means any of the following acts:

    (a) any illegal act of violence or detention, or any act of depredation, committed for private ends and directed against a ship, or against persons or property on board such ship, in a place within a Contracting Party's jurisdiction over such offenses;

    (b) any act of voluntary participation in the operation of a ship with knowledge of facts making it a ship for armed robbery against ships;

    (c) any act of inciting or of intentionally facilitating an act described in subparagraph (a) or (b).

Article 2: General Provisions

1.   The Contracting Parties shall, in accordance with their respective national laws and regulations and subject to their available resources or capabilities, implement this Agreement, including preventing and suppressing piracy and armed robbery against ships, to the fullest extent possible.

2.   Nothing in this Agreement shall affect the rights and obligations of any Contracting Party under the international agreements to which that Contracting Party is party, including the UNCLOS, and the relevant rules of international law.

3.   Nothing in this Agreement shall affect the immunities of warships and other government ships operated for noncommercial purposes.

4.   Nothing in this Agreement, nor any act or activity carried out under this Agreement shall prejudice the position of any Contracting Party with regard to any dispute concerning territorial sovereignty or any issues related to the law of the sea.

5.   Nothing in this Agreement entitles a Contracting Party to undertake in the territory of another Contracting Party the exercise of jurisdiction and performance of functions which are exclusively reserved for the authorities of that other Contracting Party by its national law.

6.   In applying paragraph 1 of Article 1, each Contracting Party shall give due regard to the relevant provisions of the UNCLOS without prejudice to the rights of the third Parties.

Article 3: General Obligations

1. Each Contracting Party shall, in accordance with its national laws and regulations and applicable rules of international law, make every effort to take effective measures in respect of the following:
    (a) to prevent and suppress piracy and armed robbery against ships;
    (b) to arrest pirates or persons who have committed armed robbery against ships;
    (c) to seize ships or aircraft used for committing piracy or armed robbery against ships, to seize ships taken by and under the control of pirates or persons who have committed armed robbery against ships, and to seize the property on board such ships; and
    (d) to rescue victim ships and victims of piracy or armed robbery against ships.
2. Nothing in this Article shall prevent each Contracting Party from taking additional measures in respect of subparagraphs (a) to (d) above in its land territory.

PART II: INFORMATION SHARING CENTER

Article 4: Composition

1. An Information Sharing Center, hereinafter referred to as "the Center," is hereby established to promote close cooperation among the Contracting Parties in preventing and suppressing piracy and armed robbery against ships.
2. The Center shall be located in Singapore.
3. The Center shall be composed of the Governing Council and the Secretariat.
4. The Governing Council shall be composed of one representative from each Contracting Party. The Governing Council shall meet at least once every year in Singapore, unless otherwise decided by the Governing Council.
5. The Governing Council shall make policies concerning all the matters of the Center and shall adopt its own rules of procedure, including the method of selecting its Chairperson.
6. The Governing Council shall take its decisions by consensus.
7. The Secretariat shall be headed by the Executive Director who shall be assisted by the staff. The Executive Director shall be chosen by the Governing Council.
8. The Executive Director shall be responsible for the administrative, operational and financial matters of the Center in accordance with the policies as determined by the Governing Council and the provisions of this Agreement, and for such other matters as determined by the Governing Council.
9. The Executive Director shall represent the Center. The Executive Director shall, with the approval of the Governing Council, make rules and regulations of the Secretariat.

Article 5: Headquarters Agreement

1.   The Center, as an international organization whose members are the Contracting Parties to this Agreement, shall enjoy such legal capacity, privileges and immunities in the Host State of the Center as are necessary for the fulfillment of its functions.
2.   The Executive Director and the staff of the Secretariat shall be accorded, in the Host State, such privileges and immunities as are necessary for the fulfillment of their functions.
3.   The Center shall enter into an agreement with the Host State on matters including those specified in paragraphs 1 and 2 of this Article.

Article 6: Financing

1.   The expenses of the Center, as provided for in the budget decided by the Governing Council, shall be provided by the following sources:
     (a)   Host State financing and support;
     (b)   Voluntary contributions from the Contracting Parties;
     (c)   Voluntary contributions from international organizations and other entities, in accordance with relevant criteria adopted by the Governing Council; and
     (d)   Any other voluntary contributions as may be agreed upon by the Governing Council.
2.   Financial matters of the Center shall be governed by a Financial Regulation to be adopted by the Governing Council.
3.   There shall be an annual audit of the accounts of the Center by an independent auditor appointed by the Governing Council. The audit report shall be submitted to the Governing Council and shall be made public, in accordance with the Financial Regulation.

Article 7: Functions

The functions of the Center shall be:
     (a)   to manage and maintain the expeditious flow of information relating to incidents of piracy and armed robbery against ships among the Contracting Parties;
     (b)   to collect, collate and analyze the information transmitted by the Contracting Parties concerning piracy and armed robbery against ships, including other relevant information, if any, relating to individuals and transnational organized criminal groups committing acts of piracy and armed robbery against ships;
     (c)   to prepare statistics and reports on the basis of the information gathered and analyzed under subparagraph (b), and to disseminate them to the Contracting Parties;

(d) to provide an appropriate alert, whenever possible, to the Contracting Parties if there is a reasonable ground to believe that a threat of incidents of piracy or armed robbery against ships is imminent;

(e) to circulate requests referred to in Article 10 and relevant information on the measures taken referred to in Article 11 among the Contracting Parties;

(f) to prepare nonclassified statistics and reports based on information gathered and analyzed under subparagraph (b) and to disseminate them to the shipping community and the International Maritime Organization; and

(g) to perform such other functions as may be agreed upon by the Governing Council with a view to preventing and suppressing piracy and armed robbery against ships.

Article 8: Operation

1. The daily operation of the Center shall be undertaken by the Secretariat.
2. In carrying out its functions, the Center shall respect the confidentiality of information provided by any Contracting Party, and shall not release or disseminate such information unless the consent of that Contracting Party is given in advance.
3. The Center shall be operated in an effective and transparent manner, in accordance with the policies made by the Governing Council, and shall avoid duplication of existing activities between the Contracting Parties.

PART III: COOPERATION THROUGH THE INFORMATION SHARING CENTER

Article 9: Information Sharing

1. Each Contracting Party shall designate a focal point responsible for its communication with the Center, and shall declare its designation of such focal point at the time of its signature or its deposit of an instrument of notification provided for in Article 18.
2. Each Contracting Party shall, upon the request of the Center, respect the confidentiality of information transmitted from the Center.
3. Each Contracting Party shall ensure the smooth and effective communication between its designated focal point, and other competent national authorities including rescue coordination centers, as well as relevant nongovernmental organizations.
4. Each Contracting Party shall make every effort to require its ships, ship owners, or ship operators to promptly notify relevant national authorities including focal points, and the Center when appropriate, of incidents of piracy or armed robbery against ships.

5. Any Contracting Party which has received or obtained information about an imminent threat of, or an incident of, piracy or armed robbery against ships shall promptly notify relevant information to the Center through its designated focal point.
6. In the event that a Contracting Party receives an alert from the Center as to an imminent threat of piracy or armed robbery against ships pursuant to subparagraph (d) of Article 7, that Contracting Party shall promptly disseminate the alert to ships within the area of such an imminent threat.

Article 10: Request for Cooperation

1. A Contracting Party may request any other Contracting Party, through the Center or directly, to cooperate in detecting any of the following persons, ships, or aircraft:
    (a) pirates;
    (b) persons who have committed armed robbery against ships;
    (c) ships or aircraft used for committing piracy or armed robbery against ships, and ships taken by and under the control of pirates or persons who have committed armed robbery against ships; or
    (d) victim ships and victims of piracy or armed robbery against ships.
2. A Contracting Party may request any other Contracting Party, through the Center or directly, to take appropriate measures, including arrest or seizure, against any of the persons or ships mentioned in subparagraph (a), (b), or (c) of paragraph 1 of this Article, within the limits permitted by its national laws and regulations and applicable rules of international law.
3. A Contracting Party may also request any other Contracting Party, through the Center or directly, to take effective measures to rescue the victim ships and the victims of piracy or armed robbery against ships.
4. The Contracting Party which has made a direct request for cooperation pursuant to paragraphs 1, 2 and 3 of this Article shall promptly notify the Center of such request.
5. Any request by a Contracting Party for cooperation involving extradition or mutual legal assistance in criminal matters shall be made directly to any other Contracting Party.

Article 11: Cooperation by the Requested Contracting Party

1. A Contracting Party, which has received a request pursuant to Article 10, shall, subject to paragraph 1 of Article 2, make every effort to take effective and practical measures for implementing such request.
2. A Contracting Party, which has received a request pursuant to Article 10, may seek additional information from the requesting Contracting Party for the implementation of such request.

3.   A Contracting Party, which has taken measures referred to in paragraph 1 of
      this Article, shall promptly notify the Center of the relevant information on
      the measures taken.

PART IV: COOPERATION

Article 12: Extradition

A Contracting Party shall, subject to its national laws and regulations,
endeavor to extradite pirates or persons who have committed armed robbery
against ships, and who are present in its territory, to the other Contracting
Party which has jurisdiction over them, at the request of that Contracting
Party.

Article 13: Mutual Legal Assistance

A Contracting Party shall, subject to its national laws and regulations,
endeavor to render mutual legal assistance in criminal matters, including the
submission of evidence related to piracy and armed robbery against ships, at
the request of another Contracting Party.

Article 14: Capacity Building

1.   For the purpose of enhancing the capacity of the Contracting Parties to pre-
      vent and suppress piracy and armed robbery against ships, each Contracting
      Party shall endeavor to cooperate to the fullest possible extent with other
      Contracting Parties which request cooperation or assistance.
2.   The Center shall endeavor to cooperate to the fullest possible extent in pro-
      viding capacity building assistance.
3.   Such capacity building cooperation may include technical assistance such as
      educational and training programs to share experiences and best practices.

Article 15: Cooperative Arrangements

Cooperative arrangements such as joint exercises or other forms of cooperation,
as appropriate, may be agreed upon among the Contracting Parties concerned.

Article 16: Protection Measures for Ships

Each Contracting Party shall encourage ships, ship owners, or ship operators, where appropriate, to take protective measures against piracy and
armed robbery against ships, taking into account the relevant international

standards and practices, in particular, recommendations adopted by the International Maritime Organization.

PART V: FINAL PROVISIONS

Article 17: Settlement of Disputes

Disputes arising out of the interpretation or application of this Agreement, including those relating to liability for any loss or damage caused by the request made under paragraph 2 of Article 10 or any measure taken under paragraph 1 of Article 11, shall be settled amicably by the Contracting Parties concerned through negotiations in accordance with applicable rules of international law.

Article 18: Signature and Entry into Force

1. This Agreement shall be open for signature at the depositary referred to in paragraph 2 below by the People's Republic of Bangladesh, Brunei Darussalam, the Kingdom of Cambodia, the People's Republic of China, the Republic of India, the Republic of Indonesia, Japan, the Republic of Korea, the Lao People's Democratic Republic, Malaysia, the Union of Myanmar, the Republic of the Philippines, the Republic of Singapore, the Democratic Socialist Republic of Sri Lanka, the Kingdom of Thailand, the Socialist Republic of Viet Nam.
2. The Government of Singapore is the depositary of this Agreement.
3. This Agreement shall enter into force 90 days after the date on which the tenth instrument of notification by a State listed in paragraph 1, indicating the completion of its domestic requirements, is submitted to the depositary. Subsequently it shall enter into force in respect of any other State listed in paragraph 1 above 30 days after its deposit of an instrument of notification to the depositary.
4. The depositary shall notify all the States listed in paragraph 1 of the entry into force of this Agreement pursuant to paragraph 3 of this Article.
5. After this Agreement has entered into force, it shall be open for accession by any state not listed in paragraph 1. Any State desiring to accede to this Agreement may so notify the depositary, which shall promptly circulate the receipt of such notification to all other Contracting Parties. In the absence of a written objection by a Contracting Party within 90 days of the receipt of such notification by the depositary, that State may deposit an instrument of accession with the depositary, and become a party to this Agreement 60 days after such deposit of instrument of accession.

Article 19: Amendment

1. Any Contracting Party may propose an amendment to this Agreement, any time after the Agreement enters into force. Such amendment shall be adopted with the consent of all Contracting Parties.

2. Any amendment shall enter into force 90 days after the acceptance by all Contracting Parties. The instruments of acceptance shall be deposited with the depositary, which shall promptly notify all other Contracting Parties of the deposit of such instruments.

Article 20: Withdrawal

1. Any Contracting Party may withdraw from this Agreement at any time after the date of its entry into force.
2. The withdrawal shall be notified by an instrument of withdrawal to the depositary.
3. The withdrawal shall take effect 180 days after the receipt of the instrument of withdrawal by the depositary.
4. The depositary shall promptly notify all other Contracting Parties of any withdrawal.

Article 21: Authentic Text

This Agreement shall be authentic in the English language.

Article 22: Registration

This Agreement shall be registered by the depositary pursuant to Article 102 of the Charter of the United Nations.

IN WITNESS WHEREOF, the undersigned, being duly authorized thereto by their respective Governments, have signed this Agreement.

THE BATAM JOINT STATEMENT OF THE 4TH TRIPARTITE MINISTERIAL MEETING OF THE LITTORAL STATES ON THE STRAITS OF MALACCA AND SINGAPORE
Batam, Indonesia
August 2, 2005*

1. The Minister of Foreign Affairs of Indonesia, H.E. Dr. N. Hassan Wirajuda, Minister of Foreign Affairs of Malaysia, Hon. Dato' Seri Syed Hamid Albar, and Minister for Foreign Affairs of Singapore, H.E. George Yeo, met in Batam, on August 1–2, 2005, to discuss matters pertaining to the safety of

*http://app.mfa.gov.sg/internet/press/view_press.asp?post_id=1406

navigation, environmental protection and maritime security in the Straits of Malacca and Singapore.

2. The Foreign Ministers of Malaysia and Singapore appreciated the initiative of the Foreign Minister of Indonesia for convening this timely Meeting in view of the current challenges faced by the littoral States and user States of the Straits.

3. The Ministers noted the series of Tripartite Ministerial Meetings of the Straits of Malacca and Singapore as well as Meetings at the technical level held annually within the context of the Tripartite Technical Experts Group (TTEG) on safety of navigation and Revolving Fund Committee (RFC) in dealing with issues of environmental protection in the Straits of Malacca and Singapore.

4. The Ministers reaffirmed the sovereignty and sovereign rights of the Littoral States over the Straits of Malacca and Singapore, defined under UNCLOS 1982 as straits used for international navigation. As such, the primary responsibility over the safety of navigation, environmental protection, and maritime security in the Straits of Malacca and Singapore lies with the Littoral States.

5. The Ministers emphasized that whatever measures undertaken in the Straits should be in accordance with international law including UNCLOS 1982. In this regard they acknowledged the interest of user States and relevant international agencies and the role they could play in respect of the Straits.

6. The Ministers recognized the importance of the Tripartite Ministerial Meeting on the Straits of Malacca and Singapore in providing the overall framework for cooperation. They agreed that the Ministers and the Senior Officials should meet on a more regular basis to address relevant issues in a timely manner. Such meetings may include, if necessary, representatives of other relevant agencies of the respective Littoral States.

7. The Ministers recognized the importance of engaging the states bordering the funnels leading to the Straits of Malacca and Singapore, and the major users of the Straits. In this regard, the Ministers supported continuing discussion on the overall subject of maritime security in the Southeast Asian region within the framework of ASEAN and the ASEAN Regional Forum (ARF).

8. The Ministers acknowledged the good work carried out by the Tripartite Technical Experts Group (TTEG) on Safety of Navigation in the Straits of Malacca and Singapore. They also recognized the efforts of the Revolving Fund Committee (RFC) in dealing with issues of environmental protection in the Straits. In this regard, the Ministers welcomed the convening of the 30th TTEG on Safety of Navigation Meeting scheduled to be held in Penang, Malaysia, in September 2005.

9. The Ministers encouraged cooperation between Littoral States and the International Maritime Organization (IMO) to put in place the Pilot Project of Marine Electronic Highway (MEH) as a step forward for the enhancement of the safety of navigation and environmental protection in the Straits. The Ministers also took note of the forthcoming establishment of the ReCAAP Information Sharing Center in Singapore. In this regard the Ministers of Indonesia and Malaysia indicated their respective countries' preparedness to cooperate with the Center.

10. The Ministers supported the convening of the Chiefs of Defence Forces of Malaysia, Indonesia, Singapore, and Thailand Informal Meeting (CDF-MIST

Informal Meeting) in Kuala Lumpur on August 1–2, 2005, and encouraged them to further strengthen their cooperation.

11. The Ministers acknowledged that the littoral States should address the issue of maritime security comprehensively which includes trans-boundary crimes such as piracy, armed robbery and terrorism. The Ministers also recognized the need to address the issue of trafficking in persons and smuggling of people, weapons, and other trans-boundary crimes through appropriate mechanisms.

12. The Ministers agreed to establish a TTEG on Maritime Security to complement the works of the existing TTEG on Safety of Navigation and the Revolving Fund Committee.

13. Bearing in mind the responsibility and burden of littoral States and the interests of user States in maintaining the safety of navigation, environmental protection and maritime security, the Ministers welcomed the assistance of the user States, relevant international agencies, and the shipping community in the areas of capacity building, training and technology transfer, and other forms of assistance in accordance with UNCLOS 1982. In this regard they also welcomed closer collaboration between littoral States and the international community.

14. The Ministers expressed regret at Lloyds' categorization of the Straits of Malacca and Singapore as a high-risk zone for piracy and terrorism without consulting and taking into account the existing efforts of the littoral States to deal with the problems of safety of navigation and maritime security. The Ministers urged the Committee to review its risk assessment accordingly.

15. The Ministers welcomed the forthcoming "Meeting on the Straits of Malacca and Singapore: Enhancing Safety, Security and Environmental Protection" in collaboration with the International Maritime Organization to be held on September 7–8, 2005, in Jakarta, Indonesia.

FACTSHEET ON THE REGIONAL COOPERATION AGREEMENT ON COMBATING PIRACY AND ARMED ROBBERY AGAINST SHIPS IN ASIA (RECAAP)
ReCAAP Information Sharing Center
November 29, 2006*

What is ReCAAP?

1. The Regional Cooperation Agreement on Combating Piracy and Armed Robbery against Ships in Asia (ReCAAP) is the first regional government-to-government agreement to promote and enhance cooperation against piracy and armed robbery in Asia.

2. Proposed by the then Japanese Prime Minister Junichiro Koizumi in October 2001, the ReCAAP initiative aims to enhance multilateral cooperation

---

*http://app.mot.gov.sg/data/ReCAAP%20factsheet%20_Nov06_%20%5BFINAL%5Das%2 0of%20281106.pdf

amongst 16 regional countries, namely the ASEAN 10 plus Japan, China, Republic of Korea, India, Sri Lanka and Bangladesh to combat sea piracy and armed robbery against ships in the region. After three years of negotiations, the ReCAAP Agreement was finalized in November 2004 in Tokyo. Singapore is the depositary of the ReCAAP Agreement, which was open for signature on February 28, 2005.

3. The ReCAAP Agreement entered into force on September 4, 2006. To date, fourteen (14) countries have signed and ratified the ReCAAP Agreement, namely, Bangladesh, Brunei, Cambodia, China, India, Japan, Republic of Korea, Laos, Myanmar, the Philippines, Singapore, Sri Lanka, Thailand, and Vietnam. Malaysia and Indonesia have also indicated their preparedness to cooperate with the ReCAAP Information Sharing Centre (ISC). This commitment was first made in August 2005 at the 4th Tripartite Ministerial Meeting of the Littoral States of the Straits of Malacca and Singapore held in Batam, and was most recently reiterated at the International Maritime Organisation (IMO) Meeting on the Straits of Malacca and Singapore held in Kuala Lumpur in September 2006. Singapore looks forward to the signature and ratification by the remaining ReCAAP countries in due course.

4. The significance of the ReCAAP Agreement has been recognized by regional and international organizations. For example, the ASEAN Regional Forum (ARF) Intersessional Support Group Meeting on Confidence Building and Preventive Diplomacy held on October 18–19, 2005, noted the importance of agreements such as ReCAAP in enhancing maritime security in the region. The September 2005 IMO Meeting on the Straits of Malacca and Singapore held in Jakarta noted the importance of ReCAAP in addressing piracy and armed robbery against ships, and the entry into force of ReCAAP on September 4, 2006. The launch of the ISC in Singapore in November was subsequently welcomed at the September 2006 IMO Meeting on the Straits of Malacca and Singapore held in Kuala Lumpur. The Plenary of the 60th session of the United Nations General Assembly also adopted Resolution 60/30 of November 29, 2005, on Oceans and the Law of the Sea, which welcomed "the progress in regional cooperation" through the ReCAAP Agreement and urged States to "give urgent attention to adopting, concluding and implementing cooperation agreements at the regional level in high risk areas."

What does ReCAAP consist of?

5. The ReCAAP Agreement sets out obligations undertaken by member countries to effect measures to prevent and suppress piracy and armed robbery against ships. It also lays out a framework for cooperation among member countries, based on three main pillars of information sharing, capacity building, and operational cooperation, with information sharing as the main pillar. Sharing of piracy and armed robbery information can help improve operational cooperation when responding to incidents as well as enable the development of more effective prevention measures.

6. As a platform for cooperation, the ReCAAP countries will establish an Information Sharing Centre (ISC). The ISC was officially launched on November

29, 2006, in Singapore by Mr. Raymond Lim, Minister for Transport and Second Minister for Foreign Affairs. The Headquarters Agreement, which establishes the ReCAAP ISC as an independent, international body, was signed by Minister Lim (representing the government of Singapore), and Mr. Yoshiaki Ito, the Executive Director of the ReCAAP ISC.

7. The ISC is an international organization and includes representatives from ReCAAP member countries. This is the first time that regional governments have institutionalized their cooperation in combating piracy and armed robbery against ships in the form of a permanent body with full-time staff. Singapore will be the host of the ISC.

8. The ISC will undertake the following activities:
   - facilitate communications, information exchange and operational cooperation between the participating governments to improve incident response by member countries;
   - collate and prepare statistics and analysis of the piracy and sea robbery situation in the Asia region, and
   - support capacity building efforts.

9. Through the above activities, the ReCAAP ISC will help to improve the national response and capability of member countries to prevent and suppress piracy and sea robbery in the region. Through its periodic reports made available to the public, the ISC will contribute to the pool of information which shipowners and shipmasters access to help them take preventive measures against piracy and armed robbery attacks in regional waters.

SINGAPORE—HOST OF THE INFORMATION SHARING CENTRE (ISC)

10. As an independent international organization, the ISC will have its own premises situated in the NOL Building along Alexandra Road. ST Electronics has also been appointed to develop the Information Network (IFN) System to support the communication flow and exchange between ISC and the ReCAAP member countries. Details of the IFN system can be found in Annex A.

11. A training workshop was recently held on October 2–4, 2006, to conduct training on the IFN for the Focal Points (e.g., national coast guard, maritime authority), which were designated by each individual ReCAAP member country as the points of contact for the ISC. This was followed by the Pre-Governing Council Preparatory Meeting on October 5–6, 2006, which was held to finalize preparations for the first Governing Council Meeting on November 28–30, 2006. The Governing Council comprises one representative from each ReCAAP Contracting Party, and oversees policies guiding the work of the ReCAAP ISC. The Governing Council representative for the Republic of Singapore is the Chief Executive of the Maritime and Port Authority of Singapore, BG (NS) Tay Lim Heng.

12. The expenses of the ISC will be funded largely by voluntary contributions from the ReCAAP member countries. As the host, Singapore has generously

contributed towards the operations of the ISC. For example, Singapore has borne the entire startup costs of the ISC, including the development of the IFN and provision of suitable premises to house the ISC. The start-up costs of the ISC are estimated to be about S$2.2 million.

13.   In addition, Singapore will be contributing towards the annual running costs of the ISC, such as the rental, maintenance and utility charges. Singapore will also be bearing the salaries of the staff of the ISC who are Singapore citizens or permanent residents. Singapore's annual contribution to the ISC is estimated to be about S$1.5 million.

The IFN System is a 24-hour, secure, Web-based information system that supports the ISC in the collection, organization, analysis, and sharing of piracy and armed robbery information among ReCAAP member countries. It links up the ReCAAP Information Sharing Centre (ISC) in Singapore with the designated Focal Points of ReCAAP member countries to enable the dissemination and exchange of information. These Focal Points (e.g., national coast guard, maritime authority) are designated by each individual ReCAAP member country as the points of contact for the ISC. When a piracy or sea robbery incident occurs, the victim reports to the closest Focal Point, which would respond to the incident as well as submit an incident report to the ISC through the IFN. The ISC would be able to communicate with this Focal Point and other Focal Points via the IFN, as well as disseminate alerts to other Focal Points. The shipping community can gain access to information on incidents through the ISC Web site.

COUNTERTERRORISM IN MARITIME OPERATIONS

Philip Ruddock
Attorney General, Australia
Port and Maritime Security and Counterterrorism Summit 2007,
Langham Hotel, Melbourne, Australia
May 1, 2007*

ACKNOWLEDGMENTS

Firstly, may I acknowledge the traditional owners of the land we meet on—and pay my respects to their elders, both past and present.

---

*http://www.ag.gov.au/agd/WWW/MinisterRuddockHome.nsf/Page/Speeches_2007_
Speeches_1_May_2007_-_Speech_-_Port_and_Maritime_Security_and_Counter
-Terrorism_Summit_2007

OTHER ACKNOWLEDGMENTS

- Commodore Lee Cordner, AM, Summit Chair and Principal Research Fellow at the Australian National Centre for Ocean Resources and Security
- Mr. Hartmut Hesse, Senior Deputy Director Operational Safety and Human Element Subdivision, International Maritime Organisation
- Rear Admiral Geoff Smith, Chief Executive Officer, Sydney Ferries Corporation
- Ms. Elizabeth Kelly, Executive Director, AusCheck
- Mr. Andrew Tongue, Deputy Secretary, Department of Transport & Regional Services
- Distinguished guests, including those from overseas.
- Ladies and Gentlemen

INTRODUCTION

1. When people think of maritime terrorism they are likely to picture speed-boats packed with explosives and driven into the sides of ships. We all remember when suicide bombers drove a boat into the USS *Cole* in 2000, killing seventeen sailors. Another shocking target is ordinary commuter vessels carrying people to work or on family visits. One such vessel was *Super-Ferry 14*, which was set alight in the Philippines after a planted device exploded on February 27, 2004. One hundred and sixteen people died in that terrorist attack.

2. Or people might remember the many cases of high-powered weapons smuggled around the world in ordinary containers looking like legitimate shipping.

3. These are the high-profile cases of maritime terrorism that fix in people's minds.

4. But protecting our vital maritime infrastructure and resources from terrorism means focusing on the whole environment, not just the sea or ships or ports. It means examining a range of policies and issues which may be less enthralling than incidents on the high seas.

5. We must look at every possible vulnerability at the local, national, and international level. Then we must develop solutions to those weaknesses and negotiate their implementation. Our national security depends on the government ensuring that terrorists face a multitude of barriers to give our country and our interests the best possible protection.

6. However, the government cannot do this alone.

7. As the Australian Strategic Policy Institute found in a 2005 analysis, there is a risk of a terrorist attack on Australia's maritime interests.

8. Thankfully, terrorists have been less attracted to maritime assets than to some others. But this is no reason for complacency.

9. An attack on a maritime target in Australia would have serious consequences—for individuals, for business, and the entire economy as a whole.

10. The maritime sector is vast, complex and in a constant state of change. It encompasses assets on the high seas, in ports and on land. That means there are three different environments in which to consider a variety of necessary protective measures.
11. It is difficult, but it is a challenge the government has met and will continue to meet. Our seaports and maritime infrastructure are key components of our national economy, and we must protect them to safeguard our nation and our prosperity.

AUSTRALIAN GOVERNMENT ACTION

12. Since September 11, 2001, the Australian government has taken significant steps to increase our national security.
13. We have put in place a wide range of measures—both at the national and industry-specific level—to help keep your industry safe. They are also aimed at keeping the economic benefits flowing to the wider community.
14. We have spent over $8.3 billion on more than 200 individual national security related measures to improve our safety. These measures are part of a comprehensive, multilayered response which has seen every aspect of our national security assessed and improved.

MARITIME SECURITY REGIME

15. The Australian government has put in place a robust and world-class maritime security regime to help safeguard our maritime transport system and offshore facilities.
16. My colleague the Honorable Mark Vaile, Minister for Transport and Regional Services, yesterday discussed some of these industry-specific measures in detail.
17. You have heard from a number of agencies within my portfolio including the Australian Security Intelligence Organisation, the Australian Crime Commission, and the Australian Customs Service. These agencies are working to protect the maritime industry.
18. In addition, my Department is leading some of the key activities that are integral to counter terrorism and other criminal activity in the maritime industry, such as background checking initiatives.

AUSCHECK

19. In recent years we have introduced a range of measures at airports—and more recently at port facilities—designed to control access. One of the most important security tasks has focused on background checking.

20. As you will all know, the Maritime Security Identification Card was introduced on January 1. It provides proof that the holder has an operational need to be in a maritime security zone. It also proves the holder has no relevant criminal record or adverse security assessment.

21. As I foreshadowed at this conference last year, the government has established the Australian Background Checking Service—known as AusCheck.

22. AusCheck's work will contribute to improving the security of one of the largest maritime domains in the world.

23. Australians depend on that security for about $188 billion of seaborne trade every year. Document Verification Service

24. To further strengthen our security framework, we are also establishing a national Document Verification Service. The Service will be managed by my Department. It will form a central component of our National Identity Security Strategy.

25. The Service will allow authorized government agencies to check key identity documents online and in real-time. It will check whether the document being presented and the information recorded by the agency are an exact match. Importantly, there will be a cross-check function to detect stolen or fraudulent documents.

26. Organized crime and terrorist groups both seek to exploit the use of false and stolen identities. The Report of the 9/11 Commission in the United States says travel documents are as important as weapons to terrorists. Identity fraud has suddenly become a much bigger problem for us all.

27. The proliferation of false identity documents makes it very hard for background checking systems to work effectively.

28. The new Document Verification Service will make it extremely difficult for people to present false identification. As a result, industry can be confident of even greater surety in background checking. And all Australians will be better protected from criminals using their identities for illegal purposes.

BIG PICTURE INITIATIVES

29. The Maritime Security Identification Card Scheme and the Document Verification Service are just two examples of how the government is working to protect Australia's maritime industry. Effective counterterrorism arrangements in this industry are also dependent on a strong foundation. That foundation is provided by the wider security framework within Australia and the region.

30. The Australian government's response to terrorism operates at three levels— the international, the national and the local.

31. It is a response which builds on the success of our existing structures and administrative arrangements.

32. It is through a series of complementary measures that the maritime industry and the broader Australian interest are best protected.

INTERNATIONAL COOPERATION

33. Internationally, we are working with other countries to target terrorists. We do this directly through military operations—including in Afghanistan and Iraq—multilaterally through international forums, and on a bilateral basis.
34. We are working with other countries and international institutions to track down terrorists, deny them bases of operation, and prevent them planning, financing, and launching attacks. We have improved intelligence gathering and sharing, implemented tighter passport and border controls, and increased protection of offshore facilities. As I told you last year, I signed two protocols to an international convention—the Suppression of Unlawful Acts Against the Safety of Maritime Navigation Convention—in 2005. The protocols strengthen the original Convention to provide an appropriate response to the increasing risks posed to maritime navigation by international terrorism.
35. As of February, 18 states had signed the two 2005 protocols. One will come into effect once 12 states have ratified it. The other will come into effect with three ratifications and the entry into force of the first protocol. Australia has begun the process of ratifying the protocols, and I have encouraged other States to do the same.
36. As well, we are improving anti–money laundering and money-tracing measures to locate and freeze terrorists' funds.

NATIONAL LEVEL

37. At the national level, the Commonwealth, together with the states and territories, has established a nationwide, cooperative counterterrorism framework.
38. We have national laws dealing specifically with terrorist offenses. We have strengthened the powers of our security authorities to detain and question people who may have information about terrorist activities. We have also given our law enforcement agencies the power to detain people to prevent an imminent terrorist attack.
39. We have developed new institutional arrangements to fight terrorism. But in focusing on the protection of people, we have not neglected the risk to our economy.

BUSINESS COMMUNITY CONSULTATION/CRITICAL INFRASTRUCTURE PROTECTION

40. Australian businesses are the government's key partners in Australia's national counterterrorism strategy.
41. This is particularly true of businesses involved in critical sectors. These include vital services like transport, telecommunications, energy utilities and

the banking and finance industries. These services are critical to the running of other businesses and the economy as a whole—and, because of their importance to the nation, could be an attractive target for terrorists.

42. The Commonwealth, in partnership with the states and territories, has cataloged our critical infrastructure and identified those at greatest risk. Very few of them are owned by government. In fact, in some areas, up to 90 percent of them are owned or operated on a commercial basis. And it is these businesses that are primarily responsible for protecting the assets.

43. The Australian government actively engages the private sector to develop long-term approaches that both protect Australia's economic interests and leverage business expertise and capabilities to help to counter terrorism.

44. We have put in place a range of consultative bodies and forums. We have established the Trusted Information Sharing Network for Critical Infrastructure Protection as a forum in which the owners and operators of critical infrastructure work together to share information on security issues.

45. There are currently nine industry sector advisory groups covering the range of Australia's critical infrastructure, including a group that focuses on transport matters.

46. We have also established a high-level Business-Government Advisory Group on National Security. This group gives business leaders the opportunity to raise security issues at the highest levels with myself and other senior ministers. It also helps clarify the way business and government can continue to work together to effectively ensure our nation's security.

47. The Australian government believes that the best results for national security will be achieved through cooperation.

BUSINESS PROTECTION STRATEGIES

48. In government, we are doing everything we can to get the legislative protections right. We are also giving industry whatever information and practical assistance we can. But ultimately, because you are the people who know and understand your business, the security of your business is in your hands.

49. You are the ones who must make sure the correct security measures are in place.

50. Implementing security measures is really nothing more than good business planning. It means employing risk management strategies, fostering a security culture and putting good business continuity plans in place. These are hardly radical management theories. They simply represent the basics of good business practice.

ROLE OF BUSINESS LEADERS

51. Finally, risk management and other security measures will not work without the vision and drive of business leaders. You set the tone for your organizations.

Good security is not an end in itself. It is good business and, although it is a cost, it indirectly leads to profit.

CONCLUSION

52. Australia faces a very real threat from terrorists—and it is a threat that is unlikely to change any time soon.
53. In government, we are constantly reviewing our laws and our policies to ensure that we are doing everything we can to keep Australia safe.
54. However, I must again stress that terrorism cannot be countered by governments alone. We need the help of all Australians—including those of you in the maritime industry. We need you to look at your own industry and business, assess the risks, and take what measures you can to safeguard your operations.

Together, we can keep Australians safe and maintain our economic prosperity.

Africa

PIRATES PURSUE AMERICAN SHIP
U.S. Overseas Security Advisory Council, Safety & Security,
Sub-Saharan Africa—Somalia
December 22, 2006*

An OSAC constituent contributed to the following report:

An American-owned ship was pursued by suspected pirates on December 19 in the Indian Ocean. The ship was 120 miles off the coast of Somalia when another vessel approached them, claiming to be in distress. The distress message came at approximately 5:30 P.M., from a distance of 5 miles off the starboard bow. The crew began tracking the signal of the allegedly distressed vessel but did not change course.

The American ship caught sight of the other vessel within 5 minutes. Due to the frequency of pirate attacks in the waters of Somalia, the vessel's relative high speed and interceptive course, the distress claims of the vessel became suspect. From the American ship, the vessel looked to be in sound condition; there appeared to be a group of men on deck. These factors caused the American ship's captain to put the bridge watch on notice and order the house to be locked down. The course was altered as well; the American ship

---

*https://www.osac.gov/Reports/report.cfm?contentID=60901

headed farther out to sea, as the suspect vessel was small and pirate vessels often are unable to pursue after reaching a certain distance from their home port, due to fuel concerns.

By 6:00 P.M., the American ship began to pull away from the suspect vessel, and within 15 minutes there was a distance between them of approximately two miles. The suspect vessel appeared to have slowed, but continued in pursuit of the American ship. The American ship again headed further away from the Somali shoreline, heading east at maximum speed. The suspect vessel then faded from sight. Throughout the entire period, the suspect vessel had been calling for the American ship to stop and come to their position. According to the Americans, the radio calls sounded as though they were using more than one radio, and that there was more than one caller.

This incident is significant because it marks only the second time in over six months that a western ship has reported suspecting itself as the target of pirates off the coast of Somalia. Through approximately May 2006, the Somali waters were generally considered the second-worst in the world for piracy, after Indonesia's Malacca Straits. The U.S. government has issued successive warnings for ships plying the Indian Ocean, with the most recent warning recommending vessels stay 200 nautical miles from the coast. However, the Islamic Courts Union announced in late spring that piracy would not be tolerated, as it was un-Islamic and punishable under Shari'a Law. Since that time, suspected acts of reported piracy appear to have diminished in frequency.

COORDINATED ACTION URGED AS PIRACY THREATENS
UN LIFELINE TO SOMALIA
Joint Communiqué, IMO Briefing 23,
International Maritime Organization
July 10, 2007*

The heads of two United Nations agencies today made a joint call for concerted and coordinated international action to address the threat of piracy and armed robbery against ships in waters off the coast of Somalia, amid growing concern about the perils it poses for commercial shipping, fishing and other vessels and the delivery of humanitarian assistance needed by hundreds of thousands of Somali men, women and children.

The secretary-general of the International Maritime Organization (IMO), Efthimios E. Mitropoulos, and the Executive Director of the UN World Food

---

*International Maritime Organization (IMO), www.imo.org.

Programme (WFP), Josette Sheeran, warned that the actions of pirates operating in the waters off Somalia threaten the sea-lanes in the region and could endanger the fragile supply line for food assistance to Somalis whose lives have been shattered by more than 15 years of civil conflict, political instability and recurring natural disasters.

Last month, the IMO Council, meeting in London, shared the concerns expressed by Secretary-General Mitropoulos and agreed with his proposals for further action to engage the international community in addressing the continuing incidence of acts of piracy and armed robbery in the region and, in particular, against ships carrying humanitarian aid to Somalia.

The IMO Council accordingly authorized Mr. Mitropoulos to request United Nations Secretary-General Ban Ki-moon to bring the piracy situation off Somalia, once again, to the attention of the UN Security Council, so that, in turn, the Security Council requests the Transitional Federal government of Somalia to take appropriate action. Such action could include giving consent to ships—as defined in Article 107 of the United Nations Convention on the Law of the Sea—to enter the country's territorial waters when engaging in operations against pirates or suspected pirates and armed robbers endangering the safety of life at sea.

Delivering supplies to Somalia, both commercial goods and humanitarian aid, has been a logistical and security challenge ever since the collapse of the last national government in 1991. Roadblocks controlled by militia groups across the country have hampered deliveries by road. Transportation by sea should, in principle, be both cheaper and safer, but a recent increase in the frequency of attacks by pirates appears to have led to higher shipping costs and a dramatic reduction in the use of cargo vessels, particularly those employed in moving food assistance to Somalia from ports in Kenya and elsewhere in Africa.

"Close to 80 percent of WFP's assistance to Somalia is shipped by sea but, because of piracy, we have seen the availability of ships willing to carry food to the country cut by half," said WFP Executive Director Sheeran. "Pirates may have a romantic image on the silver screen these days, but the picture might not be quite so pretty from the point of view of someone stuck in a camp for internally displaced people in Somalia, dependent on food assistance for survival. Much more has to be done to address this problem of piracy and, at WFP, we are much encouraged by the actions that IMO has taken recently for that purpose."

So far this year there have been 15 attacks on vessels in or near Somali waters, which carry some of the highest risks of piracy in the world. Two of these attacks involved WFP-contracted ships, and in one of these two incidents, a security guard was killed.

WFP aims to provide food assistance to 1 million people in Somalia this year, at a time when the country is once again plagued by brutal civil conflict. Forecast crop failures in the south and central parts of the country, already hit by alarming levels of malnutrition, are raising fears of food shortages and rising prices, both of which could be ameliorated by securing an uninterrupted supply line.

"The continuing incidence of acts of piracy and armed robbery in these waters is of great concern," IMO Secretary-General Mitropoulos said. "In conjunction with other multifaceted initiatives recently taken by IMO to address the issue effectively, this latest high-level approach to the Security Council, through Mr. Ban, will, I believe, help considerably in alleviating the situation, especially if support and assistance to ships is enhanced; and if administrations and the shipping industry implement effectively the guidance that IMO has issued and the notices promulgated regularly by naval operations' centers."

A new request from the UN Security Council would be in line with its Presidential Statement of March 15, 2006, issued after the matter had first been brought to its attention following adoption of resolution A.979(24) by the IMO Assembly. The 2006 Presidential Statement encouraged UN member states with naval vessels and military aircraft operating in international waters and airspace adjacent to the coast of Somalia, to be vigilant for any incident of piracy therein and to take appropriate action to protect merchant shipping (in particular ships being used to transport humanitarian aid) against any such act, in line with relevant international law.

Subsequently, there had been a much-welcomed reduction in acts of piracy and armed robbery off Somalia, due, to a large extent, to the support provided by naval assets in the region, as a consequence of the well-established liaison by IMO and WFP with relevant naval operations' centers.

However, as a result of the renewed rise in attacks on ships in recent months, IMO has lately taken a number of steps, including intensifying its existing coordination mechanism with WFP and the navies operating in the western Indian Ocean region, with a view to ensuring that the tracking of and, where necessary, the provision of assistance to merchant shipping is maintained and further strengthened.

IMO has also recently issued a Maritime Safety Committee (MSC) circular (MSC.1/Circ.1233) warning maritime interests of what continues to be a worrying situation off Somalia and inviting governments and organizations concerned to implement effectively the guidance to administrations, industry, and crew issued previously by IMO.

Additionally, in the context of the United Nations Open-ended Informal Consultative Process on Oceans and the Law of the Sea, IMO has requested the inclusion, within this year's related General Assembly resolution, of a renewed call for all concerned to continue their co operation in combating acts of piracy and armed robbery and in ensuring the early release of ships and persons held hostage as a consequence of such acts.

"We would like to see a more coordinated and robust approach to dealing with the problem of piracy, from the Transitional Federal Government in Somalia, from neighboring countries that have influence, and from the African Union," said Sheeran. "WFP is grateful for the continuing presence in the seas off Somalia of naval forces from several nations. They have been helpful on occasion in the past and they offer a potential deterrence to pirates. But we need to explore how these resources can be brought more heavily into play to protect shipping and, thereby, the delivery by sea of life-saving humanitarian assistance."

AFRICA COMMAND: A HISTORIC OPPORTUNITY FOR ENHANCED ENGAGEMENT—IF DONE RIGHT

Dr. J. Peter Pham
Director, the Nelson Institute for International and Public Affairs,
James Madison University
Before the House Committee on Foreign Affairs,
Subcommittee on Africa and Global Health
August 2, 2007*

I am honored by the invitation to appear today before the Subcommittee on Africa and Global Health and am grateful for the opportunity to add my voice to those of my distinguished colleagues on a subject which I have studied, written about, and advocated on behalf of, for a number of years: a United States Department of Defense regional unified combatant command for Africa that offers the potential for sustained engagement of a region where America has very real strategic interests.

SETTING THE CONTEXT OF THE NEW ENGAGEMENT

I beg the Subcommittee's indulgence to observe that we as a nation have indeed all come a very long way in recent years in our perceptions of Africa—some of us perhaps more than others. With the anniversary on March 6 of this year of the independence of Ghana, we also mark the fiftieth anniversary of the beginning of the wave of national sovereignty that swept across sub-Saharan Africa in the wake of the Second World War. At that time, however, no part of the region was included in any U.S. military command's Area of Responsibility (AOR) except for several North African countries which five years earlier had been tacked onto the U.S. European Command (EUCOM). The rest of the continent was left unaccounted for the rest of the decade until 1960 when, following then-Vice President Richard Nixon's extensive tour of the continent, President Dwight D. Eisenhower put the then Atlantic Command (LANTCOM) in charge of security planning for sub-Saharan Africa just as he had previously created the Africa Bureau within the State Department to coordinate diplomatic initiatives. Two years later, President John F. Kennedy transferred sub-Saharan Africa into the Strike Command (STRICOM) AOR. From that time until the present, responsibility for defense planning affecting the continent has shifted a number of times as administrations came and went and geopolitical perceptions evolved over the course of the Cold War and its aftermath.

Just three years ago, when writing on the subject of a possible regional command for Africa, I was still being counseled by one editor to make sure that I couched the whole proposal as a hypothetical in the conditional tense.[1] And going back a little farther to 2000, I can recall that a number of Africa's friends—some of whom are in this room today—were quite disappointed when a certain Republican presidential candidate responded negatively to a question from PBS's Jim Lehrer about whether Africa fit into his definition of the strategic interests of the United States: "At some point in time the president's got to clearly define what the national strategic interests are, and while Africa may be important, it doesn't fit into the national strategic interests, as far as I can see them."[2]

Yet almost seven years to the day later, on February 6, 2007, President George W. Bush announced the establishment of a U.S. Africa Command (AFRICOM), directing the Department of Defense to stand it up by October 2008 and entrusting the new structure with the mission to "enhance our efforts to bring peace and security to the people of Africa and promote our common goals of development, health, education, democracy, and economic growth in Africa" by strengthening bilateral and multilateral security cooperation with African states and creating new opportunities to bolster their capabilities.[3]

I rehearse this history in order to lend some perspective to just how extraordinary the decision to set up AFRICOM as America's sixth regional command really is. As former Assistant Secretary of State for International Organizations Princeton N. Lyman, who previously served as U.S. ambassador to South Africa and to Nigeria, has observed, the apparent strategic neglect of Africa nonetheless sadly reflects "what [has] in fact been the approach of both Democratic and Republican administrations for decades."[4] Historically, with the exception of Cold War period when concerns about Soviet attempts to secure a foothold on the continent drove U.S. policy, America generally perceived Africa as secondary to its foreign policy and other strategic objectives. Thus, more often than not, American perspectives on Africa were framed almost exclusively in terms of preoccupation over the humanitarian consequences of poverty, war, and natural disaster. Alas, as noble as these moral impulses have been, they lacked the "staying power" needed to sustain a long-term commitment. Rightfully, many of our African friends viewed us as well-meaning but unreliable.

I would argue, however, that three factors have providentially come together which cumulatively have the potential to significantly alter the course of the relationship between the United States and the African continent as a whole as well as with its individual sovereign states. First, in the wake of 9/11, analysts and policymakers have shifted to a more strategic view of Africa in terms of U.S. national interests. Second, independent of our interests and actions, Africans themselves have increasingly expressed the desire and, more importantly, demonstrated the political will, to tackle the continent's myriad challenges of disease, poverty, ethnic tension, religious extremism, bad governance, lack of security, etc., although they still need outside assistance. Third, we have come to recognize a commonality between our strategic interests and the interests of Africans in enhanced security, stability, and development.

RECOGNIZING OUR STRATEGIC INTERESTS

Broadly conceived, there are three major areas in which Africa's significance for America—or at least the public recognition thereof—has been amplified in recent years. The first is Africa's role in the "Global War on Terror" and the potential of the poorly governed spaces of the continent to provide facilitating environments, recruits, and eventual targets for Islamist terrorists who threaten Western interests in general and those of the United States in particular—and, in some regions like the Horn of Africa and Sahel, this has already become reality. The second important consideration is Africa's abundant natural resources, particularly those in its burgeoning energy sector. The third area of interest remains the humanitarian concern for the devastating toll which conflict, poverty, and disease, especially HIV/AIDS, continue to exact in Africa.

Concerns about Terrorism

There is no denying that U.S. security policy, both currently and for the foreseeable future will be heavily influenced by the "Global War on Terrorism," the "Long War," or whatever the designation du jour for the fight against the threat of transnational Islamist terrorism happens to be. The 2002 National Security Strategy of the United States of America rightly acknowledged that "weak states . . . can pose as great a danger to our national interests as strong states. Poverty does not make poor people into terrorists and murderers. Yet poverty, weak institutions, and corruption can make weak states vulnerable to terrorist networks and drug cartels within their borders."[5] With the possible exception of the Greater Middle East, nowhere is this analysis truer than Africa where, as the document went on to acknowledge, regional conflicts arising from a variety of causes, including poor governance, external aggression, competing claims, internal revolt, and ethnic and religious tensions all "lead to the same ends: failed states, humanitarian disasters, and ungoverned areas that can become safe havens for terrorists."[6]

While the terrorist attacks by al-Qaeda on the U.S. embassies in Dar es Salaam Tanzania, and Nairobi, Kenya, in 1998, and on an Israeli-owned hotel in Mombasa, Kenya, and, simultaneously, on an Israeli commercial airliner in 2002 have underscored the deadly reality of the terrorist threat in Africa, perhaps the most eloquent reminder of the particular vulnerability of the continent to terrorism comes from the terrorists themselves. In June 2006, a new online magazine for actual and aspiring global jihadis and their supporters, Sada al-Jihad ("Echo of Jihad"), which took the place of Sawt al-Jihad ("Voice of Jihad") as the publication of al-Qaeda in Saudi Arabia after Saudi authorities finally came around to shutting down the presses of latter, featured an article by one Abu Azzam al-Ansari entitled "Al-Qaeda is Moving to Africa."[7] Abu Azzam was remarkably frank:

There is no doubt that al-Qaeda and the holy warriors appreciate the significance of the African regions for the military campaigns against the Crusaders. Many people sense that this continent has not yet found its proper and expected role and the next stages of the conflict will see Africa as the battlefield.

With a rather commendable analytical rigor surprisingly free from ideological rancor, Abu Azzam then proceeded to enumerate and evaluate what he perceived to be significant advantages to al-Qaeda shifting terrorist operations to Africa, including: the fact that jihadi doctrines have already been spread within the Muslim communities of many African countries; the political and military weakness of African governments; the wide availability of weapons; the geographical position of Africa vis-à-vis international trade routes; the proximity to old conflicts against "Jews and Crusaders" in the Middle East as well as new ones like Darfur, where the author almost gleefully welcomed the possibility of Western intervention; the poverty of Africa which "will enable the holy warriors to provide some finance and welfare, thus, posting there some of their influential operatives"; the technical and scientific skills that potential African recruits would bring to the jihadi cause; the presence of large Muslim communities, including ones already embroiled conflict with Christians or adherents of traditional African religions; the links to Europe through North Africa "which facilitates the move from there to carry out attacks"; and the fact that Africa has a wealth of natural resources, including hydrocarbons and other raw materials, which are "very useful for the holy warriors in the intermediate and long term." Abu Azzam concluded his assessment on an ominous note:

In general, this continent has an immense significance. Whoever looks at Africa can see that it does not enjoy the interest, efforts, and activity it deserves in the war against the Crusaders. This is a continent with many potential advantages and exploiting this potential will greatly advance the jihad. It will promote achieving the expected targets of Jihad. Africa is a fertile soil for the advance of jihad and the jihadi cause.

It would be a mistake to dismiss Abu Azzam's analysis as devoid of operational effect. Shortly before the publication of the article, an Islamist movement whose leaders included a number of figures linked to al-Qaeda, the Islamic Courts Union, seized control of the sometime Somali capital of Mogadishu and subsequently overran most of the former state which—with the exception of the northern Republic of Somaliland where the inhabitants have tried to reassert the sovereignty they possessed before joining Somalia in a disastrous union and have, by and large, succeeded[8]—has been without an effective government since 1991.[9] Although forceful intervention by neighboring Ethiopia in late December 2006 dislodged the Islamists, Somalia's internationally recognized but utterly ineffective "Transitional Federal Government" has yet to assert itself in the face of a growing insurgency which has adopted the same nonconventional tactics that foreign jihadis and Sunni Arab insurgents have used to great effect in Iraq.[10] Considerable evidence has emerged of links between the Somali Islamists and fugitive al-Qaeda leaders in Pakistan, not least of which was the capture and subsequent transfer last June to the U.S. detention facility at Guantánamo Bay of Abdullahi Sudi Arale, who was apparently dispatched from Pakistan to Somalia in September 2006 and who, according to a Pentagon statement, "played a significant role in the reemergence" of the militants after their initial rout.[11]

Another al-Qaeda "franchise" has sought to reignite conflict in Algeria and spread it to the Sahel, the critical boundary region where sub-Saharan Africa meets North Africa and where vast empty spaces and highly permeable borders are readily exploitable by local and international militants alike both as a base for recruitment and training and as a conduit for the movement of personnel and materiel. Last year members of the Algerian Islamist terrorist group Salafist Group for Preaching and Combat (usually known by its French acronym GSPC) formally pledged allegiance to Osama bin Laden and al-Qaeda and began identifying themselves in communiqués as "Al-Qaeda Organization in the Islamic Maghreb." The link to al-Qaeda was confirmed by bin Laden's deputy Ayman al-Zawahiri who, in the "commemorative video" the terrorist network issued on the fifth anniversary of the 9/11 attacks, declared: "Our mujahid Sheikh and the Lion of Islam, Osama bin Laden, . . . has instructed me to give the good news to Muslims in general and my mujahidin brothers everywhere that the Salafist Group for Preaching and Combat has joined al-Qaeda organization."[12] The Egyptian terrorist hailed the "blessed union" between the GSPC and al-Qaeda, pledging that it would "be a source of chagrin, frustration and sadness for the apostates [of the regime in Algeria], the treacherous sons of [former colonial power] France," and urging the group to become "a bone in the throat of the American and French crusaders" in the region and beyond. Last April, al-Qaeda's new affiliate claimed credit for a pair of bomb blasts—one close to the prime minister's office, the other near a police station—that rocked Algiers, killing two dozen people and wounding more than a hundred, shattering the calm that the Algerian capital had enjoyed since the conclusion of the civil war of the 1990s which claimed at least 150,000 lives.[13]

Perhaps most menacing over the long term, however, is an increasingly apparent willingness on the part of transnational Islamist terror networks to not only exploit the grievances which might be nursed by some African Muslim communities, but also to reach out to non-Muslim militants to make common cause against their mutual enemies. Although there is no shortage of violent non-Muslim groups in sub-Saharan Africa, the region has long been plagued by a number of indigenous Islamist groups like the Eritrean Islamic Jihad, the Ogaden National Liberation Front (ONLF) in Ethiopia, and the Allied Democratic Forces/National Army for the Liberation of Uganda (ADF/NALU).[14] More recently, evidence has emerged that outside forces have been providing these groups with strategic guidance, tactical assistance, and operational planning. For example, the ONLF has been battling successive Ethiopian governments for years with the goal of splitting the ethnic Somali region from the country. However, it was only within the last year that the group acquired from somewhere the wherewithal to mount the most spectacular attack within Ethiopia since the fall of the Derg dictatorship in 1991.[15]

In addition to shelter, recruits, and opportunities to terrorists, terrorist groups have also profited from the weak governance capacities of African states not only to raise money by soliciting sympathizers, but also to trade in gemstones and other natural resources either as a means to launder and make money as al-Qaeda did with Sierra Leonean "conflict diamonds" through the good offices of then–Liberian president Charles Taylor. Former Washington Post correspondent Douglas Farah, for example, has reported on how al-Qaeda procured somewhere between $30 million and $50 million worth of diamonds through this channel in the month before the September 11 attacks, while I have documented how Hezbollah has used the extensive Lebanese Shī'a communities in places like Sierra Leone, Liberia, and Guinea to make money in an illicit market estimated by the United Nations to worth between $170 million and $370 million.[16]

Energy and Maritime Security

In his 2006 State of the Union address, President Bush called for the United States to "replace more than 75 percent of our oil imports from the Middle East by 2025" and to "make our dependence on Middle Eastern oil a thing of the past."[17] According to the Department of Energy's Energy

Information Administration, America has already advanced significantly in its effort to wean itself from dependency on hydrocarbons originating in the volatile Persian Gulf, thanks in large measure to the abundant energy resources of Africa. This past March, Nigeria edged past Saudi Arabia to become America's third largest supplier, delivering 41,717,000 barrels of oil that month compared to the desert kingdom's 38,557,000. When one adds Angola's 22,542,000 barrels to the former figure, the two African states alone now supply more of America's energy needs than Saudi Arabia, Iraq, Kuwait, and the United Arab Emirates combined.[18] This milestone is all the more remarkable when one considers that the campaign of bombings and kidnappings carried out over the course of the last two years by the relatively small Movement for the Emancipation of the Niger Delta (MEND), a militant group fighting the Nigerian government over the oil-rich Delta region's underdevelopment, environmental degradation, and political marginalization, has had the cumulative effect of cutting Nigeria's total oil production by almost one-third.[19]

This natural wealth makes Africa an inviting target for the attentions of the People's Republic of China, whose dynamic economy, averaging 9 percent growth per annum over the last two decades, has an almost insatiable thirst for oil as well as a need for other natural resources to sustain it. China is currently importing approximately 2.6 million barrels of crude per day, about half of its consumption; more than 765,000 of those barrels—roughly a third of its imports—come from African sources, especially Sudan, Angola, and Congo (Brazzaville). Is it any wonder, then, that apart from the Central Eurasian region on its own northwestern frontier, perhaps no other foreign region rivals Africa as the object of Beijing's sustained strategic interest in recent years? Last year the Chinese regime published the first ever official white paper elaborating the bases of its policy toward Africa. This year, ahead of his 12-day, eight-nation tour of Africa—the third such journey since he took office in 2003—Chinese President Hu Jintao announced a 3-year, $3 billion program in preferential loans and expanded aid for Africa. These funds come on top of the $3 billion in loans and $2 billion in export credits that Hu announced in October 2006 at the opening of the historic Beijing summit of the Forum on China-Africa Cooperation (FOCAC) which brought nearly fifty African heads of state and ministers to the Chinese capital. Intentionally or not, many analysts expect that Africa—especially the states along its oil-rich western coastline—will increasingly becoming a theatre for strategic competition between the United States and its only real near-peer competitor on the global stage, China, as both countries seek to expand their influence and secure access to resources.[20] In connection with this, an additional security worry is China's increasing arms exports to Africa, especially as weapons are flowing to despotic regimes and fueling simmering conflicts even as they diminish further what little leverage Western governments and international organization—to say nothing of African ones—have with recalcitrant regimes.[21]

Yet for all its global importance as well as strategic significance for U.S. national interests, Africa's waters—especially the Gulf of Guinea, the Gulf of Aden and other waters off Somalia, and the "Swahili Coast" of East Africa— seen comparatively few resources poured into maritime security, a deficit which only worsens when one considers the scale of the area in question and the magnitude of the challenges faced. Depending on how one chooses to define the Gulf of Guinea region, the nearly 3,500 miles of coastline running in an arc from West Africa to Angola, for example, are highly susceptible to piracy, criminal enterprises, and poaching—in addition to the security challenge presented by the oil production facilities, both onshore and offshore, and the transport of the natural resources thus derived.[22]

The International Maritime Bureau's Piracy and Armed Robbery against Ships Report covering the first quarter of 2007, for instance, noted that while the number of reported attacks declined significantly compared to just one year before, the figure for incidents off the coast of Nigeria doubled.[23] At the same time, the Gulf of Guinea's oil-producing states have long been a plagued by "illegal bunkering," the tapping of pipelines for oil which is eventually loaded on to tankers which sell the crude to refineries elsewhere at a considerable profit. This highly organized and far-reaching activity—at one point, two Nigerian admirals were court-martialed for their involvement in one infamous 2004 incident involving the disappearance of a tanker with 11,000 barrels of oil—has grown increasingly deadly as energy prices surge upward and the criminal syndicates involved have acquired ever more sophisticated arms. There is also an increasing drug trade through the subregion: Nigeria is the transshipment point for approximately one-third of the heroin seized by authorities in the United States and more than half of the cocaine seized by South African officials, while European law enforcement officials report that poorly scrutinized West Africa has become the major conduit for drugs shipped to their countries by Latin American cartels.[24]

In addition to their vast hydrocarbon reserves, the waters of the Gulf of Guinea contain some of the richest fisheries in the world. Yet, according to a 2005 report commissioned by the British Department for International Development (DFID) and the Norwegian Agency for Development Cooperation (NORAD), illegal, unreported, or unlicensed (IUU) fishing—often by large foreign commercial trawlers—cost countries in the Gulf of Guinea more than $375 million annually. In addition to the obvious economic impact of the loss of the value of the catches to the countries affected, IUU fishing also carries indirect costs in terms of losses to industries upstream and downstream from fishing itself—to say nothing of damage to the ecosystem.[25]

In response to these challenges, the United States 2005 National Strategy for Maritime Security declared that:

> assisting regional partners to maintain the maritime sovereignty of their territorial seas and internal waters is a longstanding objective of the United States and contributes directly to the partners' economic development as well as their ability to combat unlawful or hostile exploitation by a variety of threats. For example, as a result of our active discussions with African partners, the United States is now appropriating funding for the implementation of border and coastal security initiatives along the lines of the former Africa Coastal Security (ACS) Program. Preventing unlawful or hostile exploitation of the maritime domain requires that nations collectively improve their capability to monitor activity throughout the domain, establish responsive decision-making architectures, enhance maritime interdiction capacity, develop effective policing protocols, and build intergovernmental cooperation. The United States, in cooperation with its allies, will lead an international effort to improve monitoring and enforcement capabilities through enhanced cooperation at the bilateral, regional, and global level.[26] [. . .]*

FINDING COMMON GROUND WITH AFRICANS AND WITH OURSELVES

Given what I outlined earlier, it is not surprising that the most recent iteration of the National Security Strategy of the United States of America, a document which identified the international counterterrorism effort as the country's top national security priority, affirmed that "Africa holds growing geo-strategic importance and is a high priority of this Administration."[27] However, the 2006 National Security Strategy also, quite appropriately in my judgment, went out of its way to state that "our security depends on partnering with Africans."

I have already noted the significant achievements of the current administration with regard to assistance toward Africa, including the Millennium Challenge Corporation, the President's Emergency Plan for AIDS Relief (PEPFAR), and the union of position of director of U.S. Foreign Assistance with that of administrator of the U.S. Agency for International Development (USAID) in the person with the rank of deputy secretary of state. These initiatives build upon the foundation of the African Growth and Opportunity Act (AGOA), originally signed in the previous administration, which has created some significant openings for some African countries.

---

* The following sections of the original work have been omitted from this compilation, because we believe that they were not relevant to the purposes of this book: the subsection titled "Humanitarian Challenges" (under the section "Recognizing our Strategic Interests") and the section titled "Acknowledging Increased African Leadership."

However, given the looming nature of the terrorist threat as well as the newly recognized geostrategic importance of Africa, it is not surprising that the U.S. military has also taken the lead in America's new engagement across the continent.

To date, the largest commitment has been the Combined Joint Task Force-Horn of Africa (CJTF-HOA), a unit created by the U.S. Central Command (CENTCOM) in late 2002 and based since May 2003 at a former French Foreign Legion outpost in Djibouti, Camp Lemonier. The approximately 1,500 personnel from each branch of the U.S. military, American civilian employees, and coalition forces, who make up CJTF-HOA have as their mission "detecting, disrupting and ultimately defeating transnational terrorist groups operating in the region" of Djibouti, Ethiopia, Eritrea, Kenya, Seychelles, Somalia, and Sudan (as well as Yemen across the Gulf of Aden).[28] CJTF-HOA pursues its objective of enhancing the long-term stability of its area of responsibility (AOR) by a combination of civil-military operations and supporting international governmental and nongovernmental organizations, including advisors who have assisted the African Union Mission in Sudan (AMIS). The task force also undertakes more traditional military-to-military training and other collaborative efforts, including some which certainly enabled Ethiopian forces to launch their offensive against the Somali Islamists last year. In certain exceptional circumstances when actionable intelligence was available, the physical proximity of CJTF-HOA to the front lines has enabled the United States to quickly and directly engage against high-value terrorist targets, as was the case last January when an Air Force AC-130 gunship launched a strike against what was described as "principal al-Qaeda leadership" in southern Somalia[29] or in June when the guided-missile destroyer USS *Chafee* shelled an al-Qaeda cell in the northern part of the country, killing six foreign terrorists.

At the same time CENTCOM was developing its Djibouti-based task force, the State Department launched a similar multilateral program, the Pan-Sahel Initiative (PSI), a modest effort to provide border security and other counterterrorism assistance to Chad, Mali, Mauritania, and Niger using personnel from U.S. Army Special Forces attached to the Special Operations Command Europe (SOCEUR) of the U.S. European Command (EUCOM). As a follow-up to PSI, the State Department–funded Trans-Sahara Counterterrorism Initiative (TSCTI) was launched in 2005 with support from the Department of Defense's Operation Enduring Freedom–Trans Sahara (OEF-TS). TSCTI added Algeria, Nigeria, Morocco, Senegal, and Tunisia to the original four PSI countries. In addition to the Pentagon-led efforts, the Sahel countries have also received support from State Department programs—especially the Anti-Terrorism Assistance (ATA) program and the Terrorist Interdiction Program (TIP)—and other U.S. government agencies, including USAID and the Department of the Treasury.

These efforts in the Sahelian subregion have already borne fruit. For example, Amari Saïfi, a former Algerian army officer-turned-GSPC leader better known by his nom de guerre Abderrazak al-Para ("the paratrooper") who was responsible for the daring 2003 kidnapping of 32 European tourists (they were ransomed for $6 million), was himself captured after an unprecedented chase involving personnel from seven countries who pursued him across the open deserts of Mali, Niger, and Chad (the hunt was directed by U.S. Navy P-3C Orion long range surveillance aircraft); Saïfi now serves a life sentence in far-less-open confines of an Algerian prison.[30]

Although the United States has historically deployed naval forces to Africa only to rescue stranded expatriates—Commodore Matthew Calbraith Perry's Cape Verde–based transatlantic slave trade–interdicting Africa Squadron in the 1840s being a notable exception—EUCOM's naval component, U.S. Naval Forces Europe (NAVEUR), has taken the lead in maritime engagement in the Gulf of Guinea. In late 2005, the dock landing ship USS *Gunston Hall* and the catamaran *HSV-2 Swift* conducted 5 weeks of joint drills with forces from several West African nations, including Ghana, Guinea, and Senegal. In early 2006, the submarine tender USS *Emory S. Land* deployed to the region with some 1,400 sailors and Marines to boost maritime security and strengthen partnerships, calling on ports from Senegal to Angola. And last November, the Department of State and the Department of Defense cosponsored a ministerial-level conference in Cotonou, Benin, on "Maritime Safety and Security in the Gulf of Guinea" which included representatives from eleven Gulf of Guinea countries as well as delegates from the United States, Europe, Senegal, South Africa, the African Union, and regional and international organizations. This fall the USS *Fort McHenry* will be in the Gulf of Guinea on an extended 6-month deployment as part of a multinational maritime-security-and-safety initiative that partners with West African countries to train teams from 11 African countries along to gulf, helping them to build their security capabilities, especially maritime domain awareness. NAVEUR's commander, Admiral Henry G. "Harry" Ulrich III, has described the *Fort McHenry*'s mission, which he characterized as within "the spirit of AFRICOM and the initial operating capacity of AFRICOM," as "the tipping point for us [which will] move this whole initiative of maritime safety and security ahead."[31] [. . .]

PUBLIC ANNOUNCEMENT
East Africa Consular Affairs Bulletins,
U.S. Overseas Security Advisory Council
August 31, 2007*

This Public Announcement is being reissued to remind Americans of the continuing potential for terrorist actions against U.S. citizens in East Africa,

---

*https://www.osac.gov/Reports/report.cfm?contentID=72989

particularly along the East African coast, to alert Americans to continuing sporadic violence in Somalia, and to note a number of incidents of maritime piracy near the horn of Africa and the southern Red Sea. This supersedes the Public Announcement of January 4, 2007, and expires on February 29, 2008.

A number of al-Qaida operatives and other extremists are believed to be operating in and around East Africa. As a result of the recent conflict and continuing tension in Somalia, some of these individuals have sought to relocate elsewhere in the region, and others may seek to do so. Americans considering travel to the region and those already there should review their plans carefully, remain vigilant with regard to their personal security, and exercise caution. Terrorist actions may include suicide operations, bombings, kidnappings, or targeting maritime vessels. Terrorists do not distinguish between official and civilian targets. Increased security at official U.S. facilities has led terrorists to seek softer targets such as hotels, beach resorts, prominent public places, and landmarks. In particular, terrorists may target civil aviation and seaports. Americans in remote areas or border regions where military or police authority is limited or nonexistent could also become targets.

Americans considering seaborne travel near the Horn of Africa or in the southern Red Sea should exercise extreme caution, as there have been several incidents of armed attacks, robberies, and kidnappings for ransom at sea by pirates during the past several years. Merchant vessels continue to be hijacked in Somali territorial waters, while others have been hijacked as far as 200 nautical miles off the coast of Somalia in international waters.

The U.S. government maritime authorities advise mariners to avoid the port of Mogadishu, and to remain at least 200 nautical miles off the coast of Somalia. In addition, when transiting around the Horn of Africa or in the Red Sea, it is strongly recommended that vessels travel in convoys, and maintain good communications contact at all times . . .

South America & the Caribbean

NAVAL FORCES FROM EIGHT COUNTRIES TRAIN TO PROTECT PANAMA CANAL
Press Release, Embassy of the United States,
Panama
August 10, 2004*

Naval forces from eight countries begin this week PANAMAX 2004, a maritime exercise in which the multinational forces plan and coordinate a coalition response to a security threat against the Panama Canal.

---

*http://panama.usembassy.gov/panama/Panamax.html

PANAMAX is conducted under the direction of Commander U.S. Naval Forces Southern command and involves personnel, aircraft and ships from Argentina, Chile, Colombia, Dominican Republic, Honduras, Panama, Peru, and the United States and observers from Ecuador. The participants organized into Task Force 138 will conduct the weeklong exercise, which includes operations on the high seas, coast, and land.

"The great interest of the nations in the region to participate and expand this exercise is a clear indication of the importance that they place in Panama Canal and its security," said Rear Adm. Vinson E. Smith, Commander Task Force 138, the multinational naval force of the Americas. "Likewise, Panamanian government agencies and services are involved in the exercise ready to assume their role in the exercise scenario."

On its second year, PANAMAX has also increased its complexity. This year's scenario includes multiple seaborne threats approaching the Panama Canal from the Caribbean Sea and the Eastern Pacific. To respond to these threats, the multinational task force is tasked to detect, monitor, and interdict suspicious vessels and to hand them over to the Panamanian National Maritime Service as the ships approach the country's territorial waters.

"The complex no-notice scenario and the multinational involvement make this realistic exercise very challenging. We will be planning and responding exactly like we would in an actual crisis," said Commodore Dave Costa, Commander Destroyer Squadron (CDS) Six, in charge of the forces operating in the Caribbean Sea, which include the guided missile frigate USS *Crommelin* (FFG 37) and the Colombian ship *ARC Almirante Padilla*.

The forces operating in the Pacific will be led by Chilean Captain Francisco Alvayay and include USS *John L. Hall* (FFG 32), the Peruvian ships *BAP Mariategui* and *BAP Herrera*, the Chilean ships *BACH Zenteno* and *BACH Macalbi*, and the U.S. Coast Guard cutter USCG *Legare*.

In addition, the Panamanian National Maritime Service and National Air Service will lead the coastal, and land and air operations coordinating efforts with Panamanian National Security Council, the National Police, and the Panama Canal Authority among others.

The exercise scenario was designed by expert naval planners from the participating nations in an effort to develop combined responses in the defense of hemispheric security. The exercise supports two objectives: first ensure freedom of navigation and, second, increase interoperability among nations with critical interest in the Panama Canal.

The Panama Canal is perhaps the most crucial piece of infrastructure in the flow of goods and commerce in the Western Hemisphere. Hundreds of ships transit the canal every year carrying more than 235 million tons of exports and imports, which sustain the economies of all the nations in the region.

ARGENTINA BECOMES THE FIRST SOUTH AMERICAN
COUNTRY TO SIGN CONTAINER SECURITY INITIATIVE
DECLARATION OF PRINCIPLES
U.S. Customs and Border Protection,
Office of Public Affairs
May 11, 2005*

Washington, D.C.—U.S. Customs and Border Protection (CBP) announced that Argentina is the first South American country to participate in the Container Security Initiative (CSI). By signing the declaration of principles on May 9, 2005, U.S. Ambassador to Argentina Lino Gutierrez and Dr. Alberto R. Abad, Federal Administrator of National Revenue of the Argentine Republic, enable all cargo destined for the United States through the port of Buenos Aires to be targeted and prescreened for terrorists and terrorist weapons. On hand to support the signing was Ambassador Cresencio (Cris) Arcos, Director, International Affairs, from the Department of Homeland Security, and Dr. Ricardo Echegarray, Director General of Argentine Customs.

"The port of Buenos Aires is one of the leading ports in South America. I applaud the government of Argentina for assuming a leadership role in the Container Security Initiative," said CBP Commissioner Robert C. Bonner. "CSI strengthens our ability to prevent terrorists and their weapons from entering the United States. By working closely with our host nations, CBP officers are able to identify containers bound for U.S. seaports that pose a potential threat for terrorism. I am particularly pleased to expand the CSI security blanket to South America."

Buenos Aires, Argentina, is located at the river Rio de la Plata and by open sea. The expansion of CSI to Buenos Aires will provide a strategic advantage for targeting containers transshipped through the port.

"Argentina's commitment to the Container Security Initiative today is a praiseworthy act of regional leadership," Ambassador Arcos said. "It will invigorate ocean-bound commerce worldwide and bolster efforts to keep the Hemisphere secure."

CSI is the only multinational program in place in the world today that is protecting global trade lanes from being exploited and disrupted by international terrorists. By collaborating with foreign customs administrations, CBP is working towards a safer, more secure world trading system. Under CSI, CBP has entered into bilateral partnerships with other

---

*http://www.cbp.gov/xp/cgov/newsroom/news_releases/archives/2005_press_releases/052005/05112005.xml

administrations to identify high-risk cargo containers and to prescreen them before they are loaded on vessels destined for the United States. Today, 22 administrations have committed to joining CSI and are at various stages of implementation.

On average, every day about 25,000 seagoing containers are offloaded at America's seaports. Commissioner Bonner, confirmed by Congress shortly after 9/11, made maritime cargo security one of his top priorities. The Container Security Initiative was launched in January 2002. CSI has been accepted globally as a bold and revolutionary initiative to secure maritime cargo shipments against the terrorist threat.

The 36 operational ports in Europe, Asia, Africa, the Middle East, and North America include Halifax, Montreal, and Vancouver, Canada; Rotterdam, The Netherlands; Le Havre and Marseille, France; Bremerhaven and Hamburg, Germany; Antwerp and Zeebrugge, Belgium; Singapore; Yokohama, Tokyo, Nagoya, and Kobe, Japan; Hong Kong; Göteborg, Sweden; Felixstowe, Liverpool, Southampton, Thamesport, and Tilbury, United Kingdom; Genoa, La Spezia, Naples, Gioia Tauro and Livorno, Italy; Busan, Korea; Durban, South Africa; Port Klang and Tanjung Pelepas, Malaysia; Piraeus, Greece; Algeciras, Spain; Laem Chabang, Thailand; Dubai, United Arab Emirates; and Shanghai, China.

CSI will continue to expand to strategic locations around the world. The World Customs Organization (WCO), the European Union (EU), and the G8 support CSI expansion and have adopted resolutions implementing CSI security measures introduced at ports throughout the world.

INFORMATION ON PORT SECURITY IN THE CARIBBEAN BASIN

Steven Caldwell
Director, Homeland Security and Justice Issues,
General Accountability Office
Government Accountability Office Report Summary
June 29, 2007*

Referred to as our "third border," the Caribbean Basin has significant maritime links with the United States.[32] Given these links and the region's proximity, the United States is particularly interested in ensuring that the ports in the Caribbean Basin—through which goods bound for this country's ports and cruise ships carrying its citizens must travel—are secure.

Section 233 (c) of the Security and Accountability for Every Port Act of 2006 (SAFE Port Act)[33] requires GAO to report on various security-related

---

*http://www.gao.gov/new.items/d07804r.pdf

aspects of Caribbean Basin ports. Our specific objectives were to identify and describe the

- threats and security concerns in the Caribbean Basin related to port security,
- actions that foreign governments and local stakeholders have taken in the Caribbean Basin to implement international port security requirements and the challenges that remain,
- activities reported to be under way by U.S. government agencies to enhance port security in the Caribbean Basin, and
- potential economic impacts of port security and terrorist attacks in the Caribbean Basin.

To determine the threats and security concerns in the Caribbean Basin related to port security, we interviewed officials from federal agencies, international organizations and associations, and various stakeholders (such as facility operators and government officials of Caribbean countries) involved in port security in the region. To determine the actions taken by Caribbean Basin countries to implement international port security requirements and the challenges they face, we visited several Caribbean nations and reviewed information provided by agencies and organizations working in the region. To determine the activities under way by U.S. government agencies to enhance port security in the Caribbean Basin, we met with agency officials and reviewed pertinent documents. Finally, to identify the potential economic impacts of port security in the Caribbean Basin, we met with officials from the countries we visited, as well as from U.S. agencies and international organizations, and reviewed various analyses by a government agency and nongovernmental researchers. Because the mandate gave us a limited time frame within which to complete our work, this report is descriptive in nature and does not provide a detailed analysis of the actions taken or efforts made regarding port security in the Caribbean Basin. Enclosure II describes our scope and methodology in more detail.

Between March 29 and April 13, 2007, we briefed your offices on the results of our work to address these objectives. This report summarizes the information provided during those discussions and provides the detailed handouts in enclosure I. Additional information received from the agencies since the briefings were presented is contained in the body and agency comments section of this document. We conducted our work from October 2006 through June 2007 in accordance with generally accepted government auditing standards.

SUMMARY

Although intelligence sources report that no specific, credible terrorist threats to maritime security exist in the Caribbean Basin, the officials we spoke to indicated that there are a number of security concerns that could affect port security in the region. Caribbean ports contain a variety of facilities such as cargo facilities, cruise ship terminals, and facilities that handle petroleum products and liquefied natural gas. Additionally, several Caribbean ports are among the top cruise ship destinations in the world. Given the volume and value of this maritime trade, the facilities and infrastructure of the maritime transportation system may be attractive targets for a terrorist attack. Our prior work on maritime security issues has revealed that the three most likely modes of attack in the port environment are a suicide attack using an explosive-laden vehicle or vessel, a standoff attack using small arms or rockets, and the traditional armed assault. Beyond the types of facilities and modes of attack to be considered, officials we spoke to identified a number of overarching security concerns that relate to the Caribbean Basin as a whole. Among these concerns are (1) the level of corruption that exists in some Caribbean nations to undermine the rule of law in these countries, (2) organized gang activity occurring in proximity to or within port facilities, and (3) the geographic proximity of many Caribbean countries, which has made them transit countries for cocaine and heroin destined for U.S. markets. Other security concerns in the Caribbean Basin mentioned by U.S. agency officials include stowaways, illegal migration, and the growing influence of Islamic radical groups and other foreign terrorist organizations.

Foreign governments and local stakeholders in the Caribbean Basin have taken a number of steps to implement the International Ship and Port Facility Security (ISPS) Code, although challenges for further progress remain.[34] The U.S. Coast Guard has visited a number of Caribbean Basin countries to observe the security and antiterrorism measures put in place at their ports to determine the degree to which the ISPS Code has been implemented. Final reports from these visits have been issued for 14 of the 29 Caribbean Nations included in this report. Most of the countries were found to have "substantially implemented the ISPS Code." Even so, the Coast Guard also found that facilities within some countries needed to make improvements or take additional measures. According to a Coast Guard official, although the Coast Guard cannot require the facilities to make improvements to respond to Coast Guard's findings, improvements have been made in order to avoid potential difficulties in conducting trade with the United States. We also visited five countries in the region and found that security measures were generally in place, although there were areas of concern, such as maintaining access controls, conducting security plan exercises, and maintaining security records.[35] Our discussions with facility operators as well as government officials and a regional association during these visits revealed that challenges exist, such as obtaining additional training for their security personnel and funding for the further enhancement of port security measures in the region.

Several U.S. agencies reported being involved in activities in the Caribbean Basin that could help enhance port security in the region. Through its embassies, the Department of State serves as the lead coordinator of the activities of other U.S. federal agencies in the Caribbean nations. The State Department has also been involved through the Organization of American States to coordinate and fund projects to improve maritime security. The Coast Guard is involved in the region through its International Port Security Program to assess the effectiveness of antiterrorism measures in place in other countries. The Coast Guard monitors the implementation of ISPS Code requirements in these countries and provides them with best practices to help them improve port security. The Coast Guard also has a Port State Control (PSC) program in which officials board and inspect foreign vessels arriving at U.S. ports to ensure that the vessels are complying with security standards. To address a potential mass migration event from a Caribbean nation such as Haiti or Cuba, the Department of Homeland Security (DHS) has developed a plan that involves dozens of federal, state, and local agencies. Customs and Border Protection, another DHS component, has provided training assistance to a number of Caribbean nations and is also operating its Container Security Initiative in the Bahamas, the Dominican Republic, Honduras, and Jamaica. Under this initiative, Customs and Border Protection staff are placed at foreign seaports to screen containers for weapons of mass destruction. Related to the security of containers in the ports, the Department of Energy (DOE) also has efforts under way in the Caribbean Basin related to its Megaports Initiative, which provides equipment to scan containers for nuclear and radiological materials. This initiative is currently operational in the Bahamas and is expected to eventually operate in other countries as well. The U.S. Agency for International Development (USAID), already active throughout the Caribbean because of its role in administering assistance programs, also has directly contributed funds toward a project to help Haiti comply with the requirements of the ISPS Code. The Department of Defense (DOD), through its Southern Command (SOUTHCOM), is active in the Caribbean through its Enduring Friendship program, which seeks to achieve regional security cooperation and build maritime security capabilities. Finally, there are several interagency efforts under way in the region to help secure cargo and counter illicit trafficking, migration, and narco-terrorism operations. For example, one effort involves coordinating the efforts of Coast Guard, Customs and Border Protection, Immigration and Customs Enforcement, and the U.S. Attorney's Office to target illegal migration and narco-trafficking near Puerto Rico and the U.S. Virgin Islands.

Although the potential economic impact of port security (or lack thereof) in the Caribbean Basin is difficult to determine, our review of analyses performed by a government agency and nongovernmental researchers identified a number of factors that could influence the economic impact of port security and a terrorist attack in the maritime domain. These factors include (1) the target of the attack, (2) the tactics employed and objectives of the attack, (3) the amount of destruction caused by the attack, and (4) the ability to recover from the disruption or loss of facilities resulting from the attack. As part of an effective risk management approach—a framework that can aid in determining which vulnerabilities should be addressed in ways within available resources—government officials and port stakeholders must determine which security measures to implement by considering their benefits and costs with these factors in mind. To address the risk posed by vessels seeking entry into the United States from foreign ports that do not maintain effective antiterrorism measures as determined through the country visits completed under the International Port Security Program, the U.S. Coast Guard is authorized to take certain actions such as boarding vessels or conducting inspections of vessels. These actions can result, for example, in costs to shippers and others because of time lost while the vessel is boarded or being inspected. From July 10, 2006, when the Coast Guard began data measurements of its activities with these vessels, to April 2007, only two vessels have been subjected to a boarding offshore by Coast Guard officials prior to gaining entry to a U.S. port solely because they arrived from a Caribbean Basin port facility deemed by the Coast Guard as not maintaining effective antiterrorism measures. To determine the potential costs of such boardings, we talked with a variety of maritime stakeholders in the region, such as facility operators and a shipping association, who indicated that such boardings have not been a significant source of delay or financial loss for their businesses. Thus the economic impact on the maritime industry—of actions taken to date by the Coast Guard in response to security problems at Caribbean Ports—appears to be insignificant.

AGENCY COMMENTS

We provided a draft of this report to the Department of Defense, the Department of Energy, the Department of Homeland Security and its component agencies (the Coast Guard, Customs and Border Protection, and Immigration and Customs Enforcement), the Department of State, and the U.S. Agency for International Development for their review and comment. We received technical comments from the Department of Defense and the Coast Guard, which we incorporated where appropriate. The Department of Homeland Security and the U.S. Agency for International Development provided formal written comments, which are presented in enclosures III and IV. These comments and the supplemental comments provided by the Coast Guard, Immigration and Customs Enforcement, and the Department of State are discussed below. The Department of Energy did not provide comments on the report.

In its comments, the Department of Homeland Security suggested that additional information be included on other Customs and Border Protection programs and initiatives under way in the region. CBP officials subsequently provided the following information on two of these programs:

- The Caribbean Corridor Initiative: Established in April 2005, this is a multia-gency initiative that targets drug trafficking in the Eastern and Central Caribbean areas. The mission of this operation is to identify, disrupt, and dis-mantle South American drug trafficking organizations that utilize the mar-itime domain to smuggle narcotics into and throughout the Caribbean. The agencies that are part of this initiative include Customs and Border Protection (CBP), Immigration and Customs Enforcement (ICE), the Drug Enforcement Administration, the Federal Bureau of Investigation, the U.S. Coast Guard Investigative Services (USCIS), and the U.S. Attorney for the District of Puerto Rico. Under this initiative, CBP has provided training to countries in the region on the use of cargo scanning technologies and identifying fraudulent documents.
- The Secure Freight Initiative: Formally initiated in December 2006, this initia-tive will fuse commercial data from the supply chain, information on the ves-sel and crew, information about cargo movement and integrity, and an integrated foreign and domestic radiography and radiation detection scan to create an enhanced risk assessment for the maritime domain.

Coast Guard officials commented that the individuals involved in the recent JFK International Airport terrorist plot were from Trinidad and Guyana and are believed to have been in contact with that the radical Islamic group Jamaat al Muslimeen, which has been active in Trinidad. Related to the secu-rity of domestic U.S. ports, waterways and coastal areas, Coast Guard officials also noted that operational activities conducted by the Coast Guard and its federal, state, and local partners are guided by a Coast Guard operations order called Operation Neptune Shield, which contains a classified set of requirements establishing the Coast Guard's homeland security activity lev-els with performance minimums that escalate as the maritime security (MAR-SEC) level increases. Operational activities covered by this order include patrols to provide deterrence and response, boardings of vessels, escorts of selected vessels during transits, deployment of antiterrorism and counterter-rorism assets, and enforcement of security zones among other things.

ICE officials commented that the Caribbean Basin region continues to remain as a major center for drug trafficking, money laundering, and poten-tial major staging area for terrorist operations. They stated that commercial vessels departing from Colombia, Venezuela, Panama, Haiti, and the Domini-can Republic pose a direct threat to U.S. law enforcement assets assigned to the detection and monitoring of narcotics traffic and national security as well. ICE officials also stated that steps have been taken to monitor and detect high-risk shipments and containers coming from the region. In addition to these security concerns, ICE officials noted that the United States depends greatly on critical energy infrastructure located in the region and that any destabi-lization of this infrastructure could negatively affect the U.S. economy.

The Department of State stated in its comments that the threat by an explo-sive-laden vehicle to a cruise ship port facility or directly to a cruise ship should be a matter of great concern to U.S. government authorities and that U.S. citizens can be particularly vulnerable in this area. According to the State Department, such an attack can cause loss of life to American cruise line passengers and considerable economic impact on American cruise line and tourist industries in the United States. In addition, the State Department stated that compliance with the International Ship and Port Facility Security Code does not necessarily mean that a port is secure from a terrorist attack. The State Department noted that it and its contractors have witnessed open gates, poor screening of vehicles, and inadequate physical protections at ports with cruise line activity. The State Department stated that these deficiencies, coupled with poorly trained security personnel, can make cruise line terminals and cruise ships vulnerable to attack. According to the State Department, poor training of port security personnel is also an overarching security concern.

The U.S. Agency for International Development expressed agreement with the contents of this report.

We are sending copies of this report to the secretaries of the Departments of Defense, Energy, Homeland Security, and State, as well as the administrator of the U.S. Agency for International Development, and other interested congressional committees. We will also make copies available to others upon request. Additionally, this report will be available at no charge on GAO's Web site at http://www.gao.gov [. . .]

GLOBAL MULTILATERAL PERSPECTIVES

European Union (EU)

EU PRESIDENCY STATEMENT—PIRACY AT SEA

Dr. Marie Jacobsson
Alternate Head of Delegation of Sweden on behalf of the European Union
EU Statement in Discussion Panel B: Combating Piracy
and Armed Robbery at Sea, European Union at United Nations
New York City
May 10, 2001*

Mr. Co-Chairman,

I have the honor to speak on behalf of the European Union. The Central and Eastern European countries associated with the European Union Bulgaria, Czech Republic, Estonia, Hungary, Latvia, Lithuania, Poland, Romania, Slovakia, and Slovenia and the associated countries Cyprus and Malta align themselves with this statement.

---

*http://www.eu-un.europa.eu/articles/en/article_233_en.htm

"Acts of piracy and armed robbery against ships represent a serious threat to the lives of seafarers, the safety of navigation, the marine environment, and the security of coastal states. They also impact negatively on the entire maritime transport industry, leading, for example, to increases in insurance rates and even the suspension of trade." The quotation comes from the unedited text of the UN report on Oceans and the Law of the Sea, to be considered at the 56th session of the General Assembly.

It describes in two sentences why piracy and armed robbery against ships constitute a problem.

Statistics from the International Maritime Organisation shows that the number of acts of piracy and armed robbery against ships that occurred in 2000, as reported to the Organisation, was 471. That is an increase of 162 (52 percent) over the figure for 1999.

Piracy and armed robbery against ships simply makes our common maritime area for transport—the seas—an unsafe area to use.

They bring about and encourage lawlessness.

They either threaten to undermine coastal states' authority in the coastal state's own territory, or they threaten to undermine an effective global management of a global common.

They make the environment in which the crews work unsafe.

They are often a threat to the environment.

They are simply a destabilizing factor that needs to be combated!

Piracy is a crime under international law. Other acts, such as unlawful acts against the safety of maritime navigation, including armed robbery against ships, are prohibited in recent treaties. Piracy and armed robbery against ships are very often also crimes under national law. The international community as a whole has an interest in preventing and in combating such crimes. Although it is possible to assume that the flag state, the coastal state, the port state and the state of which the pirates or criminals are nationals, have a particular responsibility to combat piracy and armed robbery, preventing and combating piracy has been an obligation of all states for centuries. Article 100 of UNCLOS clearly reiterates that all states have a duty to cooperate for the repression of piracy.

Ships of all states enjoy the right of innocent passage, transit passage and archipelagic sea-lanes passage in areas under the sovereignty of a coastal state. It is clear that armed robbery against ships seriously threatens these fundamental rights.

It is, and it should remain, the prerogative of the coastal state to exercise control over its territory. The coastal states have a special responsibility to fight criminal acts in their territory. It is therefore extremely important that the coastal states concerned are encouraged to take this problem seriously, especially considering that most attacks occur within their sea territory, i.e. including internal waters and ports. However, this requires knowledge and resources.

Mr. Co-Chairman,

There is a proliferation of regional and global governmental and nongovernmental organizations that at various levels deal with the issue of piracy and armed robbery against ships, for example the International Maritime Organisation, (IMO), INTERPOL, the International Maritime Bureau of the International Chamber of Commerce (ICC-IMB), the Baltic and International Maritime Council (BIMCO), the International Chamber of Shipping (ICS), the International Transport Workers' Federation (ITF), the International Union of Marine Insurance (IUMI), the International Group of P & I Clubs (IGP & I), and numbers of others.

The International Maritime Organisation plays a vital role and the organization should remain a focal point when it comes to combating piracy. The organization has addressed the problem since 1983, when it was 'reintroduced' on the international agenda. Since then, a number of committees of the IMO have taken measures to address the problem—for example, the Maritime Safety Committee, the Legal Committee, and the Marine Environment Protection Committee.

The Maritime Safety Committee has approved for circulation a Code of Practice for the Investigation of the Crimes of Piracy and Armed Robbery Against Ships, pending its adoption by the IMO Assembly in November 2001. The IMO Subcommittee on Flag State Implementation has recently prepared a resolution in order to prevent registration of so-called phantom ships that will be presented for adoption at the IMO Assembly in November 2001.

The series of regional workshops initiated by the IMO in October 1998 in Singapore and concluded in Mumbai, India, in March 2000 have already produced positive results. Let me just mention one example, namely the problem of underreporting. Since the IMO stressed the need for all incidents to be reported, there has been an increase in reports. This, in turn, helps us to get a clearer picture of the problem.

Impressive regional efforts have been made in order to combat piracy. The initiatives taken by Japan, India, and Malaysia—for example, within the Japan-ASEAN Summit and other meetings—are commendable, as is the initiative to hold combined antipiracy exercises with other countries in the region.

States have now decided to bring up the matter in the oceans consultative process. The EU member states recognize the importance of the fact that the matter is brought up within the context of this process and welcome the inclusion on the agenda of piracy and armed robbery against ships. It is logical to discuss the matter in this context, not least since the United Nations Convention on the Law of the Sea provides for the rights and duties of all states in respect of acts of piracy.

There is a need for all UN agencies and international bodies to coordinate responses to the threat of piracy and armed robbery against ships. The matter is of concern to the IMO, the World Bank, to UNEP, to international police agencies—just to mention a few.

Mr. Co-Chairman,

It is important that states become parties to the relevant international treaties in this field, namely the 1982 UN Convention on the Law of the Sea; 1988 Convention on the Suppression of Unlawful Acts against the Safety of

Maritime Navigation and its Protocol on Suppression of Unlawful Acts against the Safety of Fixed Platforms Located on the Continental Shelf; and the UN Convention on Combating Organised Crime.

Unfortunately, this is not enough. States should also be encouraged to enact and enforce national legislation for effective implementation and enforcement of these conventions. Perhaps all states ought to review their national legislation and practice to see if they fully reflect the rights and duties embedded in these conventions.

It is, furthermore, important that the coastal states concerned make an increased effort to prevent and combat piracy and armed robbery. This should be done both by addressing the question of preventive measures to be taken in ports and by handling of reports from ships that are being attacked or have been attacked. In doing so they may seek guidance in the guidelines developed by both IMO and nongovernmental organizations.

It is also essential that those flag states whose ships are sailing in waters affected by crimes at sea, and who are the targets of piracy attacks or armed robbery, make an increased effort to advise their ships on how to take precautions against these attacks. Guidance in these matters may also be found in the guidelines developed by IMO.

But this is still not enough. Piracy is an international crime that by definition can only be committed outside of the territory of a state. Sometimes piratical acts are better described as internationally organized crime. This is particularly true in cases, which involve "phantom ships." It is also an indication of the fact that a crime must not be treated in isolation.

It is therefore of the utmost importance that cooperation between states and relevant international bodies is encouraged. We need a global management regime, and we need to make sure that measures taken by individual states are consistently enforced within the framework of international law. The World Bank and regional bodies and states should support these measures.

The IMO should be recognized as the international organization that has the primary mandate to globally deal with the problem of piracy. At the same time, regional initiatives and activities, such as the discussion in the ASEAN Regional Forum (ARF) should be strongly encouraged.

Experience has also shown that the coastal states concerned may benefit from entering into regional cooperation. Specific areas for cooperation could include capacity building in law enforcement and legislation, development of standard reporting procedures, development of both global and regional information bases and cooperation between coast guards.

Cooperation and the building of networks can also be achieved through other measures. A number of reports have shown that law enforcement officials and policy-makers from affected areas need education, and need to exchange information on experience. There is one institution that seems apt to provide a forum for such measures namely, the United Nations' World Maritime University, which is a university, established under the auspices of the IMO.

At present, the World Maritime University gives lectures on piracy in some of its courses. However, the WMU could do something on a wider scale, perhaps a weeklong seminar, to which representatives from, for example, other UN bodies such as IMO could be invited to give presentations. An alternative might be to develop and deliver education on piracy matters as a "Professional Development Course (PDC)" and invite all maritime administrations around the world to participate. The courses could also include training of investigators of piracy and armed robbery against vessels. Such a course could also serve as an international contact point for representatives from those different regions in the world that are most affected by piracy.

The EU member states suggest that the WMU should be asked whether it would be possible for the WMU to serve as a focal educational point and to commence a more organized education on the issue of piracy and armed robbery against ships.

Mr. Co-Chairman,

Let me also take the opportunity to say a few words about the work of the Comité Maritime International.

In February 2001, the Assembly of the Comité Maritime International adopted a resolution (at the XXXVII International Conference of the CMI) encouraging the Executive Council to transmit the so-called Model National Law to the Secretary-General of the IMO with a request for endorsement by the IMO Assembly.

It is, of course, to be welcomed that piracy and armed robbery against ships is now gaining more and more attention. The work by the CMI should be honored. Piracy is a truly global problem and it cuts across all sectors of society—from political to commercial, from state actors to individuals. At the same time there is a risk, given the number of fora in which piracy and armed robbery against ships is discussed, that the problem is dealt with in disparate ways and not in a particularly organized and consistent manner. The attempts to define criminal acts against ships not included in the definition of piracy in UNCLOS represent one example that needs to be discussed.

The EU member states believe that the only viable way to prevent and to combat piracy and armed robbery at sea goes through cooperation and capacity building. Moreover, the private sector should be even further associated, as appropriate, to the efforts developed by the international community.

Such cooperation should include capacity building in law enforcement, legislation, development of both regional and global information bases, regional exchanges on law enforcement and coast guard training.

The EU would like to express its concern over the current underreporting of acts of piracy and armed robbery against ships. It is important that all incidents are reported. In this context we note that there has been an increase in reporting and that it is welcome (although the incidents themselves are not). The IMO should be a focal point when receiving reports. The recording and initial examination of reports should be made by the IMO, because the IMO is an intergovernmental organization with international credibility also within the private sector. Furthermore, it is essential that all states support the initiatives taken by the IMO to prevent and combat piracy and armed robbery against ships, thereby maintaining focus on this very serious problem. The WMU should be asked to bear responsibility for the development of international education and training.

Piracy and armed robbery against ships can constitute an environmental hazard.

It is therefore important that regional emergency plans be developed.

The IMO and other organizations strongly discourage the carrying and use of firearms on board merchant vessels, and the EU supports this point of view. However, when the vessels do not carry firearms on board, the states must take their responsibility to patrol areas in which incidents are most likely to occur, and to act against the criminals. This is indeed a costly business and the lack of capacity and funds to tackle it needs to be examined and discussed, as does the matter of what could be done to build up capacity.

There are also other issues that need to be discussed, such as the need for maritime areas to be properly charted, how far an obligation for a ship to carry an Automatic Identification System (AIS) can curb criminality, and if smoother exchange control restrictions would be of help.

The EU member states are willing and prepared to commence a discussion on what measures could be taken. We look forward to a strong statement in the report of this meeting to UNGA on the importance of preventing and combating piracy, suggesting measures and decisions that could be reviewed at future meetings of the oceans consultative process and by the General Assembly. Piracy and armed robbery against ships are matters for the international community as a whole.

Thank you, Mr. Co-Chairman.

AN INTEGRATED MARITIME POLICY FOR THE EUROPEAN UNION
Communication from the Commission to the European Parliament, the Council, the European Economic and Social Committee, and the Committee of the Regions, Commission of the European Communities, Brussels
October 10, 2007*

EXECUTIVE SUMMARY

The seas are Europe's lifeblood. Europe's maritime spaces and its coasts are central to its wellbeing and prosperity—they are Europe's trade routes, climate regulator, sources of food, energy and resources, and a favored site for

---

*http://eur-lex.europa.eu/LexUriServ/site/en/com/2007/com2007_0575en01.pdf

its citizens' residence and recreation. Our interactions with the sea are more intense, more varied, and create more value for Europe than ever before. Yet the strain is showing. We are at a crossroads in our relationship with the oceans.

On the one hand technology and know-how allow us to extract ever more value from the sea, and more and more people flow to Europe's coasts to benefit from that value. On the other hand, the cumulated effect of all this activity is leading to conflicts of use and to the deterioration of the marine environment that everything else depends on. Europe must respond to this challenge; in a context of rapid globalization and climate change the urgency is great.

The European Commission has recognized this, and launched a comprehensive consultation and analysis of how Europe relates to the sea.[36] It has triggered a massive response from stakeholders that reveals clearly the enormous potential of the seas and the scale of the challenge if we are to realize that potential sustainably. It has also provided a wealth of ideas as to how Europe can rise to meet this challenge.

Building on this valuable input the Commission proposes an Integrated Maritime Policy for the European Union, based on the clear recognition that all matters relating to Europe's oceans and seas are interlinked, and that sea-related policies must develop in a joined-up way if we are to reap the desired results.

This integrated, intersectoral approach was strongly endorsed by all stakeholders. Applying it will require reinforced cooperation and effective coordination of all sea-related policies at the different decision-making levels.

An Integrated Maritime Policy will enhance Europe's capacity to face the challenges of globalization and competitiveness, climate change, degradation of the marine environment, maritime safety and security, and energy security and sustainability. It must be based on excellence in marine research, technology, and innovation and will be anchored in the Lisbon agenda for jobs and growth and the Gothenburg agenda for sustainability.

An EU Integrated Maritime Policy will:

- Change the way we make policy and take decisions—at every level compartmentalized policy development and decision-making are no longer adequate. Interactions must be understood and taken into account; common tools developed; synergies identified and exploited; and conflicts avoided or resolved.
- Develop and deliver a program of work—action under the different sectoral policies must develop in a coherent policy framework. The Action Plan accompanying this communication gives a clear idea of the variety and magnitude of the work ahead. The following projects are of particular importance:
  - A European Maritime Transport Space without barriers
  - A European Strategy for Marine Research

- National integrated maritime policies to be developed by member states
- A European network for maritime surveillance
- A road map toward maritime spatial planning by member states
- A strategy to mitigate the effects of climate change on coastal regions
- Reduction of CO2 emissions and pollution by shipping
- Elimination of pirate fishing and destructive high seas bottom trawling
- An European network of maritime clusters
- A review of EU labor law exemptions for the shipping and fishing sectors

This Communication lays the foundation for the governance framework and cross-sectoral tools necessary for an EU Integrated Maritime Policy and sets out the main actions that the Commission will pursue during the course of this mandate. These actions will be guided by the principles of subsidiarity and competitiveness, the ecosystem approach, and stakeholder participation.

NATO

COMBATING TERRORISM IN THE MEDITERRANEAN

Vice Admiral Roberto Cesaretti
Commander, NATO Operation Endeavour
NATO Review, North Atlantic Treaty Organization
Autumn 2005[*]

In the course of the past four years, NATO's first Article-5, collective-defense operation has evolved from a small-scale deployment providing a modest military presence in an important stretch of sea into a comprehensive, continuously adapting counterterrorism operation throughout the Mediterranean. In the process, the Alliance has contributed to maintaining peace, stability and security in a strategic region, obtained invaluable experience of maritime interdiction operations and developed increasingly effective intelligence-gathering and information-sharing procedures relevant to the wider struggle against international terrorism.

NATO's Standing Naval Force Mediterranean deployed in the Eastern Mediterranean on October 6, 2001, a day before the launch of the U.S.-led Operation Enduring Freedom to oust the Taliban and al-Qaida from Afghanistan. This measure, taken at the request of the United States following the September 11 terrorist attacks and NATO's invocation of Article 5 a

---

[*]http://www.nato.int/docu/review/2005/issue3/english/art4.html

day later, aimed to provide a deterrent presence and surveillance in strategic international waters at a key moment.

In the intervening years, the operation, subsequently named Active Endeavour, has become increasingly sophisticated as the Alliance has refined its counterterrorism role and integrated lessons learned in the course of the operation. In this way, Active Endeavour's mandate has been regularly reviewed and its mission and force composition adjusted to create an effective counter to terrorism throughout the Mediterranean.

In February 2003, the operation was expanded to include escorting merchant shipping from Allied states through the Straits of Gibraltar. This was a precautionary measure taken on the basis of intelligence indicating that ships passing through this extremely narrow passage were potential terrorist targets. The escorts were subsequently suspended in May 2004 as a result of a decline in the number of requests but may be reactivated at any time.

In April 2003, NATO extended Active Endeavour's scope to include compliant boarding operations, that is, boarding with the consent of the ships' masters and flag states in accordance with international law. Then in March 2004, NATO expanded Active Endeavour's area of operations to include the entire Mediterranean. As of September 15, 2005, some 69,000 ships had been "hailed" and 95 boarded. In addition, 488 noncombatant escorts had been conducted through the Straits of Gibraltar.

NEW OPERATIONAL PATTERN

In October 2004, NATO put in place a new operational pattern. Since then, the focus has been on gathering and processing information and intelligence so as to target specific vessels of interest. In this way, it is now possible to deploy surface forces as reaction units to conduct specific tasks such as tracking and boarding of vessels. The new operational pattern maintains a proactive posture. Moreover, resources may be supplemented in periodic surge operations. At these times, augmentation forces, such as one of the Standing Maritime Groups of the NATO Response Force, join Task Force Endeavour to provide an enhanced presence and more intensive surveillance capability.

Specifically, Active Endeavour is now involved in the four following areas. It is helping deter and disrupt any action supporting terrorism at or from sea; controlling "choke" points, that is the most important passages and harbors of the Mediterranean, by deploying mine-hunters from one of the Standing NATO Mine Counter-Measures Groups to carry out preparatory route surveys; providing escorts for designated vessels through the Straits of Gibraltar when necessary; and enhancing the ongoing Mediterranean Dialogue program and other NATO programs to promote bilateral and multilateral relations.

At all times, NATO units dedicated to Active Endeavour are patrolling the Mediterranean basin, collecting information and assessing the situation in their vicinity. They provide the visible presence and potential reaction forces that may respond rapidly if required.

Allied Forces Maritime Component Command HQ Naples (CC-MAR Naples) controls the operation through the Maritime Operations Centre, which works around the clock. This Operations Centre, which has close ties and exchanges information with national agencies of several NATO countries, is located close to the NATO Maritime Intelligence Coordination Centre. Another important source of information is the experimental Joint Information and Analysis Centre (JIAC). This is structured as a fusion center to collect all available information and effectively collate, analyze, and then disseminate data as actionable intelligence to the appropriate command. It is located in NATO's Joint Force Command Naples and monitors the whole area of functional responsibility. Together, these agencies provide the information and analysis that allow me as commander of Active Endeavour to direct limited resources as efficiently as possible.

Sheer physical presence goes a long way to maintaining security at sea. The Mediterranean is patrolled by frigates and corvettes specifically dedicated to Active Endeavour by Allies on a voluntary basis. They are supported by the Alliance's two maritime high-readiness forces, if and when needed. In addition to these surface units, submarines provide complementary surveillance by providing discreet monitoring of specific areas to detect suspicious behavior. Maritime patrol aircraft also provide wide area coverage across large areas, using a variety of sensors to detect and classify vessels and other objects of interest.

Active Endeavour relies heavily on the logistic support of Mediterranean Allies, using two logistic bases—Souda in Greece and Aksaz in Turkey—and other Allied ports in the Mediterranean basin.

OPERATION IN PRACTICE

Every day, merchant ships sailing through the Mediterranean are "hailed," that is, contacted and questioned, by patrolling NATO naval units and aircraft. They are asked to identify themselves and their activity. This information is then reported to both CC-MAR Naples and the NATO Shipping Centre in Northwood, England. If anything appears unusual or suspicious, teams of between 15 and 20 specially trained personnel may board the vessel to inspect documentation and cargo. If there is credible intelligence or strong evidence of any terrorist-related activity, Task Force Endeavour is ready to deploy to the area and take any necessary actions as authorized by the North Atlantic Council.

Vessel inspections are conducted with the consent of both the flag state and the ship's captain. The results are then evaluated by CC-MAR Naples. If irregularities are discovered, not necessarily related to terrorism, this information will be relayed to the appropriate law-enforcement agency in the vessel's next port of call, provided there is an established protocol with the country involved to do so. The suspect vessel will then be shadowed until action is taken by a responsible agency, or it enters a country's territorial waters on the way to a port. If a vessel refuses to be boarded, NATO will take all necessary steps to ensure that it is inspected as soon as it enters any NATO country's territorial waters.

CC-MAR Naples works closely with Allied national authorities and directly with the NATO naval forces operating in the Mediterranean. An example illustrates the potential benefits of such cooperation. In June 2003, a southern-region country reported that a vessel was operating in a suspicious manner. CC-MAR Naples disseminated this information to a wider audience to increase general awareness and in preparation for any subsequent action on the part of NATO or national authorities. Subsequently, an Ally's Coast Guard was able to use the information when it spotted the same vessel operating within its territorial waters and the national authorities decided to investigate more thoroughly.

Having a force ready at sea gives NATO the opportunity to react to a broad range of situations and emergencies, in addition to combating terrorism. This includes humanitarian, search-and-rescue and disaster-relief operations. Indeed, in this way, NATO ships and helicopters rescued 84 civilians on a stricken oil rig in high winds and heavy seas in December 2001. And in January 2002, NATO ships and helicopters provided life-saving support to 254 passengers of a sinking ship in the Eastern Mediterranean off Crete. Helicopters evacuated the passengers and the ship's hull was repaired at sea before being towed into port.

At the June 2004 NATO Summit in Istanbul, the Alliance decided to enhance Active Endeavour by inviting the participation of NATO Partners, including Mediterranean Dialogue countries. All offers of support, including those by other interested countries, are now being considered on a case-by-case basis. Offers of contributory support by Russia and Ukraine, for example, were made in 2004, and expert teams on both sides are currently working to integrate Russian and Ukrainian forces into the operation in 2006.

Three Mediterranean Dialogue countries (Algeria, Israel, and Morocco) and three Partner countries (Croatia, Georgia, and Sweden) have also indicated a desire to participate in the operation. The extent of the contribution will be tailored according to the specifics of the country concerned and optimized on the basis of the offers received and the needs of the operation.

IMPROVING INTELLIGENCE SHARING

NATO is also developing an experimental networking system to enable all Mediterranean countries to exchange information about the merchant shipping in the basin more effectively. Once approved and implemented, our understanding of the extent of illegal activities and therefore our ability to control them will be improved. The resulting picture of the merchant shipping traffic in the Mediterranean should assist law-enforcement agencies, as well as NATO forces in international waters, to act decisively against these problems.

In the same context, NATO is looking forward to including more national contributions from non-NATO, Mediterranean-rim countries. Such contributions, in addition to increasing Active Endeavour's effectiveness throughout the area of responsibility by enhancing cooperation and information sharing, will reduce the need for more dedicated assets.

Over the years, Active Endeavour has increasingly become an information and intelligence-based operation through the sharing of data gathered at sea by Allies and Mediterranean-rim countries. The level of information sharing achieved to date provides a sound foundation upon which to build in the future. The aim is to develop a much more effective information collection and analysis system and to change the character of the operation from one that is intelligence-supported to one that is intelligence-driven.

The main tool for this concept will be the JIAC, with the aim of promoting a common information collection and reporting strategy, providing analysis and warning, and advising on deployment of assets. Its establishment is meant to encourage the widest sharing of information and ensure that the JIAC output is passed in a timely manner to the countries or agencies most likely to be able to make use of it. The JIAC should help energize efforts of both NATO and individual Allies to provide usable information that contributes to the struggle against the destabilizing factors of terrorism, organized crime, and proliferation of weapons of mass destruction in the region.

The experience that NATO has acquired in Active Endeavour and other maritime interdiction operations has given the Alliance unparalleled expertise in this field. This expertise is relevant to wider international efforts to combat terrorism and, in particular, the proliferation and smuggling of weapons of mass destruction. As a result, countries involved in the Proliferation Security Initiative, a U.S.-led partnership aiming to help halt flows of dangerous technologies to and from states and nonstate actors of concern, are currently seeking to learn the lessons of NATO's maritime operations.

Active Endeavour has proved to be an effective tool in countering terrorism at and from the sea in the Mediterranean. With continuing cooperation from both military and civilian agencies in all Mediterranean countries, the day will come when NATO is only required to provide the coordination for a more holistic approach to countering terrorism, and more generally illegal activity in the area. When effective links are established and appropriate agreements put in place whereby national authorities can react upon suspicious indicators, Active Endeavour should evolve into a more routine activity involving both NATO Allies and Partners.

COMBATING TERRORISM AT SEA
NATO Active Endeavour Briefing: NATO Naval Operations, Proliferation Security
Initiative, NATO Public Diplomacy Division, North Atlantic Treaty Organization
June 2006*

NATO ships are patrolling throughout the Mediterranean monitoring shipping to help detect, deter, defend, and protect against terrorist activity.

This operation, called Active Endeavour, has evolved out of NATO's
immediate response to the terrorist attacks against the United States of
September 11, 2001. In the intervening years, the operation has developed
increasingly effective intelligence-gathering and information-sharing procedures relevant to the wider struggle against international terrorism.

"Active Endeavour has proved to be an effective tool in countering terrorism
at and from the sea in the Mediterranean," says Vice Admiral Roberto Cesaretti,
Commander of Active Endeavour. The operation has also helped NATO gain
valuable experience of maritime interdiction operations and more broadly contributed to maintaining peace, stability, and security in a strategic region.

NATO initially deployed its Standing Naval Forces to the Eastern Mediterranean on October 6, 2001, in a demonstration of Alliance resolve and soli-
darity. That was a day before the beginning of Operation Enduring Freedom,
the U.S.-led campaign to oust al-Qaida and the Taliban from Afghanistan.

The deployment was one of eight measures taken by NATO to support the
United States in the wake of the terrorist attacks of September 11, 2001, following the invocation of Article 5, NATO's collective-defense provision, for
the first time in the Alliance's history. Its aim was to provide a deterrent presence and surveillance in strategic international waters at a key moment.

The deployment, which was formally named Operation Active Endeavour
on October 26, 2001, is commanded by Allied Forces Maritime Component
Command HQ Naples (CC-MAR Naples) through the Maritime Operations
Centre and represented a milestone for the Alliance. Together with the dis-
patch of Airborne Warning and Control Systems (AWACS) aircraft to the
United States, it was the first time that NATO assets had been deployed in
support of an Article 5 operation.

Keeping the Mediterranean's busy trade routes open and safe is critical to
NATO's security. In terms of energy alone, some 65 percent of the oil and natural gas consumed in Western Europe pass through the Mediterranean each
year, with major pipelines connecting Libya to Italy and Morocco to Spain.
For this reason, NATO ships are systematically carrying out preparatory route
surveys in "choke" points as well as in important passages and harbors
throughout the Mediterranean.

---

*http://www.nato.int/docu/briefing/terrorism_at_sea2006/terrorism_at_sea2006-e.pdf

EXPANDING THE MISSION

In March 2003, Active Endeavour was expanded to include providing escorts through the Straits of Gibraltar to merchant ships from Allied states that requested them. This extension of the mission was designed to help prevent terrorist attacks such as those off Yemen on the USS *Cole* in October 2000 and on the French oil tanker *Limburg* two years later. This was a precautionary measure taken on the basis of intelligence indicating that ships passing through this extremely narrow passage were potential terrorist targets. Some 3,000 commercial shipments pass through the Straits every day. In May 2004 the escorts were suspended as a result of a declining number of requests. They may, however, be reactivated at any time.

In April 2003, NATO further expanded the mission and began boarding suspect ships. These boardings take place with the compliance of the ships' captains and flag states, in accordance with international law. In practice, merchant ships are hailed by patrolling NATO naval units and asked to identify themselves and their activity. This information is then reported to both CC-MAR Naples and the NATO Shipping Centre in Northwood, England. If irregularities are discovered, not necessarily related to terrorism, this information is relayed to the appropriate law-enforcement agency in the vessel's next port of call.

The suspect vessel will then be shadowed until action is taken by a responsible agency, or until it enters a country's territorial waters on the way to a port. In March 2004, as a result of the success of Active Endeavour in the Eastern Mediterranean, NATO extended its remit to the entire Mediterranean.

NEW OPERATIONAL PATTERN

In October 2004, NATO put in place a new operational pattern. Since then, the focus has been on gathering and processing information and intelligence so as to target specific vessels of interest.

In this way, it is now possible to deploy surface forces as reaction units to conduct specific tasks such as tracking and boarding of vessels. Augmentation forces, such as one of the Alliance's Standing Maritime Groups, may join the operation to provide an enhanced presence and more intensive surveillance capability.

Active Endeavour has over the years increasingly become an information and intelligence-based operation through the sharing of data gathered at sea by Allies and Mediterranean-rim countries. The level of information sharing achieved to date provides a sound foundation upon which to build in the future. According to Vice Admiral Cesaretti: "The aim is to develop a much more effective information collection and analysis system and to change the character of the operation from one that is intelligence-supported to one that is intelligence-driven."

NATO is also developing an experimental networking system to enable all Mediterranean countries to exchange information about merchant shipping in the basin more effectively. The resulting picture of the merchant shipping traffic in the Mediterranean should assist law-enforcement agencies, as well as NATO forces in international waters, to act against these problems.

PARTICIPATION OF NATO PARTNERS

At NATO's Istanbul Summit in June 2004, the Alliance decided to enhance Active Endeavour including through the support of NATO Partner nations and Mediterranean Dialogue countries. The Mediterranean Dialogue Programme, which was set up in 1995, seeks to contribute to regional security and stability and to achieve better mutual understanding between NATO and its Mediterranean Partners. All offers of support, including those by other interested countries, will be considered on a case-by-case basis. Following offers of support by Russia and Ukraine, agreements concerning their support to the operation were finalized in 2004. Expert NATO teams have been working with staff from both countries to prepare for the beginning of their operational contributions later in 2006 or early 2007.

Negotiations are also under way with three Mediterranean Dialogue countries—Algeria, Israel and Morocco—and two Partner countries—Georgia and Albania—which indicated a desire to support the operation. In the words of Jaap de Hoop Scheffer: "NATO is the place where common responses are being developed to the challenges posed by the spread of weapons of mass destruction and failed states and the place where common decisions are converted into common action."

BENEFITS

Although the mandate of Active Endeavour is focused on deterring and detecting terrorist-related activities, the operation has had a visible effect on security and stability in the Mediterranean that is beneficial to trade and economic activity, as well as emergencies. As of July 13, 2006, some 81,000 ships had been "hailed" and 102 boarded. In addition, 488 noncombatant escorts had been conducted through the Straits of Gibraltar. In June 2003, a southern-region country reported that a vessel was operating in a suspicious manner. CC-MAR Naples disseminated this information to a wider audience to increase general awareness and in preparation for any subsequent action on the part of NATO or national authorities. Subsequently, an Ally's Coast Guard was able to use the information when it spotted the same vessel operating within its territorial waters and the national authorities decided to investigate more thoroughly.

NATO ships and helicopters have also intervened on several occasions to rescue civilians on stricken oilrigs and sinking ships. This includes helping 84 workers to evacuate an oilrig in high winds and heavy seas in December 2001 and winching women and children off a sinking ship carrying some 250 refugees in January 2002 and helping to repair the damaged hull. The experience that NATO has accrued in Active Endeavour and other maritime interdiction operations has given the Alliance unparalleled expertise in this field. This expertise is relevant to wider international efforts to combat terrorism and, in particular, the proliferation and smuggling of weapons of mass destruction.

Although many characteristics of Active Endeavour are essentially the same as those of earlier NATO maritime missions in terms of the equipment used and activities involved, the nature of the threat is new and has required the adoption of innovative approaches. The Alliance's two maritime high-readiness frigate forces—Standing NATO Maritime Group 2 (SNMG 2, formerly STANAV-FORMED) and Standing NATO Maritime Group 1 (SNMG 1, formerly STANAV-FORLANT)—rotate on a three-monthly basis in the Mediterranean in support of Active Endeavour. These forces include ships from many NATO nations that are also deployed on a rotational basis. Allies also contribute additional forces on a voluntary basis and Active Endeavour relies heavily on the logistic support of Allies in the Mediterranean. In addition, submarines provide complementary surveillance by providing discreet monitoring of specific areas to detect suspicious behavior. Maritime patrol aircraft also provide wide area coverage across large areas, using a variety of sensors to detect and classify vessels and other objects. Spanish maritime forces play a particularly important role in escorting ships through the Straits of Gibraltar. Regular reports on the conduct of Operation Active Endeavour are provided to the UN Security Council.

NATO NAVAL OPERATIONS

Since the end of the Cold War, NATO has acquired much experience and practical expertise in naval operations, whether carried out in support of individual Allies or coalitions of Allies or under the NATO banner. The longest-duration NATO maritime missions took place during the wars of Yugoslav dissolution. Between 1992 and 1996, the Alliance helped enforce both an arms embargo against the whole of the former Yugoslavia and economic sanctions against Serbia and Montenegro, both of which were imposed by the UN Security Council. This operation, which also involved forces from the Western European Union, was originally called Maritime Monitor and then renamed Sharp Guard as the mission was expanded from surveillance to include boarding and searching of vessels. Given the many similarities with Active Endeavour, the experience gained during these years has proved extremely useful to the current operation.

PROLIFERATION SECURITY INITIATIVE

The Proliferation Security Initiative (PSI) is a response to the growing challenge posed by the proliferation of weapons of mass destruction (WMD), their delivery systems, and related materials worldwide. Launched by U.S. president George W. Bush in May 2003, it is a global partnership of countries seeking to halt the flow of dangerous technologies to and from states and nonstate actors engaged in or supporting WMD proliferation programs.

Participating countries agreed a Statement of Interdiction Principles in September 2003. These commit them to undertaking effective measures, either alone or in concert with other states, in a number of specific areas: interdicting the transfer or transport of WMD, their delivery systems and related materials to and from states and nonstate actors of proliferation concern, adopting streamlined procedures for rapid exchange of relevant information concerning suspected proliferation activity; protecting the confidential character of classified information provided by other states as part of this initiative; dedicating appropriate resources and efforts to interdiction operations and capabilities and maximizing coordination among participants in interdiction efforts; reviewing and working to strengthen relevant national legal authorities where necessary to accomplish these objectives and working to strengthen relevant international laws and frameworks in appropriate ways to support these commitments; and taking specific actions in support of interdiction efforts regarding cargoes of WMD, their delivery systems, or related materials, to the extent national legal authorities permit and consistent with their obligations under international law.

At the Istanbul Summit in June 2004, the Alliance underscored its strong support for the aims of the Proliferation Security Initiative and its Statement of Interdiction Principles, and called on partners and other countries to join in supporting and implementing the objectives of the Initiative. NATO's experience of patrolling the Mediterranean to detect and deter terrorism in Active Endeavour is highly relevant in this context.

EARLY MEASURES TO COMBAT TERRORISM

Having invoked Article 5 in response to the terrorist attacks against the United States of September 11, 2001, the Allies agreed on October 4, 2001—at the request of the United States—to take eight initial measures to implement it. Specifically, they agreed to enhance intelligence sharing and cooperation, both bilaterally and in the appropriate NATO bodies, related to the threats posed by terrorism and the actions to be taken against it; to provide individually or collectively, as appropriate and according to their capabilities, assistance to Allies and other states which are or may be subject to increased terrorist threats as a result of their support for the campaign against terrorism; and to take necessary measures to provide increased security for facilities of the United States and other Allies on their territory.

The Allies also agreed to "backfill" selected Allied assets required to support operations against terrorism; to provide blanket overflight clearances for U.S. and other Allied aircraft for military flights related to operations against terrorism; and to provide access for the United States and other Allies to ports and airfields on the territory of NATO nations for operations against terrorism. In addition, the Allies agreed to deploy part of NATO's Standing Naval Forces to the Eastern Mediterranean and AWACS planes to the United States to support operations against terrorism.

United Nations

CONVENTION ON THE HIGH SEAS
United Nations
April 29, 1958*

The States Parties to this Convention,

DESIRING to codify the rules of international law relating to the high seas,

RECOGNIZING that the United Nations Conference on the Law of the Sea, held at Geneva from February 24 to April 27, 1958, adopted the following provisions as generally declaratory of established principles of international law,

Have agreed as follows:

ARTICLE 1

The term "high seas" means all parts of the sea that are not included in the territorial sea or in the internal waters of a State.

ARTICLE 2

The high seas being open to all nations, no State may validly purport to subject any part of them to its sovereignty. Freedom of the high seas is exercised under the conditions laid down by these articles and by the other rules of international law. It comprises, inter alia, both for coastal and noncoastal States:

(1)   Freedom of navigation;
(2)   Freedom of fishing;

---

*http://untreaty.un.org/ilc/texts/instruments/english/conventions/8_1_1958_high_seas.pdf

(3)   Freedom to lay submarine cables and pipelines;

(4)   Freedom to fly over the high seas.

These freedoms, and others which are recognized by the general principles of international law, shall be exercised by all States with reasonable regard to the interests of other States in their exercise of the freedom of the high seas.

ARTICLE 3

1.   In order to enjoy the freedom of the seas on equal terms with coastal States, States having no seacoast should have free access to the sea. To this end States situated between the sea and a State having no seacoast shall by common agreement with the latter, and in conformity with existing international conventions, accord:
     (a)   To the State having no seacoast, on a basis of reciprocity, free transit through their territory; and
     (b)   To ships flying the flag of that State treatment equal to that accorded to their own ships, or to the ships of any other States, as regards access to seaports and the use of such ports.
2.   States situated between the sea and a State having no seacoast shall settle, by mutual agreement with the latter, and taking into account the rights of the coastal State or State of transit and the special conditions of the State having no seacoast, all matters relating to freedom of transit and equal treatment in ports, in case such States are not already parties to existing international conventions.

ARTICLE 4

Every State, whether coastal or not, has the right to sail ships under its flag on the high seas.

ARTICLE 5

1.   Each State shall fix the conditions for the grant of its nationality to ships, for the registration of ships in its territory, and for the right to fly its flag. Ships have the nationality of the State whose flag they are entitled to fly. There must exist a genuine link between the State and the ship; in particular, the State must effectively exercise its jurisdiction and control in administrative, technical, and social matters over ships flying its flag.
2.   Each State shall issue to ships to which it has granted the right to fly its flag documents to that effect.

ARTICLE 6

1. Ships shall sail under the flag of one State only and, save in exceptional cases expressly provided for in international treaties or in these articles, shall be subject to its exclusive jurisdiction on the high seas. A ship may not change its flag during a voyage or while in a port of call, save in the case of a real transfer of ownership or change of registry.
2. A ship which sails under the flags of two or more States, using them according to convenience, may not claim any of the nationalities in question with respect to any other State and may be assimilated to a ship without nationality.

ARTICLE 7

The provisions of the preceding articles do not prejudice the question of ships employed on the official service of an intergovernmental organization flying the flag of the organization.

ARTICLE 8

1. Warships on the high seas have complete immunity from the jurisdiction of any State other than the flag State.
2. For the purposes of these articles, the term "warship" means a ship belonging to the naval forces of a State and bearing the external marks distinguishing warships of its nationality, under the command of an officer duly commissioned by the government and whose name appears in the Navy List, and manned by a crew who are under regular naval discipline.

ARTICLE 9

Ships owned or operated by a State and used only on government non-commercial service shall, on the high seas, have complete immunity from the jurisdiction of any State other than the flag State.

ARTICLE 10

1. Every State shall take such measures for ships under its flag as are necessary to ensure safety at sea with regard inter alia to:
    (a) The use of signals, the maintenance of communications and the prevention of collisions;

   (b) The manning of ships and labor conditions for crews taking into account the applicable international labor instruments;

   (c) The construction, equipment, and seaworthiness of ships.

2.   In taking such measures each State is required to conform to generally accepted international standards and to take any steps which may be necessary to ensure their observance.

ARTICLE 11

1.   In the event of a collision or of any other incident of navigation concerning a ship on the high seas involving the penal or disciplinary responsibility of the master or of any other person in the service of the ship, no penal or disciplinary proceedings may be instituted against such persons except before the judicial or administrative authorities either of the flag State or of the State of which such person is a national.

2.   In disciplinary matters, the State which has issued a master's certificate or a certificate of competence or license shall alone be competent, after due legal process, to pronounce the withdrawal of such certificates, even if the holder is not a national of the State which issued them.

3.   No arrest or detention of the ship, even as a measure of investigation, shall be ordered by any authorities other than those of the flag State.

ARTICLE 12

1.   Every State shall require the master of a ship sailing under its flag, in so far as he can do so without serious danger to the ship, the crew, or the passengers,

   (a) To render assistance to any person found at sea in danger of being lost;

   (b) To proceed with all possible speed to the rescue of persons in distress if informed of their need of assistance, in so far as such action may reasonably be expected of him;

   (c) After a collision, to render assistance to the other ship, her crew and her passengers and, where possible, to inform the other ship of the name of his own ship, her port of registry and the nearest port at which she will call.

2.   Every coastal State shall promote the establishment and maintenance of an adequate and effective search and rescue service regarding safety on and over the sea and where circumstances so require by way of mutual regional arrangements cooperate with neighboring States for this purpose.

ARTICLE 13

Every State shall adopt effective measures to prevent and punish the transport of slaves in ships authorized to fly its flag and to prevent the unlawful use of its flag for that purpose. Any slave taking refuge on board any ship, whatever its flag, shall ipso facto be free.

ARTICLE 14

All States shall cooperate to the fullest possible extent in the repression of piracy on the high seas or in any other place outside the jurisdiction of any State.

ARTICLE 15

Piracy consists of any of the following acts:

(1) Any illegal acts of violence, detention or any act of depredation, committed for private ends by the crew or the passengers of a private ship or a private aircraft, and directed:
   (a) On the high seas, against another ship or aircraft, or against persons or property on board such ship or aircraft;
   (b) Against a ship, aircraft, persons or property in a place outside the jurisdiction of any State;
(2) Any act of voluntary participation in the operation of a ship or of an aircraft with knowledge of facts making it a pirate ship or aircraft;
(3) Any act of inciting or of intentionally facilitating an act described in subparagraph 1 or subparagraph 2 of this article.

ARTICLE 16

The acts of piracy, as defined in article 15, committed by a warship, government ship or government aircraft whose crew has mutinied and taken control of the ship or aircraft are assimilated to acts committed by a private ship.

ARTICLE 17

A ship or aircraft is considered a pirate ship or aircraft if it is intended by the persons in dominant control to be used for the purpose of committing one of the acts referred to in article 15. The same applies if the ship or aircraft has been used to commit any such act, so long as it remains under the control of the persons guilty of that act.

ARTICLE 18

A ship or aircraft may retain its nationality although it has become a pirate ship or aircraft. The retention or loss of nationality is determined by the law of the State from which such nationality was derived.

ARTICLE 19

On the high seas, or in any other place outside the jurisdiction of any State, every State may seize a pirate ship or aircraft, or a ship taken by piracy and under the control of pirates, and arrest the persons and seize the property on board. The courts of the State which carried out the seizure may decide upon the penalties to be imposed, and may also determine the action to be taken with regard to the ships, aircraft or property, subject to the rights of third parties acting in good faith.

ARTICLE 20

Where the seizure of a ship or aircraft on suspicion of piracy has been effected without adequate grounds, the State making the seizure shall be liable to the State the nationality of which is possessed by the ship or aircraft for any loss or damage caused by the seizure.

ARTICLE 21

A seizure on account of piracy may only be carried out by warships or military aircraft, or other ships or aircraft on government service authorized to that effect.

ARTICLE 22

1. Except where acts of interference derive from powers conferred by treaty, a warship which encounters a foreign merchant ship on the high seas is not justified in boarding her unless there is reasonable ground for suspecting:
    (a) That the ship is engaged in piracy; or
    (b) That the ship is engaged in the slave trade; or
    (c) That though flying a foreign flag or refusing to show its flag, the ship is, in reality, of the same nationality as the warship.
2. In the cases provided for in subparagraphs (a), (b) and (c) above, the warship may proceed to verify the ship's right to fly its flag. To this end, it may send a boat under the command of an officer to the suspected ship. If suspicion remains after the documents have been checked, it may proceed to a further examination on board the ship, which must be carried out with all possible consideration.
3. If the suspicions prove to be unfounded, and provided that the ship boarded has not committed any act justifying them, it shall be compensated for any loss or damage that may have been sustained.

ARTICLE 23

1. The hot pursuit of a foreign ship may be undertaken when the competent authorities of the coastal State have good reason to believe that the ship has violated the laws and regulations of that State. Such pursuit must be commenced when the foreign ship or one of its boats is within the internal waters or the territorial sea or the contiguous zone of the pursuing State, and may only be continued outside the territorial sea or the contiguous zone if the pursuit has not been interrupted. It is not necessary that, at the time when the foreign ship within the territorial sea or the contiguous zone receives the order to stop, the ship giving the order should likewise be within the territorial sea or the contiguous zone. If the foreign ship is within a contiguous zone, as defined in article 24 of the Convention on the Territorial Sea and the Contiguous Zone, the pursuit may be undertaken only if there has been a violation of the rights for the protection of which the zone was established.

2. The right of hot pursuit ceases as soon as the ship pursued enters the territorial sea of its own country or of a third State.

3. Hot pursuit is not deemed to have begun unless the pursuing ship has satisfied itself by such practicable means as may be available that the ship pursued or one of its boats or other craft working as a team and using the ship pursued as a mother ship are within the limits of the territorial sea, or as the case may be within the contiguous zone. The pursuit may be commenced only after a visual or auditory signal to stop has been given at a distance that enables it to be seen or heard by the foreign ship.

4. The right of hot pursuit may be exercised only by warships or military aircraft, or other ships or aircraft on government service specially authorized to that effect.

5. Where hot pursuit is effected by an aircraft:
   (a) The provisions of paragraph 1 to 3 of this article shall apply mutatis mutandis;
   (b) The aircraft giving the order to stop must itself actively pursue the ship until a ship or aircraft of the coastal State, summoned by the aircraft, arrives to take over the pursuit, unless the aircraft is itself able to arrest the ship. It does not suffice to justify an arrest on the high seas that the ship was merely sighted by the aircraft as an offender or suspected offender, if it was not both ordered to stop and pursued by the aircraft itself or other aircraft or ships that continue the pursuit without interruption.

6. The release of a ship arrested within the jurisdiction of a State and escorted to a port of that State for the purposes of an enquiry before the competent authorities may not be claimed solely on the ground that the ship, in the course of its voyage, was escorted across a portion of the high seas, if the circumstances rendered this necessary.

7. Where a ship has been stopped or arrested on the high seas in circumstances that do not justify the exercise of the right of hot pursuit, it shall be compensated for any loss or damage that may have been thereby sustained.

ARTICLE 24

Every State shall draw up regulations to prevent pollution of the seas by the discharge of oil from ships or pipelines or resulting from the exploitation and exploration of the seabed and its subsoil, taking account of existing treaty provisions on the subject.

ARTICLE 25

1. Every State shall take measures to prevent pollution of the seas from the dumping of radioactive waste, taking into account any standards and regulations that may be formulated by the competent international organizations.
2. All States shall cooperate with the competent international organizations in taking measures for the prevention of pollution of the seas or airspace above resulting from any activities with radioactive materials or other harmful agents.

ARTICLE 26

1. All States shall be entitled to lay submarine cables and pipelines on the bed of the high seas.
2. Subject to its right to take reasonable measures for the exploration of the continental shelf and the exploitation of its natural resources, the coastal State may not impede the laying or maintenance of such cables or pipelines.
3. When laying such cables or pipelines the State in question shall pay due regard to cables or pipelines already in position on the seabed. In particular, possibilities of repairing existing cables or pipelines shall not be prejudiced.

ARTICLE 27

Every State shall take the necessary legislative measures to provide that the breaking or injury by a ship flying its flag or by a person subject to its jurisdiction of a submarine cable beneath the high seas done willfully or through culpable negligence, in such a manner as to be liable to interrupt or obstruct telegraphic or telephonic communications, and similarly the breaking or injury of a submarine pipeline or high-voltage power cable, shall be a punishable offense. This provision shall not apply to any break or injury caused by persons who acted merely with the legitimate object of saving their lives or their ships, after having taken all necessary precautions to avoid such break or injury.

ARTICLE 28

Every State shall take the necessary legislative measures to provide that, if persons subject to its jurisdiction who are the owners of a cable or pipeline beneath the high seas, in laying or repairing that cable or pipeline, cause a break in or injury to another cable or pipeline, they shall bear the cost of the repairs.

ARTICLE 29

Every State shall take the necessary legislative measures to ensure that the owners of ships who can prove that they have sacrificed an anchor, a net or any other fishing gear, in order to avoid injuring a submarine cable or pipeline, shall be indemnified by the owner of the cable or pipeline, provided that the owner of the ship has taken all reasonable precautionary measures beforehand.

ARTICLE 30

The provisions of this Convention shall not affect conventions or other international agreements already in force, as between States Parties to them.

ARTICLE 31

This Convention shall, until October 31, 1958, be open for signature by all States Members of the United Nations or of any of the specialized agencies, and by any other State invited by the General Assembly of the United Nations to become a Party to the Convention.

ARTICLE 32

This Convention is subject to ratification. The instruments of ratification shall be deposited with the Secretary-General of the United Nations.

ARTICLE 33

This Convention shall be open for accession by any States belonging to any of the categories mentioned in article 31. The instruments of accession shall be deposited with the Secretary-General of the United Nations.

ARTICLE 34

1. This Convention shall come into force on the 30th day following the date of deposit of the 22nd instrument of ratification or accession with the Secretary-General of the United Nations.
2. For each State ratifying or acceding to the Convention after the deposit of the 22nd instrument of ratification or accession, the Convention shall enter into force on the 30th day after deposit by such State of its instrument of ratification or accession.

ARTICLE 35

1. After the expiration of a period of 5 years from the date on which this Convention shall enter into force, a request for the revision of this Convention may be made at any time by any Contracting Party by means of a notification in writing addressed to the Secretary-General of the United Nations.
2. The General Assembly of the United Nations shall decide upon the steps, if any, to be taken in respect of such request.

ARTICLE 36

The Secretary-General of the United Nations shall inform all States Members of the United Nations and the other States referred to in article 31:

(a) Of signatures to this Convention and of the deposit of instruments of ratification or accession, in accordance with articles 31, 32 and 33; (b) Of the date on which this Convention will come into force, in accordance with article 34; (c) Of requests for revision in accordance with article 35.

ARTICLE 37

The original of this Convention, of which the Chinese, English, French, Russian and Spanish texts are equally authentic, shall be deposited with the Secretary-General of the United Nations, who shall send certified copies thereof to all States referred to in article 31.

IN WITNESS WHEREOF the undersigned Plenipotentiaries, being duly authorized thereto by their respective governments, have signed this Convention.

DONE at Geneva, this 29th day of April, 1958.

UNITED NATIONS CONVENTION ON THE LAW OF THE SEA
OVERVIEW AND FULL TEXT
United Nations, Office of Legal Affairs, Division for
Ocean Affairs and the Law of the Sea
December 10, 1982*

AN OVERVIEW

The United Nations Convention on the Law of the Sea lays down a comprehensive regime of law and order in the world's oceans and seas establishing rules governing all uses of the oceans and their resources. It enshrines the notion that all problems of ocean space are closely interrelated and need to be addressed as a whole.

The Convention was opened for signature on December 10, 1982, in Montego Bay, Jamaica. This marked the culmination of more than 14 years of work involving participation by more than 150 countries representing all regions of the world, all legal and political systems, and the spectrum of socioeconomic development. At the time of its adoption, the Convention embodied in one instrument traditional rules for the uses of the oceans and at the same time introduced new legal concepts and regimes and addressed new concerns. The Convention also provided the framework for further development of specific areas of the law of the sea.

The Convention entered into force in accordance with its article 308 on November 16, 1994, 12 months after the date of deposit of the sixtieth instrument of ratification or accession. Today, it is the globally recognized regime dealing with all matters relating to the law of the sea.

The Convention (full text) comprises 320 articles and nine annexes, governing all aspects of ocean space, such as delimitation, environmental control, marine scientific research, economic and commercial activities, transfer of technology, and the settlement of disputes relating to ocean matters.

Some of the key features of the Convention are the following:

- Coastal States exercise sovereignty over their territorial sea which they have the right to establish its breadth up to a limit not to exceed 12 nautical miles; foreign vessels are allowed "innocent passage" through those waters;
- Ships and aircraft of all countries are allowed "transit passage" through straits used for international navigation; States bordering the straits can regulate navigational and other aspects of passage;

---

*http://www.un.org/Depts/los/convention_agreements/convention_overview_convention.
htm

- Archipelagic States, made up of a group or groups of closely related islands and interconnecting waters, have sovereignty over a sea area enclosed by straight lines drawn between the outermost points of the islands; all other States enjoy the right of archipelagic passage through such designated sea-lanes;
- Coastal States have sovereign rights in a 200-nautical mile exclusive economic zone (EEZ) with respect to natural resources and certain economic activities, and exercise jurisdiction over marine science research and environmental protection;
- All other States have freedom of navigation and overflight in the EEZ, as well as freedom to lay submarine cables and pipelines;
- Landlocked and geographically disadvantaged States have the right to participate on an equitable basis in exploitation of an appropriate part of the surplus of the living resources of the EEZs of coastal States of the same region or sub-region; highly migratory species of fish and marine mammals are accorded special protection;
- Coastal States have sovereign rights over the continental shelf (the national area of the seabed) for exploring and exploiting it; the shelf can extend at least 200 nautical miles from the shore, and more under specified circumstances;
- Coastal States share with the international community part of the revenue derived from exploiting resources from any part of their shelf beyond 200 miles;
- The Commission on the Limits of the Continental Shelf shall make recommendations to States on the shelf's outer boundaries when it extends beyond 200 miles;
- All States enjoy the traditional freedoms of navigation, overflight, scientific research, and fishing on the high seas; they are obliged to adopt, or cooperate with other States in adopting measures to manage and conserve living resources;
- The limits of the territorial sea, the exclusive economic zone and continental shelf of islands are determined in accordance with rules applicable to land territory, but rocks which could not sustain human habitation or economic life of their own would have no economic zone or continental shelf;
- States bordering enclosed or semi-enclosed seas are expected to cooperate in managing living resources, environmental and research policies, and activities;
- Landlocked States have the right of access to and from the sea and enjoy freedom of transit through the territory of transit States;
- States are bound to prevent and control marine pollution and are liable for damage caused by violation of their international obligations to combat such pollution;
- All marine scientific research in the EEZ and on the continental shelf is subject to the consent of the coastal State, but in most cases they are obliged to grant consent to other States when the research is to be conducted for peaceful purposes and fulfils specified criteria;
- States are bound to promote the development and transfer of marine technology "on fair and reasonable terms and conditions," with proper regard for all legitimate interests;

- States Parties are obliged to settle by peaceful means their disputes concerning the interpretation or application of the Convention;
- Disputes can be submitted to the International Tribunal for the Law of the Sea established under the Convention, to the International Court of Justice, or to arbitration. Conciliation is also available and, in certain circumstances, submission to it would be compulsory. The Tribunal has exclusive jurisdiction over deep seabed mining disputes.

MARITIME SECURITY, ISPS CODE IMPLEMENTATION, COSTS, AND RELATED FINANCING

UNCTAD Secretariat
United Nations Conference on Trade and
Development, United Nations
March 14, 2007*

EXECUTIVE SUMMARY

On July 1, 2004, the 2002 amendments to the 1974 International Convention for the Safety of Life at Sea (SOLAS) and the new International Ship and Port Facility Security Code (ISPS Code), entered into force and became mandatory for all SOLAS member states. The SOLAS amendments and the ISPS Code (hereinafter the ISPS Code) impose wide-ranging obligations on governments, shipping companies, and port facilities. Implementing these obligations entails costs and potential economic implications.

Against this background, UNCTAD conducted a global study based on a set of questionnaires designed to obtain first hand information from all affected parties. The main objective was to establish the range and order of magnitude of the ISPS Code–related expenditures made from 2003 through 2005 and to gain insight into the financing mechanisms adopted or envisaged. In addition the study sought to clarify matters relating to the implementation process, level of compliance and other less easily quantifiable impacts. Due to limited responses received from the shipping sector the report presents responses received from ports and governments only.

A. Ports' Questionnaire

A total of 55 completed questionnaires were received from respondent ports spread over all regions, the majority of which were in developed countries.

---

*http://www.unctad.org/en/docs/sdtetlb20071_en.pdf

Together respondent ports that provided information on cargo throughput handle about 16 percent of the global port cargo throughput (tonne), based on 2004 world seaborne trade figures, and approximately 24 percent of the global container port throughput (TEU).[37]

Implementation, Supplementary Measures, and Level of Compliance

Full compliance seems to have been achieved with no major difficulties. The mandatory requirements in Part A of the ISPS Code are largely fulfilled on the basis of the guidance contained in Part B of the Code. In many cases additional measures, either government- or industry-driven, have been adopted.

Cost of Compliance

Reported initial cost figures for respondent ports range between a low of US$3,000 and a high of US$35,500,000, while reported annual costs range between US$1,000 and US$19,000,000.

Unit costs and averages have been assessed on the basis of a number of parameters. These include respondent ports' annual revenues, cargo throughput (tonnes and TEUs), ship calls, and number of ISPS port facilities. The unit cost analysis revealed the presence of important cost differentials between respondent ports, especially between larger and smaller ports. In other words, relative costs appear to be substantially higher for smaller respondent ports.

As to the manner in which costs are distributed among various cost headings, responses received suggest that, on average, expenditures on equipment absorb the largest share of the initial costs followed by expenditures on infrastructure and to a lesser extent other cost headings. With respect to the annual costs, on average, personnel and staff time represent, by far, the largest share of the ISPS Code–related costs. Other cost headings take up a smaller share of the annual costs.

Global initial and annual costs were also estimated on the basis of data on costs provided, as well as reported cargo throughput (tonnes and TEUs) and number of ISPS port facilities. The share of relevant respondent ports of world seaborne trade measured in tonnes is estimated to about 13 percent, while their share of global container port throughput and total number of declared ISPS port facilities is estimated to approximately 16 percent and 6 percent, respectively.[38] Bearing in mind the limitations that may characterize such calculations, the estimated global port-related costs of the ISPS Code range between approximately US$1.1 billion and US$2.3 billion initially and approximately US$0.4 billion and US$0.9 billion annually thereafter. These costs are equivalent to increases in international maritime freight payments of about 1 percent with respect to the initial expenditure and 0.5 percent with respect to the annual expenditure.[39]

Financing the ISPS Code–Related Costs

A number of respondent ports have implemented or plan to implement cost-recovery schemes. Where applicable, ports seem to favor levying security charges on several port users, but particularly cargo and containerized traffic. In general, less than full recovery of both initial and annual costs is expected. As to security charges applied, responses received did not shed much light on the criteria used for setting the basis and the levels of the charges.

The survey also revealed that some ports had received public funding and assistance. Where applicable, assistance included governmental grants and cost-sharing agreements, mainly for respondent ports located in developed regions. Respondent ports in developing countries appear to have benefited mainly from technical assistance and capacity building provided by international organizations.

Ports' Perception of Other Effects

Ports seem to have accepted the ISPS Code objectives as legitimate and reported an overall positive impression of the new security regime, especially in terms of increasing awareness, streamlining processes, standardizing risk assessment, and improving business practices. Respondent ports that emphasized the negative impact associated with the Code appeared particularly concerned about operational interferences, as well as cost implications and related funding requirements. In this respect, some respondent ports have called for assistance.

As to the Code's impact on various port performance measures, such as efficiency, use of information and communication technologies (ICTs) and throughput growth, respondent ports' perceptions appeared rather positive. Some respondent ports, however, reported experiencing increased delays and few noted a decrease in competitiveness, while many said the ISPS Code had no impact at all.

B. Governments' Questionnaire

A total of 45 responses were received from governments located in countries representing about 24 percent of the United Nations membership. Responses received span all regions with the exception of North America and Oceania.

Implementation Process and Compliance

All respondent governments are Contracting States to the SOLAS Convention and most have delegated certain security duties to Recognized Security Organizations (RSOs). Most respondent governments reported that they had relied on dedicated legislative and regulatory instruments to ensure national implementation of the Code, including the monitoring of initial and subsequent compliance.

With few exceptions, including in relation to resource limitations, governments reported that compliance with the ISPS Code by their respective national ports and shipping sectors had been achieved with no major difficulties. Compliance with the mandatory provisions of Part A of the Code has mainly been achieved on the basis of the guidance provided in Part B of the Code. The majority of respondent governments indicated that additional measures affecting their respective national ports and the shipping sectors had been adopted to supplement the ISPS Code requirements.

Implementation and Compliance Costs

Reported initial cost figures range between US$13,500 and US$50 million per respondent government, while annual costs range between US$1,500 and US$27 million. This provides an indication of the range of ISPS Code–related expenditures on the part of governments. However, the limitations that characterize data on costs obtained require that these be considered as broadly indicative only.

Financing Governments' ISPS Code–Related Costs

There are various approaches and degrees of external support to SOLAS contracting governments, because not all respondent governments have benefited or expect to benefit from assistance. Assistance received by governments took mainly the form of capacity building, technical assistance, and grants. As to cost-recovery, for the majority of respondent governments costs appear not to be recovered through user fees or charges. That being said, where applicable, the favored approach for governments appears to be the application of fees for the issuance and renewal of certificates as well as for audits.

Governments' Financial Assistance to Their National Ports

Some respondent governments have assisted or plan to provide assistance to their respective national ports. Grants and cost-sharing arrangements appear to be the most common type of assistance provided by governments to their respective national ports. Some governments have also provided technical assistance to their ports.

Governments' Perception of the ISPS Code's Overall Impact

Summarizing the overall impact of the ISPS Code on their respective countries, a significant majority of respondent governments highlighted the positive impact of the new IMO security regime. Some argued, however, that it was expensive to implement and that additional guidance was required. Others had a negative perception of the Code due to their resource limitations. In this respect, a number of respondent governments, especially from countries of developing Africa stressed the need for international assistance and cooperation [. . .][40]

International Maritime Organization

MEASURES TO PREVENT UNLAWFUL ACTS AGAINST PASSENGERS AND CREWS ON BOARD SHIPS
International Maritime Organization
September 26, 1986*

At its 53rd session (MSC 53/24, paragraph 17.3), the Maritime Safety Committee approved the measures to prevent unlawful acts against passengers and crews on board ships (MSC 53/24, annex 14), the text of which is attached hereto.

These measures are intended to assist member governments when reviewing and strengthening, as necessary, port and onboard security in accordance with resolution A. 584(14). Member governments are requested to bring the measures to the attention of concerned organizations and interested parties.

***

ANNEX 14
MEASURES TO PREVENT UNLAWFUL ACTS AGAINST
PASSENGERS AND CREWS ON BOARD SHIPS

1 INTRODUCTION

1.1 Assembly resolution A.584(14) directed that internationally agreed measures should be developed, on a priority basis, by the Maritime Safety Committee to ensure the security of passengers and crews on board ships and authorized the

---

*International Maritime Organization (IMO), www.imo.org.

Maritime Safety Committee to request the secretary-general to issue a circular containing information on the agreed measures to governments, organizations concerned and interested parties for their consideration and adoption.

1.2 The text of Assembly resolution A.584(14) is attached at appendix 1.

2 DEFINITIONS

For the purpose of these measures:

1. DESIGNATED AUTHORITY means the organization or organizations or the administration or administrations identified by or within the government as responsible for ensuring the development, implementation and maintenance of port facility security plans or flag State ship security plans, or both.
2. PORT FACILITY means a location within a port at which commercial maritime activities occur affecting ships covered by these measures.
3. PASSENGER TERMINAL means any area within the port facility which is used for the assembling, processing, embarking, and disembarking of passengers and baggage.
4. PORT FACILITY SECURITY PLAN means a comprehensive written plan for port facility which identifies, inter alia, regulations, programs, measures, and procedures necessary to prevent unlawful acts which threaten the passengers and crews on board ships.
5. PORT FACILITY SECURITY OFFICER means the person in a port responsible for the development, implementation, and maintenance of the port facility security plan and for liaison with the ships' security officers.
6. OPERATOR means the company or representative of the company which maintains operational control over the ship while at sea or dockside.
7. SHIP SECURITY PLAN means a written plan developed under the authority of the operator to ensure the application of measures on board ship which are designed to prevent unlawful acts that threaten passengers and crews on board ships.
8. OPERATOR SECURITY OFFICER[41] means the person designated by the operator to develop and maintain the ship security plan and liaise with the port facility security officer.
9. SHIP SECURITY OFFICER[42] means the master or the person on board the ship responsible to the master and operator for onboard security, including implementation and maintenance of the ship security plan and for liaison with the port facility security officer.

3 GENERAL PROVISIONS

3.1 Governments, port authorities, administrations, ship owners, operators, shipmasters, and crews should take all appropriate measures against unlawful acts threatening passengers and crews on board ships.

The measures implemented should take into account the current assessment of the likely threat together with local conditions and circumstances.

3.2 It is desirable that there be appropriate legislation or regulations which, inter alia, could provide penalties for persons gaining or attempting to gain unauthorized access to the port facility and persons committing unlawful acts against passengers or crews on board ships. Governments should review their national legislation, regulations, and guidance to determine their adequacy to maintain security on board ships.

3.3 The measures contained in this document are intended for application to passenger ships engaged on international voyages[43] of 24 hours or more and the port facilities that serve them. Certain measures may, however, also be appropriate for application to other ships or port facilities if the circumstances so warrant.

3.4 Governments should identify a designated authority responsible to ensure the development, implementation, and maintenance of ship and port facility security plans. The designated authority should coordinate with other relevant domestic agencies to ensure that specific roles and functions of other agencies and departments are agreed and implemented.

3.5 Governments should notify the Secretary-General of progress made in the implementation of security measures. Any useful information, which might assist other governments in their implementation of measures, on any difficulties and problems which arose and were overcome during implementation of the security measures, should be forwarded with the notification. The designated authority should cooperate with similar authorities of other governments in the exchange of appropriate information.

3.6 Governments concerned with an act of unlawful interference should provide the Organization with all pertinent information concerning the security aspects of the act of unlawful interference as soon as practicable after the act is resolved. Further information and a reporting format is given in appendix 2.

3.7 In the process of implementing these measures, all efforts should be made to avoid undue interference with passenger services and take into account applicable international conventions.

3.8 Governments and port authorities should ensure the application of these measures to ships in a fair manner.

4 PORT FACILITY SECURITY PLAN

4.1 Each port facility should develop and maintain an appropriate port facility security plan adequate for local circumstances and conditions and adequate for the anticipated maritime traffic and the number of passengers likely to be involved.

4.2 The port facility security plan should provide for measures and equipment as necessary to prevent weapons or any other dangerous devices, the carriage of which is not authorized, from being introduced by any means whatsoever on board ships.

4.3   The port facility security plan should establish measures for the prevention of unauthorized access to the ship and to restricted areas of the passenger terminal.

4.4   The port facility security plan should provide for the evaluation, before they are employed, of all persons responsible for any aspect of security.

4.5   A port facility security officer should be appointed for each port facility. The port facility security plan should identify the security officer for that port facility.

4.6   The responsibilities of the port facility security officer should include, but not be limited to:

   .1   conducting an initial comprehensive security survey in order to prepare a port facility security plan, and thereafter regular subsequent security inspections of the port facility to ensure continuation of appropriate security measures;

   .2   implementing the port facility security plan;

   .3   recommending modifications to the port facility security plan to correct deficiencies and satisfy the security requirements of the individual port facility;

   .4   encouraging security awareness and vigilance;

   .5   ensuring adequate training for personnel responsible for security;

   .6   maintaining records of occurrences of unlawful acts which affect the operations of the port facility;

   .7   coordinating implementation of the port facility security plan with the competent operator security officers; and

   .8   coordinating with other national and international security services, as appropriate.

4.7   Security measures and procedures should be applied at passenger terminals in such a manner as to cause a minimum of interference with, or delay to, passenger services, taking into account the ship security plan.

5 SHIP SECURITY PLAN

5.1   A ship security plan should be developed for each ship. The plan should be sufficiently flexible to take into account the level of security reflected in the port facility security plan for each port at which the ship intends to call.

5.2   The ship security plan should include measures and equipment as necessary to prevent weapons or any other dangerous devices, the carriage of which is not authorized, from being introduced by any means whatsoever on board a ship.

5.3   The ship security plan should establish measures for the prevention of unauthorized access to the ship and to restricted areas on board.

5.4   A ship security officer should be appointed on each ship. The ship security plan should identify the ship security officer.

5.5   The operator security officer should be responsible for, but not be limited to:

   .1   conducting an initial comprehensive security survey and thereafter regular subsequent inspections of the ship;

   .2   developing and maintaining the ship security plan;

   .3   modifying the ship security plan to correct deficiencies and satisfy the security requirements of the individual ship;

.4   encouraging security awareness and vigilance;

.5   ensuring adequate training for personnel responsible for security; and

.6   coordinating implementation of the ship security plan with the competent port facility security officer.

5.6   The ship security officer should be responsible for, but not limited to:

.1   regular inspections of the ship;

.2   implementing and maintaining the ship security plan;

.3   proposing modifications to the ship security plan to correct deficiencies and satisfy the security requirements of the ship;

.4   encouraging security awareness and vigilance on board;

.5   ensuring that adequate training has been provided for personnel responsible for security;

.6   reporting all occurrences or suspected occurrences of unlawful acts to the port facility security officer and ensuring that the report is forwarded, through the master, to the operator for submission to the ship's flag State's designated authority; and

.7   coordinating implementation of the ship security plan with the competent port facility security officer.

CONVENTION FOR THE SUPPRESSION OF UNLAWFUL ACTS AGAINST THE SAFETY OF MARITIME NAVIGATION
International Maritime Organization
March 10, 1988[*]

INTRODUCTION

Concern about unlawful acts which threaten the safety of ships and the security of their passengers and crews grew during the 1980s, with reports of crews being kidnapped, ships being hi-jacked, deliberately run aground or blown up by explosives. Passengers were threatened and sometimes killed.

In November 1985 the problem was considered by IMO's 14th Assembly and a proposal by the United States that measures to prevent such unlawful acts should be developed by IMO was s ipported.

RESOLUTION A.584(14)

The Assembly adopted resolution A.584(14) "Measures to prevent unlawful acts which threaten the safety of ships ?¨⁚ ⱨ the security of their passengers

[*]International Maritime Organization (IMO), www.imo.r .g.

and crew," which notes "with great concern the danger to passengers and crews resulting from the increasing number of incidents involving piracy, armed robbery and other unlawful acts against or on board ships, including small craft, both at anchor and under way."

The IMO Assembly directed the Maritime Safety Committee to develop, on a priority basis, detailed and practical technical measures, including both shoreside and shipboard measures, to ensure the security of passengers and crews on board ships. The measures were to take into account the work of the International Civil Aviation Organization (ICAO) in the development of standards and recommended practices for airport and aircraft security.

In December 1985 further support came from the United Nations General Assembly which called upon IMO "to study the problem of terrorism aboard or against ships with a view to making recommendations on appropriate measures."

MSC CIRCULAR

The MSC in 1986 issued a Circular (MSC/Circ.443) on Measures to prevent unlawful acts against passengers and crews on board ships—which states that governments, port authorities, administrations, shipowners, shipmasters, and crews should take appropriate measures to prevent unlawful acts which may threaten passengers and crews. The Circular gives guidelines on measures that can be taken—with application to passenger ships engaged on international voyages of 24 hours or more and port facilities that service them.

In November 1986 the governments of Austria, Egypt, and Italy proposed that IMO prepare a convention on the subject of unlawful acts against the safety of maritime navigation 'to provide for a comprehensive suppression of unlawful acts committed against the safety of maritime navigation which endanger innocent human lives, jeopardize the safety of persons and property, seriously affect the operation of maritime services and thus are of grave concern to the international community as a whole."

CONVENTION AIMS

The proposal was supported, and in March 1988 a conference was held in Rome which adopted the Convention for the Suppression of Unlawful Acts against the Safety of Maritime Navigation.

The main purpose of the convention is to ensure that appropriate action is taken against persons committing unlawful acts against ships. These include the seizure of ships by force; acts of violence against persons on board ships; and the placing of devices on board a ship which are likely to destroy or damage it.

The convention obliges contracting governments either to extradite or prosecute alleged offenders.

AMENDMENT PROCEDURE

IMO may convene a conference of States parties to the Convention for the purpose of revising or amending the convention, at the request of one-third or 10 states parties, whichever is the highest.

2005 PROTOCOLS

Adoption: October 14, 2005

Entry into force: The amended Convention for the Suppression of Unlawful Acts Against the Safety of Maritime Navigation will enter into force 90 days after the date on which 12 States have either signed it without reservation as to ratification, acceptance, or approval or have deposited an instrument of ratification, acceptance, approval, or accession with the secretary-general.

The amended Protocol requires ratification from three States that are also party to the SUA Convention, but it cannot come into force unless the 2005 SUA Convention is already in force.

Status: see Status of Conventions

Amendments to the Convention for the Suppression of Unlawful Acts (SUA) Against the Safety of Maritime Navigation, 1988 and its related Protocol, were adopted by the Diplomatic Conference on the Revision of the SUA Treaties held October 10–14, 2005. The amendments were adopted in the form of Protocols to the SUA treaties (the 2005 Protocols).

2005 PROTOCOL TO THE SUA CONVENTION

Among the unlawful acts covered by the SUA Convention in Article 3 are the seizure of ships by force; acts of violence against persons on board ships; and the placing of devices on board a ship which are likely to destroy or damage it.

The 2005 Protocol to the SUA Convention adds a new Article 3bis, which states that a person commits an offense within the meaning of the Convention if that person unlawfully and intentionally:

- when the purpose of the act, by its nature or context, is to intimidate a population, or to compel a government or an international organization to do or to abstain from any act;

- uses against or on a ship or discharging from a ship any explosive, radioactive material, or BCN (biological, chemical, nuclear) weapon in a manner that causes or is likely to cause death or serious injury or damage;
- discharges, from a ship, oil, liquefied natural gas, or other hazardous or noxious substance, in such quantity or concentration that causes or is likely to cause death or serious injury or damage;
- uses a ship in a manner that causes death or serious injury or damage;
- transports on board a ship any explosive or radioactive material, knowing that it is intended to be used to cause, or in a threat to cause, death or serious injury or damage for the purpose of intimidating a population, or compelling a government or an international organization to do or to abstain from doing any act;
- transports on board a ship any BCN weapon, knowing it to be a BCN weapon;
- any source material, special fissionable material, or equipment or material especially designed or prepared for the processing, use or production of special fissionable material, knowing that it is intended to be used in a nuclear explosive activity or in any other nuclear activity not under safeguards pursuant to an IAEA comprehensive safeguards agreement; and
- transports on board a ship any equipment, materials, or software or related technology that significantly contributes to the design, manufacture, or delivery of a BCN weapon, with the intention that it will be used for such purpose.

The transportation of nuclear material is not considered an offense if such item or material is transported to or from the territory of, or is otherwise transported under the control of, a state party to the Treaty on the Nonproliferation of Nuclear Weapons (subject to conditions).

Under the new instrument, a person commits an offense within the meaning of the Convention if that person unlawfully and intentionally transports another person on board a ship knowing that the person has committed an act that constitutes an offense under the SUA Convention or an offense set forth in any treaty listed in the Annex. The Annex lists nine such treaties.

The new instrument also makes it an offense to unlawfully and intentionally injure or kill any person in connection with the commission of any of the offenses in the Convention; to attempt to commit an offense; to participate as an accomplice; to organize or direct others to commit an offense; or to contribute to the commissioning of an offense.

A new Article requires Parties to take necessary measures to enable a legal entity (this could be a company or organization, for example) to be made liable and to face sanctions when a person responsible for management of control of that legal entity has, that capacity, committed an offense under the Convention.

BOARDING PROVISIONS

Article 8 of the SUA Convention covers the responsibilities and roles of the master of the ship, flag state, and receiving state in delivering to the authorities of any state party any person believed to have committed an offense under the Convention, including the furnishing of evidence pertaining to the alleged offense.

A new Article 8bis in the 2005 Protocol covers cooperation and procedures to be followed if a state party desires to board a ship flying the flag of a state party when the requesting party has reasonable grounds to suspect that the ship or a person on board the ship is, has been, or is about to be involved in, the commission of an offense under the Convention.

The authorization and cooperation of the flag state is required before such a boarding. A state party may notify the IMO secretary-general that it would allow authorization to board and search a ship flying its flag, its cargo and persons on board if there is no response from the flag state within four hours. A state party can also notify that it authorizes a requesting party to board and search the ship, its cargo and persons on board, and to question the persons on board to determine if an offense has been, or is about to be, committed.

The use of force is to be avoided except when necessary to ensure the safety of officials and persons on board, or where the officials are obstructed to the execution of authorized actions.

Article 8bis includes important safeguards when a state party takes measures against a ship, including boarding. The safeguards include: not endangering the safety of life at sea; ensuring that all persons on board are treated in a manner which preserves human dignity and in keeping with human rights law; taking due account of safety and security of the ship and its cargo; ensuring that measures taken are environmentally sound; and taking reasonable efforts to avoid a ship being unduly detained or delayed.

EXTRADITION

Article 11 covers extradition procedures. A new Article 11bis states that none of the offenses should be considered for the purposes of extradition as a political offense. New Article 11ter states that the obligation to extradite or afford mutual legal assistance need not apply if the request for extradition is believed to have been made for the purpose of prosecuting or punishing a person on account of that person's race, religion, nationality, ethnic origin, political opinion or gender, or that compliance with the request would cause prejudice to that person's position for any of these reasons.

Article 12 of the Convention requires states parties to afford one another assistance in connection with criminal proceedings brought in respect of the offenses. A new Article 12bis cover the conditions under which a person who is being detained or is serving a sentence in the territory of one state party may be transferred to another state party for purposes of identification, testimony, or otherwise providing assistance in obtaining evidence for the investigation or prosecution of offenses.

AMENDMENT PROCEDURE

Amendments to the Articles in the Convention require acceptance by a requisite number of states. However, the Annex, which lists the treaties under which offenses can be considered for the purpose of the SUA Convention, has a special amendment procedure.

The treaties listed are as follows:

1. Convention for the Suppression of Unlawful Seizure of Aircraft, done at The Hague on December 16, 1970
2. Convention for the Suppression of Unlawful Acts against the Safety of Civil Aviation, done at Montreal on September 23, 1971
3. Convention on the Prevention and Punishment of Crimes against Internationally Protected Persons, including Diplomatic Agents, adopted by the General Assembly of the United Nations on December 14, 1973
4. International Convention against the Taking of Hostages, adopted by the General Assembly of the United Nations on December 17, 1979
5. Convention on the Physical Protection of Nuclear Material, done at Vienna on October 26, 1979
6. Protocol for the Suppression of Unlawful Acts of Violence at Airports Serving International Civil Aviation, supplementary to the Convention for the Suppression of Unlawful Acts against the Safety of Civil Aviation, done at Montreal on February 24, 1988
7. Protocol for the Suppression of Unlawful Acts against the Safety of Fixed Platforms Located on the Continental Shelf, done at Rome on March 10, 1988
8. International Convention for the Suppression of Terrorist Bombings, adopted by the General Assembly of the United Nations on December 15, 1997
9. International Convention for the Suppression of the Financing of Terrorism, adopted by the General Assembly of the United Nations on December 9, 1999

2005 PROTOCOL TO THE 1988 SUA PROTOCOL

The amendments to the 1988 Protocol for the Suppression of Unlawful Acts against the Safety of Fixed Platforms Located on the Continental Shelf reflect those in the 2005 Protocol to the SUA Convention.

New article 2bis broadens the range of offenses included in the Protocol. A person commits an offense if that person unlawfully and intentionally, when the purpose of the act, by its nature or context, is to intimidate a population, or to compel a government or an international organization to do or to abstain from doing any act, uses against or on a fixed platform or discharges from a fixed platform any explosive, radioactive material or BCN weapon in a manner that causes or is likely to cause death or serious injury or damage; or discharges from a fixed platform, oil, liquefied natural gas, or other hazardous or noxious substance, in such quantity or concentration, that it causes or is likely to cause death or serious injury or damage; or threatens, with or without a condition, as is provided for under national law, to commit an offense.

New article 2ter includes the offenses of unlawfully and intentionally injuring or killing any person in connection with the commission of any of the offenses; attempting to commit an offense; participating as an accomplice; organizing or directing others to commit an offense.

FOCUS ON IMO: PIRACY AND ARMED ROBBERY AT SEA
International Maritime Organization
January 2000*

In October 1999 the cargo ship *Alondra Rainbow* left the Indonesian port of Kuala Tanjung bound for the port of Mike in Japan. She never arrived. Instead the ship was boarded by armed pirates who put the 17 crew members in an inflatable life raft and set them adrift. Although they were passed by six ships, it was not until 11 days later that they were finally rescued by fishermen.

It must have been a terrifying experience, but the crew of the *Alondra Rainbow* were lucky. In September 1998, the Panama-registered *Tenyu* also disappeared in the Straits of Malacca while en route from Indonesia for the Republic of Korea with a cargo of aluminum ingots. She later reappeared, but with a different name and crew. It is almost certain that her original crew of 17 were murdered.

In November 1998 the bulk carrier *MV Cheung Son* was attacked by pirates in the South China Sea. Her crew of 23 were shot and their bodies thrown overboard, weighted down to make them sink. Not all did so. Fishermen off the coast of China later found six bodies in their nets, still bound and gagged.

These attacks would be shocking if they were isolated cases. But according to reports compiled by IMO, between 1984 and the end of November 1999 there had been 1,587 attacks by pirates on ships around the world. In some areas these attacks involved a disturbing increase in violence. The IMO figures show that, between June and November 1999, one security guard was killed, one crew member went missing, 13 crew members were assaulted, and 13 others were taken hostage, while two ships were hijacked or destroyed.

To most people, the surprising thing is not that piracy can be violent, but that it is happening at all. Although piracy has existed almost as long as shipping and trade, it seemed by the end of the nineteenth century that it had at last been eliminated. In more recent times it was regarded as an interesting historical problem, associated with the skull and crossbones flag, galleons of gold

---

*International Maritime Organization (IMO), www.imo.org.

and villains carrying cutlasses: wicked, but with a dash of excitement and even romance. The fact that piracy was always a crime, often vicious and usually murderous, was forgotten or ignored. In fact piracy had not disappeared. During the 1970s and 1980s attacks on merchant ships began to increase. They were often small in scale and rarely involved physical injury to those who were attacked. But it was a problem that soon could no longer be ignored.

WHAT IS PIRACY?

The following definition of piracy is contained in article 101 of the 1982 United Nations Convention on the Law of the Sea (UNCLOS):
Piracy consists of any of the following acts:
  (a) any illegal acts of violence or detention, or any act of depredation, committed for private ends by the crew or the passengers of a private ship or a private aircraft, and directed:
    (i) on the high seas, against another ship or aircraft, or against persons or property on board such ship or aircraft;
    (ii) against a ship, aircraft, persons, or property in a place outside the jurisdiction of any state;
  (b) any act of voluntary participation in the operation of a ship or of an aircraft with knowledge of facts making it a pirate ship or aircraft;
  (c) any act inciting or of intentionally facilitating an act described in subparagraph (a) or (b).
It is clear that many acts of violence against ships, especially those that occur in ports or territorial waters are not regarded as "piracy" under international law. They are therefore classified as "armed robbery."

PIRACY BECOMES A PROBLEM

In 1983 Sweden submitted a paper to the Maritime Safety Committee (MSC), IMO's most senior technical body, which stated that piratical attacks had grown to such an extent that the situation had become "alarming." Most attacks at that time were taking place at night on ships anchored off the coast of West Africa, usually waiting for a berth in port. The International Maritime Bureau, which had been established by the International Chamber of Commerce in 1979, mainly to deal with maritime fraud, said that similar attacks had been recorded as far back as 1970.

After discussing the matter, the MSC prepared a draft text that was used as the basis for a resolution adopted by the IMO Assembly when it met in November 1983 (resolution A.545(13)). The resolution notes with great concern the increasing number of incidents involving piracy and armed robbery and recognizes the grave danger to life and the grave navigational and environmental risks to which such incidents can give rise. It then "urges Governments concerned to take, as a matter of highest priority, all measures necessary to prevent and suppress acts of piracy and armed robbery from ships in or adjacent to their waters, including strengthening of security measures."

The resolution "invites Governments concerned and interested organizations to advise shipowners, ship operators, shipmasters, and crews on measures to be taken to prevent acts of piracy and armed robbery and minimize the effects of such acts." It further invites governments and organizations concerned to inform IMO of action taken to implement the aims of the resolution and recommends governments concerned to inform IMO of any act of piracy or armed robbery committed against a ship flying the flag of their country, indicating the location and circumstances of the incident.

Finally, it requests the IMO Council to keep the matter under review and take such further action as it may consider necessary in the light of developments.

In April 1984, the MSC established "Piracy and armed robbery against ships" as a separate and fixed item in its work program. The Committee decided that as a first step it would be necessary to have an indication of the scale of the problem, the areas in which attacks were prevalent and as much other information as possible. Under this agenda item, the Committee receives a summary of all reports on piracy and armed robbery against ships submitted by member governments and international organizations in consultative status.

The reports contained, where available, the names and descriptions of the ships attacked, their positions and times of attack, consequences to the crew, ship, or cargo, and actions taken by the crew and coastal states to which the incidents were reported. The reports were compiled at first twice a year and then quarterly and now they are circulated monthly, with quarterly and annual summaries. In 1986, the MSC decided that reports on piracy and armed robbery against ships received by the Secretariat, should be forwarded to the port or coastal states concerned, for comments and advice on the actions they had taken with regard to the incidents reported and that any relevant information provided by the coastal states should be reported to its future sessions.

In view of the continuing rise in the number of such unlawful acts reported and realizing that many others are not brought to the attention of the Organization, the IMO Assembly in 1991 adopted resolution A.683(17)— Prevention and suppression of acts of piracy and armed robbery against ships, which urged member governments to report to the Organization all incidents of piracy and armed robbery against ships under their flags and invited coastal states to increase their efforts to prevent and suppress such acts committed in their waters.

As at the end of November 1999, 1,587 incidents had been reported to IMO. However, IMO estimates that incidents of piracy and armed robbery against ships are underreported by a factor of two. Several reasons have been suggested, including fear that a successful act of piracy will reflect on the master's competence; concern that such a report would embarrass the state in whose territorial waters the act occurred (the coastal state); the belief that an investigation would disrupt the vessel's schedule; and the possibility that shipowners' insurance would increase.

A GLOBAL THREAT

Since piracy became a major international problem two decades ago, it has occurred in a number of areas.

West Africa

Between 1982 and 1986, West Africa—particularly Nigeria—had the highest reported number of cases of piracy and armed robbery. About 25 cases were reported annually, mainly against ships at anchor awaiting berth. Typically, a gang of up 10 people would board the ship at night, threaten the crew with knives, overpower them, and then go on to break into cargo containers and steal their contents.

Between 1984 and 1985, the Nigerian authorities, using the combined resources of the navy, police, and customs, collected enough intelligence to swoop on piracy bases and the outlets that were used for disposing of the stolen goods. The result was dramatic because by 1986, only occasional isolated incidents were reported from Lagos and Bonny ports, which had been the hot spots for such attacks. However, in 1998 22 incidents were reported in West Africa.

Malacca Strait

Prior to 1989, the Malacca Strait was considered to be relatively safe. About seven cases of piracy and armed robbery were reported annually from the area, but in 1989, the figure rose to 28 and by 1991, it had gone up to about 50 a year.

The Malacca Strait gave particular cause for concern because it is one of the busiest waterways in the world, used by up to 200 ships daily. The Strait, in some stretches, is shallow and narrow and requires precise navigation. Most of the attacks in the region were on ships underway.

The pattern used by the pirates was to board a steaming ship at night, undetected and make their way to the ship's bridge. Once there, they would overpower the officer of the navigational watch and either tie him up or handcuff him to the rail while the rest of the gang made for the master's and crew cabins to demand money and valuables. Apart from the danger to the crew of the ship under attack, there was the horrifying hazard posed by a ship often carrying dangerous cargoes, steaming at full speed, unattended, in confined waters.

At the initiative of the Secretary-General of IMO, Mr. William A. O'Neil, a Working Group composed of experts from 10 IMO member countries, including experts from the three littoral states of the Malacca Strait (Indonesia, Malaysia, and Singapore), was established in 1992, to prepare a report outlining the problem in the Strait of Malacca. Among other things, the report was to contain recommendations on safety precautions and enforcement arrangements appropriate for crews, shipowners, flag states, coastal states, and port states (individually or collectively on a regional basis) for dealing with piracy and armed robbery against ships.

Although the Working Group was instructed to focus on the situation in the areas around the Malacca Strait, it was also instructed to prepare recommendations that could be applied in other parts of the world affected by piracy and armed robbery. The Working Group visited Indonesia, Malaysia, and Singapore, between February and March 1993, and prepared a report covering navigation, radio communications, search and rescue, and piracy and armed robbery in the Malacca Strait region.

This was considered by the MSC at its 62nd session in May 1993 and two circulars were issued as a result. The first one (MSC/Circ. 622) contained recommendations to governments for preventing and suppressing piracy and armed robbery against ships. The second (MSC/Circ. 623) contains Guidance to shipowners and ship operators, shipmasters, and crews on preventing and suppressing acts of piracy and armed robber against ships (see panels for a description of the two circulars).

Later that year, the IMO Assembly adopted a new resolution A.738(18) recommending additional measures to prevent and suppress piracy and armed robbery against ships. The new resolution included the following items:

- A recommendation that masters of ships immediately report attacks or threats of attack to the nearest rescue and coordination center and request such coordination centers to immediately warn shipping in the immediate vicinity of the attack, as well as inform promptly the local security forces to implement any contingency plans they have for dealing with such incidents;
- A request that the Maritime Safety Committee to adopt a special signal for use by ships under attack or threat of attack. IMO, working in collaboration with the International Telecommunication Union (ITU) and the International Mobile Satellite Organization (Inmarsat), has included "Piracy/armed robbery attack" as a category of distress message which ships can now transmit through either their DSC (Digital Selective Calling) or Inmarsat equipment by pressing a button. The message can be received automatically by shore stations and ships in the vicinity.
- An invitation and recommendation to shipmasters to use such facilities was circulated to member governments by MSC/Circ.805 of June 6, 1997. But masters of ships under attack or threat of attack are warned about using the facility if they have been ordered by the pirates to maintain radio silence. This is

because there is equipment available capable of detecting all radio signals, including satellite communications, to which the pirates may have access.

Prior to the establishment of the Working Group, the three littoral states of the Malacca Strait (Indonesia, Malaysia, and Singapore), in response to the concerns expressed by IMO, had started implementing a coordinated patrol and other countermeasures in the region. These measures, which started in 1992, resulted in a marked decline in the number attacks in the region. In 1998 six incidents were reported in the Malacca Strait.

South China Sea

Just as the situation was improving in the Malacca Strait, it was deteriorating in the South China Sea. Statistics compiled over the 7-month period from May to December 1993 showed that 42 incidents were reported in the East and South China Sea out of 67 worldwide. Most of the attacks took place in international waters, and in some cases firearms were used.

A number of reports described persons attempting to stop and board the ships in the guise of officials or wearing uniforms. It has not been possible to confirm whether those involved were officials acting within their jurisdiction, officials acting outside their normal duties or private individuals dressed as officials. In the majority of the cases, such persons were armed with low-velocity weapons such as pistols and in a number of cases with assault rifles.

Fishing vessels, particularly around the Philippines, also received the attention of pirates and armed robbers. Very often they were waylaid by faster boats that came alongside without stopping them. The attacking boat would synchronize its speed with that of its target and the armed bandits would simply climb over the gunwale of the ship under attack, leaving some gang members in their boats as guards. The bandits operated swiftly and accurately, taking the fish catch, boat engines, fuel, personal effects, or worse, the boat itself.

Effective law enforcement is difficult in the area of the South China Sea because of its vastness (more than 200 miles wide) and the fact that it is dotted with several uninhabited islands to which the pirates can retreat. The problem has been exacerbated by the lack of cooperation, particularly exchange of information, between the law enforcement agencies of the neighboring countries and some disputes over territorial limits.

Against this background and in response to a request by the Maritime Safety Committee for a report on the situation in the South China Sea, in March 1994 IMO sent a fact-finding mission to China, the Philippines, and Hong Kong. The mission provided an opportunity to discuss with senior officials in the three countries the help which IMO could provide to their enforcement agencies in preparing measures to prevent and deal with piracy in their waters. Even so, the South China Sea remains a problem area. Of the

210 cases reported worldwide in 1998, incidents in the South China Sea accounted for 98.

South America

Attacks have been reported in various ports in South America including Colombia, Venezuela, the Guianas, and the Caribbean. A total of 38 attacks were reported in 1998. Attacks usually occur in ports or anchorages, and occasionally extreme violence has been reported.

THE SITUATION TODAY

Despite the efforts of IMO and its member states, piracy has remained a major threat to shipping in several parts of the world. In October 1998, therefore, experts were sent to Southeast Asia and Central and South America to discuss the situation and consider countermeasures.

The Southeast Asia group visited Manila (Philippines), Kuala Lumpur (Malaysia), and Jakarta (Indonesia). The mission was undertaken against some disturbing statistics showing that, over the period from 1995 to the present, 244 incidents took place in the South China Sea and Malacca Strait areas out of 715 worldwide. Of the incidents reported in the two areas:

- 86.5 percent had taken place in territorial waters or within ports;
- 56 percent concerned ships at anchor or at berth; in 23 percent of the reported incidents, violence had been used, and in 16 percent violence had been threatened.

The principal purpose of the mission was to increase awareness of the problem; impress upon the governmental representatives concerned the need for action; and, more importantly, motivate political will to act at national and regional levels.

The mission was followed up by a seminar held in Singapore in February 1999. High-level governmental representatives of the countries visited participated in the meetings, which were characterized by an open and frank exchange of views and clear expressions of political will to act at national and regional [levels].

The second mission visited the Brazilian ports of Santos and Rio de Janeiro in October 1998. Between those two visits, a seminar and workshop on piracy and armed robbery against ships was conducted in Brasilia, which was attended by representatives of the governments of Brazil, Colombia, Panama, Suriname, and Venezuela and observers from Chile, Mexico, Peru, and Uruguay.

The main objective of the Brasilia seminar was to improve safety at sea by assisting governments to implement the guidelines annexed to MSC circulars 622 and 623, which were issued in 1993 (see above). It also aimed at considering the development of cooperation agreements between neighboring countries for coordinated patrols and other appropriate measures.

During evaluation of the national reports on the piracy/armed robbery situation in their countries presented by the delegations attending the seminar and workshop, two important characteristic of the prevailing situation in Latin America, emerged:

- the modus operandi of pirates and armed robbers substantially differs from that in the Far East region with most of the attacks in Latin America taking place while ships are at berth or at anchor; and
- drug-related piracy may increase in future unless a concerted effort is promptly undertaken by the countries concerned.

The seminar and workshop, whilst recognizing that, with the involvement of a considerable number of national authorities sharing responsibility on the issue, bureaucracy was inevitable, agreed that coordination of any activity undertaken in this respect should be vigorously sought at all levels.

MSC 71: MAY 1999

The MSC discussed piracy and armed robbery at its seventy-first session in May 1999, including the outcome of the two missions to South America and Southeast Asia. It noted that the main problems in dealing with pirates and armed robbers were:

- the economic situation prevailing in the regions concerned
- resource constraints on law enforcement agencies
- lack of communication and cooperation between the agencies involved
- the time taken to respond after an incident has been reported
- general problems in reporting incidents, such as alerting the nearest coastal state as well as other ships in the area of a ship under attack or threat of attack
- timely and proper investigation of incidents
- prosecution or pirates and armed robbers when apprehended
- lack of regional cooperation

The Committee's main conclusions were incorporated into the revised MSC Circulars 622 and 623. One conclusion reached as a result of the two missions was the need for more effective action in apprehending and prosecuting pirates. The Committee agreed to develop a draft Code for the investigation of cases involving violence against crews, passengers, ships, or cargoes, to be considered at the MSC's 72nd session in May 2000.

The aim of the Code will be to promote a common approach to the investigation of cases involving violence against ships and those on board and to promote cooperation between states in the course of these investigations.

IMO RECOMMENDATIONS

Recommendations to governments for preventing and suppressing piracy and armed robbery against ships (MSC/Circ. 622/rev. 1)

The circular, first issued in 1993, was revised in 1999 on the basis of recommendations made by regional seminars in Brasilia, Brazil, in 1998 and Singapore in 1999. The circular recommends that "before embarking on any set of measures or recommendations, it is imperative for governmental or other agencies concerned to gather accurate statistics of the incidents of piracy and armed robbery against ships, to collate these statistics under both type and area and to assess the nature of the attacks with special emphasis on types of attack, accurate geographical location and modus operandi of the wrongdoers and to disseminate or publish these statistics to all interested parties in a format that is understandable and usable."

The circular says that representatives of shipowners and seafarers should also be involved in developing countermeasures. States should develop Action Plans on preventing and responding to attacks and also on dealing with any pollution that might result from an attack (for example, as a result of a collision or grounding). The necessary infrastructure and operational arrangements should be established to prevent and suppress piracy and armed robbery against ships.

An incident command system for tactical as well as operational response should be set up and be integrated with other security matters, such as smuggling, drug trafficking and terrorism. It is imperative that all attacks or threats of attacks are reported to the local rescue coordination center (RCC) or coast radio station. The RCC should in turn inform local security authorities and other ships in the area.

The recommendations go on to deal with how to investigate piracy incidents and criminal jurisdiction. They give guidance to coastal states in areas that are affected by piracy on action to be taken, including the establishment of regional agreements to facilitate a coordinated response to attacks. A draft agreement is given in an annex.

Guidance to shipowners and ship operators, shipmasters and crews on preventing and suppressing acts of piracy and armed robbery against ships (MSC/Circ.623/Rev. 1)

This recommendation was also first adopted in 1993 and revised in 1999. It outlines steps that should be taken to reduce the risk of such attacks, possible responses to them, and the vital need to report attacks, both successful and unsuccessful, to the authorities of the relevant coastal state and to the ships' own maritime administration.

The circular states that the main targets of the Southeast Asian attacker appear to be cash in the ship's safe, crew possessions and any other portable ship's equipment, even including coils of rope. In South America some piracy and armed robbery attacks are drug related. When there has been evidence of tampering with containers, it has been suggested that the raiders may initially have gained access when the ship was berthed in port and then gone over the side, with what they could carry. Thorough checking of ships' compartments and securing before leaving ports is therefore recommended.

The circular stresses the need to reduce temptation for pirates and armed robbers. The belief that large sums of cash are carried in the master's safe attracts attackers. On several occasions this belief has been justified and substantial sums have been stolen. Although carrying cash may sometimes be necessary to meet operational needs and crew requirements and to overcome exchange control restrictions in some states, it acts as a magnet for attackers and they will intimidate the master or crew members until the locations have been revealed. Shipowners should consider ways of eliminating the need to carry large sums of cash on board ship. When this need arises because of exchange control restrictions imposed by states, the matter should be referred to the ship's maritime administration to consider if representations should be made to encourage a more flexible approach as part of the international response to eliminate attacks by pirates and armed robbers.

The circular says: "Masters should bear in mind the possibility that attackers are monitoring ship-to-shore communications and using intercepted information to select their targets. Caution should, therefore, be exercised when transmitting information on cargo or valuables on board by radio in areas where attacks occur. Members of the crew going ashore in ports in affected areas should be advised not to discuss the voyage or cargo particulars with persons unconnected with the ship's business."

The circular recognizes that the "smaller crew numbers now found on board ships also favor the attacker. A small crew engaged in ensuring the safe navigation of their ship through congested or confined waters will have the additional onerous task of maintaining high levels of security surveillance for prolonged periods. Shipowners will wish to consider enhancing security watches if their ship is in waters or at anchor off ports, where attacks occur. Shipowners will wish to consider providing appropriate surveillance and detection equipment to aid their crews and protect their ships."

The circular goes on to list a series of recommended practices, which are based on reports of incidents, advice published by commercial organizations, and measures developed to enhance ship security. The extents to which the recommendations are followed or applied are matters solely for the owners or master of ships operating in areas where attacks occur.

All ships expecting to operate in waters where attacks occur should have a ship security plan, which should cover such matters as:

- the need for enhanced surveillance and the use of lighting, surveillance and detection equipment;
- crew responses, if a potential attack is detected or an attack is under way;
- the radio alarm procedures to be followed; and
- the reports to be made after an attack or an attempted attack.

Ship security plans should ensure that masters and crews are made fully aware of the risks involved during attacks by pirates or armed robbers. In particular, they should address the dangers that may arise if a crew adopts an aggressive response to an attack. Although some observers have claimed that the crews of merchant ships should be armed in areas where piracy attacks are likely, the circular states: "Aggressive responses, once an attack is underway and, in particular, once the attackers have boarded the ship, could significantly increase the risk to the ship and those on board."

The circular covers such matters as precautions in port or at anchor, watchkeeping and vigilance, communications procedures, radio watchkeeping and responses including message formats.

The circular recommends using the maximum lighting possible when operating at night and says that, on balance, the idea of a total blackout cannot be recommended. It stresses the importance of establishing secure areas which attackers will find difficult to penetrate. When the ship is underway, "masters should consider 'riding off' attackers craft by heavy wheel movements as they approach. The effect of the bow wave and wash may deter would-be attackers and make it difficult for them to attach poles or grappling irons to the ship." The use of fire hoses should be considered. "Water pressures of 80 lb per square inch and above have deterred and repulsed attackers. Not only does the attacker have to fight against the jet of water but the flow may swamp his/her boat and damage engines and electrical systems."

The circular warns that employing evasive maneuvers and hoses "could lead to reprisals by the attackers if they seize crew members and should not be engaged in unless the master is convinced he can use them to advantage and without risk to those on board."

The circular strongly discourages the use of firearms. The circular also outlines action to be taken if the attackers succeed in boarding the ship, action after an attack, and how to report incidents.

THE FUTURE

The number of acts of piracy and armed robbery against ships reported to IMO in 1998 was 210, a decrease of 42 (17 percent) over the figure for 1997. Compared to 1997, the number of incidents reported to have occurred decreased from 8 to 6 in the Malacca Strait, from 101 to 94 in the South China Sea, from 45 to 38 in South America and the Caribbean, from 41 to 25 in the

Indian Ocean, from 11 to 2 in the Mediterranean and Black Seas and from 30 to 22 in West Africa but increased from 11 to 19 in East Africa. However, the figure for 1999 is 235, an increase of 25 (11.9 percent) over the figure for 1998.

On November 16, 1999, the *Alondra Rainbow* incident—described at the beginning of this paper—was brought to a dramatic close off Goa, when the Indian Coast Guard succeeded in boarding the ship. They prevented attempts to scuttle her and so destroy evidence of the crime and 15 suspects were arrested.

However, as the Baltic and International Maritime Conference (BIMCO) has pointed out, according to information circulated by the United States Office of Naval Intelligence, the attack was not executed solely on the basis of personal gain, but rather political ambitions may have driven the forces that organized and carried out the crime. It appears that 3,000 tonnes of the cargo of aluminum had been bartered in either Cambodia or Thailand for weapons destined for use by insurgents who have been waging a long-standing action against the Sri Lankan armed forces.

There are, however, several encouraging aspects to this case. The actions taken by the Indian Coast Guard and Navy were particularly noteworthy, as were the efforts of the ICC/International Maritime Bureau's Piracy Reporting Centre which circulated information describing the hijacked vessel and coordinated the reports from ships in the area that spotted her.

BIMCO commented: "The actions of the Indian Coast Guard, Navy, and Police serve well as an example to other nations as to how piracy incidents can be dealt with in conformity with presently available international law."

Nevertheless, the incident showed that the criminals involved are becoming increasingly sophisticated—and ruthless. There is evidence that some attacks have been arranged with the connivance of organized criminal gangs, with ships being targeted because of the cargoes they carry rather than attacked at random, as seems to have been the case some years ago. Despite figures showing that the number of attacks has decreased, piracy is still a major problem, on an international scale.

THE IMB PIRACY REPORTING CENTRE

Outrage in the shipping industry at the alarming growth in piracy on the world's oceans prompted the creation of the International Maritime Bureau's Piracy Reporting Centre in October 1992. Located at IMB's Far East Regional Office in Kuala Lumpur, the center is financed by voluntary contributions from shipping and insurance companies, and its services are free of charge to all vessels irrespective of ownership or flag.

The center supplies investigating teams that respond immediately to acts of piracy and collect evidence for law enforcement agencies. This service is funded by the International Transport Workers' Federation.

Specific Piracy Reporting Centre tasks are to

- report piracy incidents and armed robbery at sea to law enforcement agencies,
- locate vessels that have been seized by pirates and recover stolen cargoes,
- help to bring pirates to justice,
- assist owners and crews of ships that have been attacked,
- collate information on piracy in all parts of the world.

The IMB Piracy Centre maintains a round-the clock watch every day of the year. In close collaboration with law enforcement, the center acts on reports of suspicious shipping movements, piracy, and armed robbery at sea anywhere in the world. The center broadcasts daily status bulletins via satellite recording pirate attacks on shipping in the East and Southeast Asian region. Quarterly reports are made available to interested bodies, including IMO.

IMO ADOPTS COMPREHENSIVE MARITIME SECURITY MEASURES
Conference of Contracting Governments to the International Convention for the Safety of Life at Sea, 1974, International Maritime Organization
December 9–13, 2002*

A new, comprehensive security regime for international shipping is set to enter into force in July 2004 following the adoption by a weeklong Diplomatic Conference of a series of measures to strengthen maritime security and prevent and suppress acts of terrorism against shipping. The Conference, held at the London headquarters of the International Maritime Organization (IMO) December 9–13, 2002, was of crucial significance not only to the international maritime community but the world community as a whole, given the pivotal role shipping plays in the conduct of world trade. The measures represent the culmination of just over a year's intense work by IMO's Maritime Safety Committee and its Intersessional Working Group since the terrorist atrocities in the United States in September 2001.

The Conference was attended by 108 contracting governments to the 1974 SOLAS Convention, observers from two IMO member states, and observers from the two IMO associate members. United Nations specialized agencies, intergovernmental organizations and nongovernmental international organizations also sent observers to the Conference.

The Conference adopted a number of amendments to the 1974 Safety of Life at Sea Convention (SOLAS), the most far-reaching of which enshrines the new International Ship and Port Facility Security Code (ISPS Code). The Code contains detailed security-related requirements for governments, port authorities, and shipping companies in a mandatory section (Part A), together with

---

Source: International Maritime Organization (IMO), www.imo.org.

a series of guidelines about how to meet these requirements in a second, non-mandatory section (Part B). The Conference also adopted a series of resolutions designed to add weight to the amendments, encourage the application of the measures to ships and port facilities not covered by the Code, and pave the way for future work on the subject.

Speaking at the end of the conference, IMO Secretary-General William O'Neil strongly urged all parties concerned to start putting in place all the necessary legislative, administrative, and operational provisions needed to give effect to the decisions of the Conference as soon as possible. In a call for continued vigilance, he added, "In the meantime, all involved in the operation of ships and ports should continue to be aware of the potential dangers to shipping through acts of terrorism and the need to be extremely vigilant and alert to any security threat they might encounter in port, at offshore terminals or when underway at sea."

The Conference has been referred to in the United Nations General Assembly. At its current session, the General Assembly adopted a resolution on "Oceans and the law of the sea," which specifically welcomed initiatives at the International Maritime Organization to counter the threat to maritime security from terrorism and encouraged states fully to support this endeavor.

The International Ship and Port Facility Security Code
The Company and the Ship
The Port Facility
Responsibilities of Contracting Governments
Amendments to SOLAS
New Chapter XI-2 (Special measures to enhance maritime security)
Resolutions adopted by the conference
Officers of the Conference

THE INTERNATIONAL SHIP AND PORT FACILITY SECURITY CODE

In essence, the Code takes the approach that ensuring the security of ships and port facilities is basically a risk management activity and that to determine what security measures are appropriate, an assessment of the risks must be made in each particular case.

The purpose of the Code is to provide a standardized, consistent framework for evaluating risk, enabling governments to offset changes in threat with changes in vulnerability for ships and port facilities.

To begin the process, each contracting government will conduct port facility security assessments. Security assessments will have three essential components. First, they must identify and evaluate important assets and infrastructures that are critical to the port facility as well as those areas or structures that, if damaged, could cause significant loss of life or damage to the port facility's economy or environment. Then, the assessment must identify the actual threats to those critical assets and infrastructure in order to prioritize security measures. Finally, the assessment must address vulnerability of the port facility by identifying its weaknesses in physical security, structural integrity, protection systems, procedural policies, communications systems, transportation infrastructure, utilities, and other areas within a port facility that may be a likely target. Once this assessment has been completed, contracting government can accurately evaluate risk.

This risk management concept will be embodied in the Code through a number of minimum functional security requirements for ships and port facilities. For ships, these requirements will include:

- ship security plans
- ship security officers
- company security officers
- certain onboard equipment

For port facilities, the requirements will include:

- port facility security plans
- port facility security officers
- certain security equipment

In addition the requirements for ships and for port facilities include:

- monitoring and controlling access
- monitoring the activities of people and cargo
- ensuring security communications are readily available

Because each ship (or class of ship) and each port facility present different risks, the method in which they will meet the specific requirements of this Code will be determined and eventually be approved by the administration or contracting government, as the case may be.

In order to communicate the threat at a port facility or for a ship, the contracting government will set the appropriate security level. Security levels 1, 2, and 3 correspond to normal, medium, and high threat situations, respectively. The security level creates a link between the ship and the port facility, because it triggers the implementation of appropriate security measures for the ship and for the port facility.

The preamble to the Code states that, as threat increases, the only logical counteraction is to reduce vulnerability. The Code provides several ways to reduce vulnerabilities. Ships will be subject to a system of survey, verification, certification, and control to ensure that their security measures are implemented. This system will be based on a considerably expanded control system as stipulated in the 1974 Convention for Safety of Life at Sea (SOLAS).

Port facilities will also be required to report certain security related information to the contracting government concerned, which in turn will submit a list of approved port facility security plans, including location and contact details to IMO.

THE COMPANY AND THE SHIP

Under the terms of the Code, shipping companies will be required to designate a Company Security Officer for the Company and a Ship Security Officer for each of its ships. The Company Security Officer's responsibilities include ensuring that a Ship Security Assessment is properly carried out, that Ship Security Plans are prepared and submitted for approval by (or on behalf of) the administration and thereafter is placed on board each ship.

The Ship Security Plan should indicate the operational and physical security measures the ship itself should take to ensure it always operates at security level 1. The plan should also indicate the additional, or intensified, security measures the ship itself can take to move to and operate at security level 2 when instructed to do so. Furthermore, the plan should indicate the possible preparatory actions the ship could take to allow prompt response to instructions that may be issued to the ship at security level 3.

Ships will have to carry an International Ship Security Certificate indicating that they comply with the requirements of SOLAS chapter XI-2 and part A of the ISPS Code. When a ship is at a port or is proceeding to a port of the contracting government, the contracting government has the right, under the provisions of regulation XI-2/9, to exercise various control and compliance measures with respect to that ship. The ship is subject to port state control inspections, but such inspections will not normally extend to examination of the Ship Security Plan itself except in specific circumstances.

The ship may, also, be subject to additional control measures if the contracting government exercising the control and compliance measures has reason to believe that the security of the ship has, or the port facilities it has served have, been compromised.

THE PORT FACILITY

Each contracting government has to ensure completion of a Port Facility Security Assessment for each port facility within its territory that serves ships engaged on international voyages. The Port Facility Security Assessment is fundamentally a risk analysis of all aspects of a port facility's operation in order to determine which parts of it are more susceptible, and/or more likely, to be the subject of attack. Security risk is seen a function of the threat of an attack coupled with the vulnerability of the target and the consequences of an attack.

On completion of the analysis, it will be possible to produce an overall assessment of the level of risk. The Port Facility Security Assessment will help determine which port facilities are required to appoint a Port Facility Security Officer and prepare a Port Facility Security Plan. This plan should indicate the operational and physical security measures the port facility should take to ensure that it always operates at security level 1. The plan should also indicate the additional, or intensified, security measures the port facility can take to move to and operate at security level 2 when instructed to do so. It should also indicate the possible preparatory actions the port facility could take to allow prompt response to the instructions that may be issued at security level 3.

Ships using port facilities may be subject to port state control inspections and additional control measures. The relevant authorities may request the provision of information regarding the ship, its cargo, passengers, and ship's personnel prior to the ship's entry into port. There may be circumstances in which entry into port could be denied.

RESPONSIBILITIES OF CONTRACTING GOVERNMENTS

Contracting governments have various responsibilities, including setting the applicable security level, approving the Ship Security Plan and relevant amendments to a previously approved plan, verifying the compliance of ships with the provisions of SOLAS chapter XI-2 and part A of the ISPS Code and issuing the International Ship Security Certificate, determining which port facilities located within their territories are required to designate a Port Facility Security Officer, ensuring completion and approval of the Port Facility Security Assessment and the Port Facility Security Plan and any subsequent amendments; and exercising control and compliance measures. They are also responsible for communicating information to the International Maritime Organization and to the shipping and port industries.

Contracting governments can designate, or establish, Designated Authorities within government to undertake their security duties and allow Recognized Security Organizations to carry out certain work with respect to port facilities, but the final decision on the acceptance and approval of this work should be given by the contracting government or the Designated Authority.

AMENDMENTS TO SOLAS

The Conference adopted a series of Amendments to the 1974 SOLAS Convention, aimed at enhancing maritime security on board ships and at ship/port interface areas. Among other things, these amendments create a new SOLAS chapter dealing specifically with maritime security, which in turn contains the mandatory requirement for ships to comply with the ISPS Code.

Modifications to Chapter V (Safety of Navigation) contain a new timetable for the fitting of Automatic Information Systems (AIS). Ships, other than passenger ships and tankers, of 300 gross tonnage and upwards but less than 50,000 gross tonnage, will be required to fit AIS not later than the first safety equipment survey after July 1, 2004, or by December 31, 2004, whichever occurs earlier. Ships fitted with AIS shall maintain AIS in operation at all times except where international agreements, rules or standards provide for the protection of navigational information."

The existing SOLAS Chapter XI (Special measures to enhance maritime safety) has been renumbered as Chapter XI-1. Regulation XI-1/3 is modified to require ships' identification numbers to be permanently marked in a visible place either on the ship's hull or superstructure. Passenger ships should carry the marking on a horizontal surface visible from the air. Ships should also be marked with their ID numbers internally.

And a new regulation XI-1/5 requires ships to be issued with a Continuous Synopsis Record (CSR), which is intended to provide an onboard record of the history of the ship. The CSR shall be issued by the administration and shall contain information such as the name of the ship and of the state whose flag the ship is entitled to fly, the date on which the ship was registered with that state, the ship's identification number, the port at which the ship is registered and the name of the registered owner(s) and their registered address. Any changes shall be recorded in the CSR so as to provide updated and current information together with the history of the changes.

NEW CHAPTER XI-2 (SPECIAL MEASURES TO ENHANCE MARITIME SECURITY)

A brand-new Chapter XI-2 (Special measures to enhance maritime security) is added after the renumbered Chapter XI-1.

This chapter applies to passenger ships and cargo ships of 500 gross tonnage and upward, including high-speed craft, mobile offshore drilling units, and port facilities serving such ships engaged on international voyages.

Regulation XI-2/2 of the new chapter enshrines the International Ship and Port Facilities Security Code (ISPS Code). Part A of this Code is mandatory and part B contains guidance as to how best to comply with the mandatory requirements.

The regulation requires administrations to set security levels and ensure the provision of security level information to ships entitled to fly their flags. Prior to entering a port, or whilst in a port, within the territory of a contracting government, a ship shall comply with the requirements for the security level set by that contracting government, if that security level is higher than the security level set by the administration for that ship.

Regulation XI-2/8 confirms the role of the Master in exercising his professional judgment over decisions necessary to maintain the security of the ship.

It says he shall not be constrained by the Company, the charterer, or any other person in this respect.

Regulation XI-2/6 requires all ships to be provided with a ship security alert system, according to a strict timetable that will see most vessels fitted by 2004 and the remainder by 2006. When activated, the ship security alert system shall initiate and transmit a ship-to-shore security alert to a competent authority designated by the administration, identifying the ship and its location and indicating that the security of the ship is under threat or has been compromised. The system will not raise any alarm on board the ship. The ship security alert system shall be capable of being activated from the navigation bridge and in at least one other location.

Regulation XI-2/10 covers requirements for port facilities, providing among other things for contracting governments to ensure that port facility security assessments are carried out and that port facility security plans are developed, implemented, and reviewed in accordance with the ISPS Code.

Other regulations in this chapter cover the provision of information to IMO, [and] the control of ships in port, (including measures such as the delay, detention, restriction of operations including movement within the port, or expulsion of a ship from port) [...].

RESOLUTIONS ADOPTED BY THE CONFERENCE

The conference adopted eleven resolutions, the main points of which are outlined below. The full text of each is available on request.

Conference resolution 1 (Adoption of amendments to the annex to the international convention for the safety of life at sea, 1974, as amended), determines that the amendments shall be deemed to have been accepted on January 1, 2004 (unless, prior to that date, more than one-third of the contracting governments to the Convention, or contracting governments the combined merchant fleets of which constitute not less than 50 percent of the gross tonnage of the world's merchant fleet, have notified their objections to the amendments), and that the amendments would then enter into force on July 1, 2004.

Conference resolution 2 (Adoption of the International Ship and Port Facility Security (ISPS) Code) adopts the International Ship and Port Facility Security (ISPS) Code, and invites contracting governments to the Convention to note that the ISPS Code will take effect on July 1, 2004, upon entry into force of the new chapter XI-2 of the Convention;

Conference resolution 3 (Further work by the international maritime organization pertaining to the enhancement of maritime security) invites the International Maritime Organization to develop, as a matter of urgency, training guidance such as model courses for ship security officers, company security officers, and port facility security officers; performance standards for ship security alarms; performance standards and guidelines for long-range ship identification and tracking systems; guidelines on control of ships; and guidelines on "recognized security" organizations, and to adopt them in time before the entry into force of the amendments to the Convention adopted by the Conference.

Conference resolution 4 (Future amendments to Chapters XI-1 and XI-2 of the 1974 SOLAS Convention on special measures to enhance maritime safety and security) recommends that future amendments to the provisions of chapters XI-1 and XI-2 of the Convention should be adopted by either the Maritime Safety Committee of the International Maritime Organization or by a conference of contracting governments to the convention.

Conference resolution 5 (Promotion of technical cooperation and assistance) strongly urges contracting governments to the convention and member states of the organization to provide, in cooperation with the organization, assistance to those states which have difficulty in meeting the requirements of the adopted amendments, and to use the Integrated Technical Co-operation Programme of the organization as one of the main instruments to obtain assistance in advancing effective implementation of, and compliance with, the adopted amendments.

It also requests the secretary-general of the organization to make adequate provision, within the Integrated Technical Co-operation Programme, to strengthen further the assistance that is already being provided and to ensure that the organization is able to address the future needs of developing countries for continued education and training and the improvement of their maritime and port security infrastructure and measures, and invites donors, international organizations and the shipping and port industry to contribute financial, human and/or in-kind resources to the Integrated Technical Co-operation Programme of the organization for its maritime and port security activities.

It also invites the secretary-general to give early consideration to establishing a Maritime Security Trust Fund for the purpose of providing a dedicated source of financial support for maritime security technical-cooperation activities and, in particular, for providing support for national initiatives in developing countries to strengthen their maritime security infrastructure and measures.

Conference resolution 6 (Early implementation of the special measures to enhance maritime security) refers to the difficulties experienced during implementation of the International Safety Management (ISM) Code and draws the attention of contracting governments and the industry to the fact that chapter XI-2 of the Convention does not provide for any extension of the implementation dates for the introduction of the special measures concerned to enhance maritime security. It urges contracting governments to take, as a matter of high priority, any action needed to finalize as soon as possible any legislative or administrative arrangements, which are required at the national level, to give effect to the requirements of the adopted amendments to the Convention relating to the certification of ships entitled to fly their flag or port facilities situated in their territory. It also recommends that contracting governments and administrations concerned designate dates, in advance of the application date of July 1, 2004, by which requests for certification should be submitted in order to allow for completion of the certification process and for companies and port facilities to rectify any noncompliance. It also recommends that contracting governments and the industry should take early appropriate action to ensure that all necessary infrastructure is in place in time for the effective implementation of the adopted measures to enhance maritime security on board ships and ashore.

Conference resolution 7 (Establishment of appropriate measures to enhance the security of ships, port facilities, mobile offshore drilling units on location, and fixed and floating platforms not covered by chapter XI-2 of the 1974 SOLAS Convention) invites contracting governments to establish, as they might consider necessary, appropriate measures to enhance the security of ships and of port facilities other than those covered by chapter XI-2 of the Convention; it also encourages contracting governments to establish and disseminate, in an appropriate manner, information to facilitate contact and liaison between company and ship security officers and the authorities responsible for the security of port facilities not covered by Chapter XI-2, prior to a ship entering, or anchoring off, such a port.

Conference resolution 8 (Enhancement of security in cooperation with the International Labour Organization) invites the ILO to continue the development of a Seafarers' Identity Document as a matter of urgency, which should cover, among other things, a document for professional purposes, a verifiable security document, and a certification information document, and invites IMO and the ILO to establish a joint ILO/IMO Working Group to undertake more detailed work on comprehensive port security requirements.

Conference resolution 9 (Enhancement of security in cooperation with the World Customs Organization) invites the WCO to consider urgently measures to enhance security throughout international closed CTU movements and requests the Secretary-General of IMO to contribute expertise relating to maritime traffic to the discussions at the WCO.

Conference resolution 10 (Early implementation of long-range ships' identification and tracking) recalls that long-range identification and tracking of ships at sea is a measure that fully contributes to the enhancement of the maritime and coastal states' security and notes that Inmarsat C polling is currently an appropriate system for long-range identification and tracking of ships. It urges governments to take, as a matter of high priority, any action needed at national level to give effect to implementing and beginning the long-range identification and tracking of ships and invites contracting governments to encourage ships entitled to fly the flag of their state to take the necessary measures so that they are prepared to respond automatically to

Inmarsat C polling, or to other available systems. It also requests governments to consider all aspects related to the introduction of long-range identification and tracking of ships, including its potential for misuse as an aid to ship targeting and the need for confidentiality in respect of the information so gathered.

Conference resolution 11 (Human element-related aspects and shore leave for seafarers) urges governments to take the human element, the need to afford special protection to seafarers and the critical importance of shore leave into account when implementing the provisions of chapter XI-2 of the Convention and the International Ship and Port Facility (ISPS) Code. It also encourages governments, member states of IMO, and nongovernmental organizations with consultative status at the organization to report to the organization any instances where the human element has been adversely impacted by the implementation of the provisions of chapter XI-2 of the Convention or the Code. It also requests the IMO Secretary-General to bring to the attention of the Maritime Safety Committee and the Facilitation Committee of the Organization any human-element-related problems, which have been communicated to the Organization as a result of the implementation of chapter XI-2 of the Convention or the Code.

IMO 2004: FOCUS ON MARITIME SECURITY
World Maritime Day 2004 Background Paper, International Maritime Organization
September 27, 2004*

HISTORY AND BACKGROUND

The vulnerability of the global transport infrastructure, both as a potential target for terrorist activity and, perhaps even more threateningly, as a potential weapon of mass destruction, was made clear in the most graphic and chilling detail in the terrorist atrocities of September 11, 2001.

Subsequently, other incidents, such as the attack on the oil tanker *Limburg* off Yemen in October 2002 and the Madrid train bombings in March 2004, demonstrated that the transport infrastructures of the world, be they national or international, were vulnerable to terrorist attacks. From the perspective of an international Organization, IMO's concern has not been so much which country might be the terrorists' next target, but rather which mode of transport would next attract their interest.

Although those tragic events horrified the civilized world, they also engendered a new and firm resolve to tackle terrorism by addressing the issue of security in the widest possible sense. Immediately after the September 11 attacks, the International Maritime Organization, as the United Nations

---

Source: International Maritime Organization (IMO), www.imo.org.

agency responsible for the safety of international shipping, mounted a swift and thorough response to the possibility of terrorist activity being directed against ships or of terrorists seeking to use ships themselves as weapons or using the proceeds of shipping activities in order to subsidize their unlawful operations. As part of this response, the end of 2002 saw the adoption of a comprehensive new regulatory regime which sets out in detail what governments, ship operators, ships' crews, port facility operators and others involved in the business of shipping should do in order to prevent and minimize this very real threat.

But, although 9/11 gave an unprecedented impetus to IMO's concern about unlawful acts that threaten the safety of ships and the security of their passengers and crews, the subject had, in fact, been addressed by IMO over the course of many years.

As long ago as in the late 1970s, IMO was forced to turn its attention to the consideration of unlawful acts such as barratry, the unlawful seizure of ships and their cargoes, and other forms of maritime fraud. Since 1982, the Organization has been monitoring acts of piracy and armed robbery against ships in various parts of the world and has taken measures to combat unlawful acts in those areas that suffer most from them. So far, it has received some 3,500 reports involving loss of ships and, in many cases, loss of life. The most disconcerting aspect is to see that the degree of violence asserted in some of the reports is on the increase.

An early catalyst in the work to combat terrorism was the *Achille Lauro* incident in 1985, in which terrorists hijacked an Italian cruise ship and killed a passenger before agreeing terms to end their siege. That same year, IMO's 14th Assembly adopted a resolution on measures to prevent unlawful acts which threaten the safety of ships and the security of their passengers and crews, inviting IMO's Maritime Safety Committee (MSC) to develop detailed and practical technical measures to ensure the security of passengers and crews on board ships, taking into account the work of the International Civil Aviation Organization in the development of standards and recommended practices for airport and aircraft security.

Furthermore, in December 1985, the UN General Assembly called on IMO to study the problem of terrorism aboard or against ships, with a view to making recommendations on appropriate measures. By the following year, the MSC had developed a series of measures to prevent unlawful acts against passengers and crews on board ships. An MSC circular gave guidelines on the steps that should be taken, with particular reference to passenger ships engaged on international voyages and the port facilities that service them.

Then, in November 1986, work began on the preparation of a convention on the subject of unlawful acts against the safety of maritime navigation and, in March 1988, a conference was held in Rome which adopted the Convention for the Suppression of Unlawful Acts against the Safety of Maritime Navigation—the so-called SUA Convention—and its protocol relating to offshore platforms "to provide for a comprehensive suppression of unlawful acts committed against the safety of maritime navigation which endanger innocent human lives, jeopardize the safety of persons and property, seriously affect the operation of maritime services and thus are of grave concern to the international community as a whole."

The main purpose of the SUA Convention is to ensure that appropriate action is taken against persons committing unlawful acts against ships, such as the seizure of ships by force, acts of violence against persons on board ships, and the placing of devices on board a ship which are likely to destroy or damage it. The Convention obliges contracting governments either to extradite or prosecute alleged offenders.

In the years since its adoption, the SUA Convention gathered widespread if not universal acceptance and received sufficient ratifications to enter into force in 1992. The recent heightened awareness of security issues has led to a dramatic increase in the number of Parties to the SUA Convention. Although in October 2001 it had been ratified by fifty-six states and the 1988 SUA Protocol by fifty-one states, by July 2004 the Convention had been ratified by 107 countries which between them were responsible for 81.52 percent of the world's merchant shipping tonnage, and the Protocol by ninety-six countries which between them were responsible for 77.66 percent of the world's tonnage.

THE 2002 INTERNATIONAL MARITIME SECURITY MEASURES

Unsurprisingly, IMO's work on maritime security intensified dramatically following the 9/11 attacks in the United States. It had become clear that the shipping industry needed a new, more stringent and more comprehensive set of measures to address the question of maritime security and IMO's secretary-general at the time, Mr. William O'Neil, initiated the process by submitting a resolution to the Organization's 22nd Assembly in November 2001. This called for a thorough review of all existing measures already adopted by IMO to combat acts of violence and crime at sea and was unanimously approved.

At the same time, contracting governments to the Safety of Life at Sea Convention attending the Assembly agreed to hold a diplomatic conference on maritime security to adopt any new regulations that might be deemed necessary to enhance ship and port security and prevent shipping from becoming a target of international terrorism. The Assembly also agreed to a significant boost to the Organization's technical cooperation program of £1.5 million, to help developing countries address maritime security issues.

The next step was the convening of an Intersessional Working Group (ISWG) on Maritime Security, which met February 11–15, 2002. It produced a series of recommendations, which were further elaborated by the May 2002 meeting of the Maritime Safety Committee (MSC 75) as well as by other IMO bodies. A second ISWG was held in September 2002, to develop the measures still further, prior to the Diplomatic Conference, which was convened in December 2002.

Detailed work was also set under way in IMO's Legal Committee, which met for its 83rd session in October 2001 and embarked on a review of the SUA Convention as a priority item in its work program over the next two years. Mindful of the fact that those responsible for perpetrating terrorist acts should not be allowed to escape prosecution and punishment, the objective of the review was to ensure that SUA Convention and its Protocol, which provide for the prosecution or extradition of alleged criminals wherever they happen to be, remain relevant in the light of the new global climate of heightened terrorist threat.

The Diplomatic Conference on Maritime Security, held at IMO's London Headquarters, was of crucial significance not only to the international maritime community but also to the world community as a whole, given the pivotal role shipping plays in the conduct of world trade. It was attended by 108 contracting governments to the 1974 SOLAS Convention, and observers from two other IMO member states and two IMO associate members. United Nations specialized agencies, intergovernmental organizations, and nongovernmental international organizations also sent observers.

The outcome of the Conference was a new, comprehensive security regime for international shipping (which entered into force on July 1, 2004), representing the culmination of just over a year's intense work by IMO's MSC and its Intersessional Working Groups. The Conference adopted a number of amendments to the 1974 Safety of Life at Sea (SOLAS) Convention, the most far-reaching of which was a new chapter XI-2 (on Special measures to enhance maritime security) which enshrines the new International Ship and Port Facility Security Code (ISPS Code). This chapter applies to passenger ships and cargo ships of 500 gross tonnage and upward, including high-speed craft and mobile offshore drilling units, and also applies to port facilities serving such ships engaged on international voyages.

The ISPS Code contains detailed security-related requirements for governments, port authorities, and shipping companies in a mandatory section (Part A), together with a series of guidelines about how to meet these requirements in a second, nonmandatory section (Part B). The Conference also adopted a series of resolutions designed to add weight to the SOLAS amendments, encourage the application of the measures to ships and port facilities not covered by the Code, and pave the way for future work on the subject.

The Conference was subsequently referred to in the United Nations General Assembly, which adopted a resolution on "oceans and the law of the sea," specifically welcoming initiatives at the International Maritime Organization to counter the threat to maritime security from terrorism and encouraged states fully to support this endeavor.

THE INTERNATIONAL SHIP AND PORT FACILITY SECURITY CODE — HOW IT WORKS

The purpose of the Code is to provide a standardized, consistent framework for port facilities. In essence, it takes the approach that ensuring the security of ships and port facilities is basically a risk management activity and that to determine what security measures are appropriate, an assessment of the risks must be made in each particular case.

To begin the process, each contracting government was required to conduct port facility security assessments. These security assessments have three essential components. First, they must identify and evaluate important assets and infrastructures critical to the port facility, as well as those areas or structures that, if damaged, could cause significant loss of life or damage to the port facility's economy or environment. Then, the assessment must consider the most likely threats to those critical assets and infrastructure in order to prioritize security measures. Finally, the assessment must address vulnerability of the port facility by identifying its weaknesses in physical security, structural integrity, protection systems, procedural policies, communications systems, transportation infrastructure, utilities, and other areas within a port facility that may be a likely target. Once this assessment has been completed, the contracting government can accurately evaluate risk.

In order to communicate the perceived threat at a port facility or for a ship, the contracting government sets the appropriate security level. Security levels 1, 2, and 3 correspond to normal, medium, and high threat situations, respectively. The security level creates a link between the ship and the port facility, because it triggers the implementation of appropriate security measures for the ship and for the port facility. As the preamble to the Code states, as threat increases, the only logical counteraction is to reduce vulnerability— and the Code provides several ways to reduce vulnerabilities, such as monitoring and controlling access, monitoring the activities of people and cargo, ensuring security communications are readily available and requiring certain types of equipment, depending on the security level in operation.

THE COMPANY AND THE SHIP

Under the terms of the ISPS Code, shipping companies are required to designate a Company Security Officer (CSO) for the company and a Ship Security Officer (SSO) for each of its ships. The CSO's responsibilities include ensuring that a Ship Security Assessment is properly carried out, that Ship Security Plans are prepared and submitted for approval by (or on behalf of) the administration and thereafter that the plan is implemented on board each ship.

The Ship Security Plan should indicate the minimum operational and physical security measures that the ship itself should implement at all times (i.e., security level 1) unless required to operate at a higher security level. The plan should also indicate the additional, or intensified, security measures the ship can take to move to and operate at security level 2 when instructed to do so. Furthermore, the plan should indicate the possible preparatory actions the ship could take to allow prompt response to instructions that may be issued to the ship at security level 3.

SHIP SECURITY OFFICER—THE ROLE OF THE MASTER?

According to the ISPS Code, it is the responsibility of the Company and the Company Security Officer to appoint the Ship Security Officer. This, naturally, has to be endorsed by the administration of the flag state and/or the Recognized Security Organization. It should be stressed that neither the drafting of the definition of the SSO, nor the provisions of the ISPS Code relating to his responsibilities, training, and so on, are aimed at preventing the master, or any other person, from being designated as SSO.

The issue of whether the master should be the SSO, given his many other responsibilities, was first raised at the IMO's Flag State Implementation meeting in March 2004, which recommended to the Maritime Safety Committee that the master could be designated and act as SSO. Two months later the MSC agreed that the definition of the SSO should be viewed in conjunction with SOLAS regulation XI-2/8 on "master's discretion for ship safety and security," which makes it clear that the master has ultimate responsibility for safety and security. Regulation XI-2/4 confirms the role of the master in exercising his professional judgment over decisions necessary to maintain the security of the ship. It states that he shall not be constrained by the company, the charterer, or any other person in this respect.

The phrase "accountable to the master," which is included in the definition of the SSO, is intended to cover those situations, for example on large passenger ships, where the SSO is not the master, by reaffirming that the master has overall responsibility for security. There is, therefore, implicitly no intention of preventing the master from assuming the duties of SSO, as this would be inconsistent with SOLAS regulation XI-2/8.

It is, of course, for national administrations to decide if they wish to impose particular restrictions on who may serve as SSOs on ships flying their flag. This should, however, not be imposed by national administrations on ships not flying their flag through port state control measures, because this is clearly the prerogative of the contracting government of the flag state concerned.

THE PORT FACILITY

Each contracting government has to ensure completion of a Port Facility Security Assessment for each port facility within its territory that serves ships engaged on international voyages. The Port Facility Security Assessment is fundamentally a risk analysis of all aspects of a port facility's operation in order to determine which parts of it are more susceptible to, or more likely to be the subject of, an attack. Security risk is seen as a function of the threat of an attack coupled with the vulnerability of the target and the consequences of an attack.

The Port Facility Security Assessment helps determine which port facilities are required to appoint a Port Facility Security Officer and prepare a Port Facility Security Plan. As with the Ship Security Plan, this is required to indicate the minimum operational and physical security measures the port facility will implement at all times (i.e. security level 1) and also to indicate the additional, or intensified, security measures the port facility can take to move to and operate at security level 2 or 3 when instructed to do so.

CONTROL AND COMPLIANCE

Under the ISPS Code, ships are required to carry an International Ship Security Certificate indicating that they comply with the requirements of SOLAS chapter XI-2 and part A of the ISPS Code. When a ship is at a port or is proceeding to a port of a contracting government, the contracting government has the right, under the provisions of regulation XI-2/9, to exercise various control and compliance measures with respect to that ship. Ships may be subject to port state control inspections, as well as to additional control measures, if the contracting government exercising the control and compliance measures has reason to believe that the security of the ship, or the port facilities that have served it, has been compromised.

The relevant authorities may request information regarding the ship, its cargo, passengers, and ship's personnel prior to the ship's entry into port, and there may be circumstances in which entry into port could be denied.

RESPONSIBILITIES OF CONTRACTING GOVERNMENTS

To summarize, contracting governments have various responsibilities, including approving the Ship Security Plan and relevant amendments to a previously approved plan, verifying the compliance of ships with the provisions of SOLAS chapter XI-2 and part A of the ISPS Code and issuing the International Ship Security Certificate, determining which port facilities located within their territory are required to designate a Port Facility Security Officer, ensuring completion and approval of the Port Facility Security Assessment and the Port Facility Security Plan and any subsequent amendments, exercising control and compliance measures and setting the applicable security level. It is also responsible for communicating information to IMO and to the shipping and port industries.

SOLAS contracting governments can designate, or establish, Designated Authorities within government to undertake their security duties and allow Recognized Security Organizations to carry out certain work with respect to port facilities, but the final decision on the acceptance and approval of this work must be given by the contracting government or the Designated Authority.

OTHER SAFETY AND SECURITY MEASURES

Although of crucial significance for the ship and port industries, the ISPS Code is far from being the only new maritime safety and security provision now in force, and it is perhaps worthwhile to summarize some of the less publicized but equally important measures aimed at enhancing safety and security on board ships and at ship/port interface areas that were adopted by the 2002 Conference.

Modifications to SOLAS chapter V (Safety of Navigation) contain a new timetable for the fitting of Automatic Information Systems (AIS). Ships, other than passenger ships and tankers, of 300 gross tonnage and upwards but less than 50,000 gross tonnage, will be required to fit AIS not later than the first safety equipment survey after July 1, 2004, or by December 31, 2004, whichever occurs earlier.

The existing SOLAS chapter XI (Special measures to enhance maritime safety) was renumbered as chapter XI-1. Regulation XI-1/3 was modified to require a ship's identification number to be permanently marked in a visible place either on the ship's hull or on its superstructure. Passenger ships should carry the marking on a horizontal surface visible from the air. Ships should also be marked with their ID numbers internally.

A new regulation XI-1/5 requires ships to be issued with a Continuous Synopsis Record (CSR), which is intended to provide an onboard record of the history of the ship. The CSR shall be issued by the administration and must contain identity-related information such as the name of the ship and of the state whose flag the ship is entitled to fly, the date on which the ship was registered with that state, the ship's identification number, the port at which the ship is registered and the name of the registered owner(s) and their registered address. Any changes shall be recorded in the CSR, so as to provide updated and current information together with the history of the changes.

As well as the ISPS Code, the brand-new chapter XI-2 (Special measures to enhance maritime security) includes a number of other important measures.

Regulation XI-2/6 requires all ships to be provided with a ship security alert system, according to a strict timetable that will see most vessels fitted by 2004 and the remainder by 2006.

When activated, the ship security alert system shall initiate and transmit a ship-to-shore security alert to a competent authority designated by the administration, identifying the ship and its location and indicating that the security of the ship is under threat or has been compromised. It must be capable of being activated from the navigation bridge and in at least one other location, but—and this is a key consideration when dangerous criminals or terrorists may be on board—the system will not raise any alarm on board the ship itself.

RESOLUTIONS ADOPTED BY THE CONFERENCE

In addition to the two resolutions introducing the ISPS Code and the other SOLAS amendments outlined above, the 2002 Diplomatic Conference also adopted nine other resolutions. Although some dealt with what are essentially administrative matters, such as entry-into-force criteria and the methods by which future amendments should be adopted, the majority addressed important, substantive issues and promise to have a strong impact in the overall endeavor to improve maritime security.

Conference resolution three, for example, set the agenda for the Organization in its future work on the subject, specifically inviting it to develop, as a matter of urgency, training guidance, such as model courses for ship security officers, company security officers and port facility security officers; performance standards for ship security alarms; performance standards and guidelines for long-range ship identification and tracking systems; guidelines on control of ships; and guidelines on "recognized security organizations," and to adopt them in time before the entry into force of the amendments to the Convention adopted by the Conference.

Another addressed the question of long-range ships' identification and tracking, which was recognized as something that could make a useful contribution to the enhancement of maritime and coastal states' security. It urged governments, as a matter of high priority, to take any action needed at national level to begin implementing long-range identification and tracking of ships and to encourage ships entitled to fly their flag to take the necessary measures to be able to respond automatically to polling. However, recognizing that there are two sides to every coin, it also requested governments to consider all aspects, including its potential for misuse (as an aid to ship targeting, for example) and the need for confidentiality in respect of the information gathered.

Among the other resolutions adopted by the conference were two addressing IMO's cooperation with other agencies on security issues, specifically the International Labour Organization (ILO) and the World Customs Organization (WCO) and we shall look at these collaborative efforts in more detail elsewhere in this paper.

IMPLEMENTATION HOLDS THE KEY

Even though every new standard adopted by IMO represents a step forward, it is virtually worthless without proper implementation. And, in this particular context, there is no doubt that the mere existence of the new regulatory maritime security regime will provide no guarantee that acts of terrorism against shipping may be prevented and suppressed. It is the wide, effective, and uniform implementation of the new measures that will ensure shipping does not become the soft underbelly of the international transport system.

One of the most important of the resolutions adopted by the conference dealt with this aspect in some detail, referring to the difficulties that had been experienced during implementation of the International Safety Management (ISM) Code and drawing the attention of contracting governments and the industry to the fact that chapter XI-2 of the SOLAS Convention did not provide for any extension of the implementation dates for the new security measures.

It urged contracting governments, as a matter of high priority, to take any action needed to finalize as soon as possible the legislative or administrative arrangements required at national level to give effect to the requirements of the adopted amendments and recommended that contracting governments and administrations should designate dates, in advance of the application date of July 1, 2004, by which requests for certification should be submitted so that the certification process could be completed in good time and for any noncompliance to be rectified.

From the outset, even before the amendments and the Code were adopted, the SOLAS contracting governments and the industry knew very well that they were bound to face a very challenging task. In the event, there were administrative bottlenecks in the run up to the deadline, and there were instances, from all sectors of the maritime community, where the necessary processes were started too late.

But, important though it undoubtedly is, the administrative process is not the most critical factor in all this. What really counts is the work that has been done on the ground: security officers appointed on ships, in companies, and in port facilities; training undertaken; security plans drawn up; awareness raised; and vigilance heightened. The real aim of IMO's security measures is to make shipping more secure, and the issuance of certificates is simply the final part of a lengthy process, every step of which is a step in the right direction.

Governments and the shipping and port industries made major efforts to improve maritime security in the weeks and months that followed the 2002 Conference leading up to the entry into force of the ISPS Code and all the related security measures. All over the world, a huge amount of work was undertaken to ensure the highest possible level of compliance. Figures made available by IMO regularly to keep the maritime community updated on progress being made indicated that more than 86 percent of ships and 69 percent of port facilities had their security plans approved by July 1, 2004.

As ever, IMO also recognized that not all its member states shared the same ability to implement the new measures and that, particularly among the developing countries, there would be shortages of expertise, manpower, and resources. Another key conference resolution addressed the vital question of technical cooperation and assistance, strongly urging contracting governments to the convention and member states of the organization to provide, in cooperation with the organization, assistance to those states which have difficulty in meeting the requirements.

It also requested the Secretary-General of the organization to make adequate provision, within the IMO's Integrated Technical Co-operation Programme, to strengthen further the assistance that was already being provided and to ensure that the organization was able to address the future needs of developing countries for continued education and training and the improvement of their maritime and port security infrastructure and measures, and invited donors, international organizations and the shipping and port industry to contribute financial, human and/or in-kind resources to the Integrated Technical Co-operation Programme of the Organization for its maritime and port security activities.

IMO actually launched its global technical cooperation program on maritime security in January 2002, 11 months before the package of new maritime security measures was adopted. The aim of the program initially was to raise awareness of maritime security threats and of the possible future regulatory measures that, at that stage, were still under development, through activities such as regional and subregional seminars, workshops, and advisory missions.

Subsequently, the emphasis has moved on to practical approaches to implementation of the new regulatory regime, with the development of training programs and materials, lesson plans and model courses. Thousands of personnel from maritime administrations, shipping companies, ports, and industry and regional organizations have already been trained as a result of IMO's activities, and the steady stream of requests to the Organization for technical assistance in the field of maritime and port security shows no sign of slowing down.

The success and continuation of IMO's work in this field depends on funding being made available to support further training activities. An International Maritime Security Trust Fund has been established, on the basis of voluntary donations, to provide a dedicated source of financial support for the maritime security technical cooperation activities and, in particular, for national initiatives in the developing regions. Secretary-General Mitropoulos has appealed to governments and industry to make contributions to the Fund in order to support the program over the coming biennium.

THE COST FACTOR

Of course, it is not just the developing countries that have had to consider resource implications in implementing the new security provisions. Significant and far-reaching measures such as these cannot be implemented without cost, and although it is impossible to put a completely accurate figure on the total cost to the industry and the various other stakeholders, there have been some attempts made to do so.

Last year, the OECD published a detailed report on the risk factors and economic impact of security in maritime transport. It reached three broad conclusions. The first was that the costs of inaction would have been potentially tremendous. A large, well-coordinated attack, it said, could have the effect of shutting down the entire maritime transport system as governments scrambled to put in place appropriate security measures—which might be drastic, such as the complete closure of some ports, and inefficient, such as duplicative and lengthy cargo checks in both originating and receiving ports. The report estimated that the cost of such an attack would likely be measured in tens of billions of dollars, and quoted a figure of up to US$58 billion for the United States alone.

The second conclusion—perhaps not surprisingly—was that some costs are more easily measured than others, and that those costs that can be measured with some precision are significantly less than the costs of doing nothing. Generally, said the report, ship-related costs tend to be relatively easy to ascertain as these involve specific equipment purchases and labor costs at known international rates. The OECD estimated the initial burden on shipowners to be at least US$1,279 million and US$730 million a year thereafter. The bulk of ship-related costs are related to management staff and security-related equipment expenses.

Estimates of port-related security costs are extremely difficult to derive, says OECD, due to uncertainty about exactly what the new measures will mean in terms of additional personnel requirements coupled with the vast differences in labor rates that apply, depending on location. Also very difficult to estimate are costs derived from procedural changes: however, OECD estimates that, for the costs that can be measured, the overall figure of slightly over US$2 billion is still substantially below the costs that might result from a major attack.

Finally, although its main focus had been on costs, the report also concluded that many of the new measures had distinct benefits that were not directly related to their antiterrorism task. These benefits related to reduced delays, faster processing times, better asset control, fewer losses due to theft, and decreased insurance costs. For example, direct savings to United States importers through a new electronic customs manifest handling system in the United States are estimated to be US$22.2 billion over 20 years while the U.S. government would make savings of US$4.4 billion over the same period, according to the report.

Aside from the OECD report, a number of individual countries have also attempted to quantify the financial costs and benefits associated with the new measures. In the United States, for example, the Commandant of the Coast

Guard has stated that the United States maritime security regulations will cost the home industry US$7 billion over the next 10 years. The regulations will affect some 10,000 United States vessels, 5,000 facilities, 361 ports, and forty offshore facilities.

And, in Australia, the government announced in the 2003–4 federal budget that it would allocate A$15.6 million over two years to tighten the country's maritime and port security by developing enabling legislation, providing guidance to industry and ensuring compliance with the ISPS Code. The government expects that the implementation costs to industry will be A$313 million in the first year with ongoing costs of up to A$96 million per year thereafter, whereas the Australian Shipowners' Association estimates that the cost for Australian flagged vessels could be between A$750,000 and A$900,000 each.

ACHIEVING A BALANCE

Throughout the development of the new security measures and the implementation process, IMO has always been at pains to stress the importance of achieving a proper balance. This has applied not just in the cost/benefit equation but in other aspects, too.

Clearly, there is an overriding imperative to find a balance between the need to implement the new security regime strictly and robustly and yet ensure that disruption to global trade, as a result of the introduction of security measures, is kept to a minimum; a balance between the traditional and legally enshrined right of ships to enjoy freedom of navigation on the high seas, and the need to make sure that strategic and potentially vulnerable sea-lanes have the special protection they may need must be established; and while tightening security provisions so that criminals and terrorists cannot gain access to ships by posing as seafarers, ensuring, at the same time, that innocent seafarers are not themselves unfairly penalized as a result.

SEAFARER ISSUES

The whole question of human-element-related aspects and, in particular, of shore leave for seafarers was dealt with in one very important conference resolution. It urged governments to take the human element, the need to afford special protection to seafarers and the critical importance of shore leave into account when implementing the new security provisions. It also encouraged governments, member states of IMO and nongovernmental organizations with consultative status at the organization to report to the organization any instances where the human element has been adversely impacted by the implementation of the provisions of chapter XI-2 of the Convention or the code and requested the IMO Secretary-General to bring to the attention of the Maritime Safety Committee and the Facilitation Committee of the organization any human element-related problems that may be reported to the organization.

This is a theme to which Secretary-General Mitropoulos has subsequently returned. Speaking at the opening of the thirty-first meeting of the IMO Facilitation Committee in July this year, he said:

> When, on the eve of the ISPS Code becoming effective, I appealed to governments and port authorities to apply the Code with a sense of pragmatism and common sense, my plea was that they should do so not only when they were dealing with ships and cargoes but also when dealing with seafarers serving on ships calling at their ports. We must not forget that it is on the seafarers, initiatives, cooperation, and constant vigilance that we rely heavily in order to prevent breaches of maritime security. Without their support and wholehearted commitment to the cause of security, the system the ISPS Code aims so meticulously to put in place will be severely weakened, to the detriment of the overall effort.

Mr. Mitropoulos added that if, on security grounds, seafarers face difficulties, such as refusal of shore leave, they may well feel somehow rejected or their services not sufficiently recognized. He pointed out how important shore leave is to hard-working professionals reaching port after days or even weeks of isolation at sea, often after having faced the elements at their full strength. He also warned that such restrictions may easily discourage prospective entrants to the maritime profession from joining ranks at a time when the industry is already short of quality officers worldwide—a situation which may worsen in the future to include shortage of ratings as well.

He concluded by appealing to governments and port authorities to treat seafarers as partners in the fight against terrorism and to facilitate their access to ports and shore facilities. "Ships' stays in port are short nowadays," he said, "and the seafarer's free time is limited, so we should provide them with every opportunity to relax and recover before they again take their ships out to sea in pursuit of their peaceful objectives in the service of world trade."

STRATEGIC SEA-LANES

In addition to seafarer issues, another concern in which finding the right balance is paramount is the importance of keeping strategically important shipping lanes secure and open to international maritime traffic, thereby ensuring the uninterrupted flow of world trade. The IMO Secretariat has taken steps to identify which areas might be particularly vulnerable and the

IMO Council, at its ninety-second meeting earlier this year, shared the concern of the Secretary-General in this respect and authorized him to work with interested parties to find ways in which they might collaborate—while always observing the sovereign rights of the coastal states concerned.

One of the world's most important, indeed truly vital, strategic shipping channels is undoubtedly the Malacca Strait. This 800 kilometer long and, in places, extremely narrow link between the Indian Ocean and the South China Sea is an artery through which runs a huge proportion of global trade. Tankers and bulk carriers move vast quantities of oil, coal, iron ore, and grain to the manufacturing centers of Southeast and Northeast Asia, while high-value manufactured goods carried in millions of containers pour back through the same outlet to feed consumer markets all over the world. Some 50,000 ship movements carrying as much as one quarter of the world's commerce and half the world's oil pass through the Malacca and Singapore Straits each year.

Any serious disruption to the flow of maritime traffic through this channel would clearly have a widespread and far-reaching detrimental effect. That is why the preservation of its integrity is such an important issue. But being a natural "choke point" for shipping makes the area particularly vulnerable, both to operational and navigational incidents and to the external threat posed by pirates and armed robbers. However, with Southeast Asia still, unfortunately, recording the highest number of pirate attacks globally, there is clearly a fear that terrorists could resort to pirate-style tactics, or even work in concert with pirates, to perpetrate their evil deeds. Although criminals and terrorists may operate in similar ways, it should be remembered that terrorists aim to use their violence in pursuit of strategic objectives and, all too frequently, mass destruction: while pirates seek private gains, terrorists pursue political ones.

Through cooperation, led by the littoral states of the Malacca and Singapore Straits, and including other user states and stakeholders—such as industry organizations—and by applying various means of state-of-the-art technology—including the utilization of the Marine Electronic Highway project, specifically designed by IMO for the Malacca Strait—it is expected that this strategic lane will continue to remain open to international navigation to serve the needs of seaborne trade and the economy—regional and global.

For IMO, balance has been a recurring theme throughout the entire process of developing and implementing the new maritime security regime. The concern had been expressed that if the focus were placed too heavily on "security" and less attention was paid to other parts of IMO's responsibilities—that is, "safety," "the environment," and the "facilitation of maritime traffic"—then shipping would not be rendered the good services it deserves. The right balance had to be struck between the various objectives involved when legislating, for example, on inspecting ships for port state control purposes; and the need for such balance has been reflected in IMO's new mission statement, which calls for "safe, secure, and efficient shipping on clean oceans."

THE WIDER PICTURE

UN Secretary-General Kofi Annan has denounced terrorism as a "global scourge with global effects," and it is very much in the spirit of international cooperation to counter this universal threat that IMO's efforts to improve maritime security should be seen. They are part of an all-embracing initiative across the UN system to tackle this invidious modern-day scourge, to which no one today is immune.

Since the 9/11 attacks in the United States, the United Nations has consistently addressed the issue of terrorism. UN Security Council resolution 1368 was adopted the day after the attacks and, since then, several more UN resolutions have been adopted to counter terrorism. In December 2002, for example, the UN General Assembly adopted a resolution on Oceans and the law of the sea which, among other things, welcomed the initiatives taken by IMO to counter the threat to maritime security from terrorism and encouraged states to support that endeavor fully.

One month later, the UN Security Council, meeting at the level of Ministers for Foreign Affairs, reaffirmed its position on terrorism and determined to counter it by a sustained, comprehensive approach involving the active participation and collaboration of all states and international and regional organizations and by redoubled efforts at the national level. The Security Council therefore called for all states to take urgent action to prevent and suppress all active and passive support to terrorism.

Security Council resolution 1456, adopted on January 20, 2003, requested states to assist each other to improve their capacity to prevent and fight terrorism and invited the Counter-Terrorism Committee (CTC) to facilitate the provision of technical and other assistance by developing targets and priorities for global action. This resolution also calls on international organizations to evaluate ways in which they can enhance the effectiveness of their action against terrorism, including establishing dialogue and exchanges of information with each other.

Furthermore, at a special meeting of the Counter-Terrorism Committee of the UN Security Council held in New York in March 2003, participants agreed that all international, regional, and subregional organizations invited had a specific role to play in enhancing the effectiveness of global action against terrorism. Although each had its own mandate and its own contribution to make, all recognized the high value of cooperation at the global level. They agreed that their coordinated approach to the suppression of terrorism would include the sharing of data and best practices and the avoidance of duplication of effort, while remaining aware of the need for respect for the rule of law and human rights' obligations.

Looking at the wider picture, UN Secretary-General Annan, in a call for a "new vision of global security," has appealed to international and regional organizations to create a new sense of common endeavor in their responses to terrorism, weapons of mass destruction and collapsing states.

At a meeting of more than 30 organizations, including NATO, Interpol and the League of Arab States, Mr. Annan said that the "unprecedented" range and diversity of challenges warranted a "new vision of global security" drawing on the "resources and legitimacy of mutually reinforcing multilateral mechanisms." He stressed that, as the world changes, our institutions ought to keep pace with those changes and we should not add to our burdens by descending into unproductive polarization.

IMO PARTICIPATION

In this context, IMO has striven to work in cooperation and collaboration with partners wherever and whenever possible. It has participated in UN-organized activities, such as the Special Meeting of the Counter-Terrorism Committee in March 2003 and the meeting of the Counter-Terrorism Action Group (established by the G-8 Leaders in June 2003 to serve as a forum for coordinating and expanding the provision of counterterrorism training and assistance) held in Washington, D.C., in February this year.

As mentioned previously two of the resolutions adopted by the 2002 maritime security conference addressed specifically IMO's work in collaboration with the World Customs Organization (WCO) and the International Labour Organization (ILO).

One invited the WCO to consider urgently measures to enhance security throughout international closed container transport unit (CTU) movements and requested the Secretary-General of IMO to contribute expertise relating to maritime traffic to the discussions at the WCO.

The importance of this work in the context of maritime security cannot be overstated: the world container fleet was estimated by Containerisation International's 2003 Yearbook at some 15,855,000 TEUs. The reported moves of containers through maritime ports were estimated at 225,300,000 TEUs in UNCTAD's "Review of Maritime Transport 2003," and experts say this figure may grow to up to 450 million TEUs by 2010. Today, according to the Lloyd's Register/Fairplay World Fleet database, the population of dedicated containerships stands at nearly 4,000 units, representing more than 100 million deadweight tonnage.

These figures show not only the importance of the sea mode of container transportation but, more significantly, the serious difficulties encountered in knowing, at any time in the transportation chain, where they are, where they are transported to, and, above all, what they contain. Containers are typically loaded some distance from seaports and terminals, hence the importance of close cooperation between all parties concerned.

Cooperation between IMO and WCO had already been established, but it was further strengthened by the signing, in July 2002, of a Memorandum of Understanding between the two Organizations to arrange for matters concerning container examination and integrity in multimodal transport as well as matters relating to the ship/port interface.

With regard to seafarer issues, the ILO was invited by a SOLAS conference resolution to continue the development of a Seafarers' Identity Document as a matter of urgency. The idea was that this document would combine, among other things, a document for professional purposes, a verifiable security document, and a certification information document. Subsequently, the 91st session of the International Labour Conference (in June 2003) adopted a new Convention on Seafarers' Identity Documents to replace the ILO Convention, which had been adopted in 1958. The new Convention establishes a more rigorous identity regime for seafarers with the aim of developing effective security from terrorism and ensuring that the world's 1.2 million seafarers will be given the freedom of movement necessary for their well-being and for their professional activities and, in general, to facilitate international commerce.

The 2002 Conference on Maritime Security also invited IMO and ILO to establish a joint Working Group to undertake more detailed work on comprehensive port security requirements. This group has developed an ILO/IMO Code of Practice on Security in Ports, which was adopted by the two Organizations earlier this year.

IN THE FUTURE

While acknowledging that after the September 11 attacks the world would not be the same again, Mr. Mitropoulos has also acknowledged that, all over the world, a huge amount of work had been undertaken in the period leading up to the entry-into-force date of the 2002 SOLAS amendments and the ISPS Code to ensure the highest possible level of compliance:

> I think we now have to look on the positive side and remember that the prime objective of this work has been to increase awareness of the real and present threat of terrorism, explain the implications of the ISPS Code and how best to implement it and, in so doing, raise the shipping industry's defenses to protect it and seaborne trade from any act of terrorism. There is no doubt that that has been done, the defenses are significantly higher than they were before, and we must now ensure that they continue to rise. While I appreciate the efforts made worldwide to achieve the set objectives, I also acknowledge with appreciation the tremendous work done by the IMO Secretariat, both at the [legislative] level and with regard to the provision of technical assistance and cooperation, to contribute to the establishment of an adequate maritime security infrastructure to keep terrorism at bay. Their commitment and dedication are most commendable.

The emphasis now must be placed on ensuring that security remains a high priority throughout the industry, even after the additional impetus given by the entry into force of the SOLAS amendments and the ISPS Code has diminished. According to the IMO secretary-general, "throughout the implementation period, IMO has repeatedly urged governments and the industry to take steps to increase awareness of the potential dangers and to encourage ships' crews to be vigilant and alert to any security threat they may encounter. Great emphasis has been placed on the entry-into-force date, but the real challenge is to ensure that, now that that date has passed, we do not allow ourselves to relax and adopt a complacent attitude."

To conclude: In the aftermath of the attacks in the United States, it seemed obvious that the global transport infrastructure was vulnerable, not simply as a target for terrorist activity but also, in the wrong hands, as a potentially highly destructive weapon. Although aircraft were the chosen weapon of the 9/11 terrorists, ships might just as easily have been selected and one only has to consider the implications of one of the mammoth cruise ships plying the seas nowadays falling into the hands of terrorists or of a laden chemical tanker being hijacked, or of even a conventional cargo ship loaded with explosives being blown up in a densely populated area or of a vital shipping channel being blocked to see how serious the consequences of terrorist action involving ships might be.

The answer to any of these nightmarish scenarios is multifaceted, embracing alertness and vigilance, training, implementation of the IMO and national security measures, and, more importantly, cooperation between governments and the industry at the national, regional, and global levels. In this way, we may hope that we never again have to witness terrorist atrocities such as those that have struck New York, Washington, Bali, Moscow, Istanbul, Baghdad, Madrid, the oil tanker *Limburg*, the USS *Cole*, and many others, and that the maritime infrastructure may never again become a victim.

PIRACY[44] AND ARMED ROBBERY AGAINST SHIPS[45] IN WATERS
OFF THE COAST OF SOMALIA
International Maritime Organization
Resolution A.[. . .][46] (25)
(Agenda item 19(a))
Adopted on November 29, 2007[*]

THE ASSEMBLY,

RECALLING Article 15(j) of the Convention on the International Maritime Organization concerning the functions of the Assembly in relation to regulations and guidelines concerning maritime safety and the prevention and control of marine pollution from ships,

---

[*]*Source:* International Maritime Organization (IMO), www.imo.org.

RECALLING ALSO article 1 of the Charter of the United Nations, which includes, among the purposes of the United Nations, the maintenance of international peace and security,

ALSO RECALLING article 100 of the United Nations Convention on the Law of the Sea (UNCLOS), which requires all states to cooperate to the fullest possible extent in the repression of piracy on the high seas or in any other place outside the jurisdiction of any state,

FURTHER RECALLING article 105 of UNCLOS which, inter alia, provides that, on the high seas or in any other place outside the jurisdiction of any state, every state may seize a pirate ship or aircraft, or a ship or aircraft taken by piracy and under the control of pirates and arrest the persons and seize the property on board, which, inter alia, enables warships, military aircraft, or other duly authorized ships or aircraft clearly marked and identifiable as being on government service to board any ship, other than a ship entitled to complete immunity in accordance with article 95 and article 96 of UNCLOS, when there are reasonable grounds for suspecting that the ship is, inter alia, engaged in piracy,

REAFFIRMING resolution A.545(13) on "Measures to prevent acts of piracy and armed robbery against ships," adopted on November 17, 1983; resolution A.683(17) on "Prevention and suppression of acts of piracy and armed robbery against ships," adopted on November 6, 1991; and resolution A.738(18) on "Measures to prevent and suppress piracy and armed robbery against ships," adopted on November 4, 1993,

BEARING IN MIND resolution A.922(22), through which the Assembly adopted the Code of Practice for the Investigation of the Crimes of Piracy and Armed Robbery against Ships ("the Code") and which, inter alia, urges governments to take action, as set out in the Code, to investigate all acts of piracy and armed robbery against ships occurring in areas or on board ships under their jurisdiction; and to report to the Organization pertinent information on all investigations and prosecutions concerning these acts,

BEARING IN MIND ALSO resolution A.979(24) on "Piracy and armed robbery against ships in waters off the coast of Somalia," by means of which the Assembly, inter alia:

- recommended a number of measures to protect ships from piracy and armed robbery attacks in waters off the coast of Somalia and by means of which the situation was brought to the attention of the Security Council of the United Nations ("the Security Council");
- requested the secretary-general to continue monitoring the situation in relation to threats to ships sailing in waters off the coast of Somalia and to report to the Council, as and when appropriate, on developments and any further actions which might be required; and
- requested the Council to monitor the situation in relation to threats to ships sailing in waters off the coast of Somalia and to initiate any actions it might

deem necessary to ensure the protection of seafarers and ships sailing in waters off the coast of Somalia,

NOTING WITH SATISFACTION the actions taken by the Council and the Secretary-General pursuant to resolution A.979(24),

CONSIDERING that the Maritime Safety Committee has approved MSC/Circ.622/Rev.1 and MSC/Circ.623/Rev.3 containing recommendations to governments and guidance to shipowners and ship operators, shipmasters and crews on preventing and suppressing acts of piracy and armed robbery against ships and has established a special signal for use by ships under attack or threat of attack,

NOTING that the General Assembly of the United Nations, at its sixty-first session, by resolution A/RES/61/222 on "Oceans and the law of the sea," adopted on December 20, 2006, inter alia:

.1   encourages states to cooperate to address threats to maritime safety and security, including piracy, armed robbery at sea, smuggling and terrorist acts against shipping, offshore installations and other maritime interests, through bilateral and multilateral instruments and mechanisms aimed at monitoring, preventing and responding to such threats;

.2   urges all states, in cooperation with the Organization, to combat piracy and armed robbery at sea by adopting measures, including those relating to assistance with capacity building through training of seafarers, port staff and enforcement personnel in the prevention, reporting and investigation of incidents, bringing the alleged perpetrators to justice, in accordance with international law, and by adopting national legislation, as well as providing enforcement vessels and equipment and guarding against fraudulent ship registration; and

.3   calls upon states to become parties to the Convention for the Suppression of Unlawful Acts against the Safety of Maritime Navigation and the Protocol for the Suppression of Unlawful Acts against the Safety of Fixed Platforms Located on the Continental Shelf; invites states to consider becoming parties to the 2005 Protocols amending those instruments; and also urges states parties to take appropriate measures to ensure the effective implementation of those instruments, through the adoption of legislation, where appropriate,

NOTING ALSO, with great concern, the increasing number of incidents of piracy and armed robbery against ships occurring in waters off the coast of Somalia, some of which have reportedly taken place more than 200 nautical miles from the nearest land,

MINDFUL OF the grave danger to life and the serious risks to navigational safety and the environment to which such incidents may give rise,

BEING PARTICULARLY CONCERNED that the Monitoring Group[47] on Somalia, in its report[48] of June 27, 2007, to the Security Council, confirmed, inter alia, that piracy and armed robbery against ships in waters off the coast of Somalia, unlike in other parts of the world, is caused by the lack of lawful administration and inability of the authorities to take affirmative action against the perpetrators, which allows the "pirate command centers" to operate without hindrance at many points along the coast of Somalia,

BEING AWARE of the serious safety and security concerns the shipping industry and the seafaring community continue to have as a result of the attacks against ships sailing in waters off the coast of Somalia referred to above,

BEING CONCERNED at the negative impact such attacks continue to have on the prompt and effective delivery of food aid and of other humanitarian assistance to Somalia and the serious threat this poses to the health and well-being of the people of Somalia,

NOTING, with appreciation, the "Subregional Seminar and Workshop on Piracy and Armed Robbery against Ships" held by IMO in Sana'a, Yemen, April 9–13, 2005, for countries in the Red Sea and Gulf of Aden region; and the follow-up meeting held in Muscat, Oman, from 14 to January 18, 2006,

BEING AWARE that the Security Council has, through resolution S/Res/1425(2002), adopted on July 22, 2002, stipulated that the arms embargo on Somalia prohibits the direct or indirect supply to Somalia of technical advice, financial and other assistance, and training related to military activities,

NOTING that the Security Council, by resolution S/Res/1766(2007) adopted on July 23, 2007, decided, inter alia, to reestablish the Monitoring Group on Somalia and directed it to continue to investigate, in coordination with relevant international agencies, all activities, including in the financial, maritime and other sectors, which generate revenues used to commit violations of the embargo on all delivery of weapons and military equipment to Somalia, which the Security Council had established by resolution S/Res/733(1992),

NOTING ALSO that the Security Council, being concerned at the continuing incidence of acts of piracy and armed robbery against ships in waters off the coast of Somalia:

.1   on March 15, 2006, in response to resolution A.979(24), through a statement[49] by the president of the Security Council, inter alia, encouraged member states of the United Nations, whose naval vessels and military aircraft operate in international waters and airspace adjacent to the coast of Somalia, to be vigilant to any incident of piracy therein and to take appropriate action to protect merchant shipping, in particular the transportation of humanitarian aid, against any such act, in line with relevant international law and further urged cooperation among all states, particularly regional states, and active prosecution of piracy offenses; and

.2   on August 20, 2007, in operative paragraph 18 of resolution S/Res/1772(2007) encouraged member states of the United Nations, whose naval vessels and military aircraft operate in international waters and airspace adjacent to the coast of Somalia, to be vigilant to any incident of piracy therein and to take appropriate action to protect merchant shipping, in particular the transportation of humanitarian aid, against any such act, in line with relevant international law,

NOTING WITH APPRECIATION the action taken by the secretary-general of the United Nations in response to the request of the Council, at its 98th session, in particular, to bring the Organization's concerns to the president of the Security Council with a request to bring them to the attention of the members of the Security Council,

RECOGNIZING that the particular character of the present situation in Somalia requires an exceptional response to safeguard the interests of the maritime community making use of the sea off the coast of Somalia,

RECOGNIZING ALSO the strategic importance of the navigational routes along the coast of Somalia for regional and global seaborne trade and the need to ensure that they remain safe at all times,

RECOGNIZING FURTHER, in view of the continued situation in Somalia giving rise to grave concern, the need for the immediate establishment of appropriate measures to protect ships sailing in waters off the coast of Somalia from piracy and armed robbery attacks,

APPRECIATING the efforts of those who have responded to calls from, or have rendered assistance to, ships under attack in waters off the coast of Somalia; acknowledging the efforts of a number of international organizations in raising awareness amongst, and providing guidance for, their respective memberships and reporting to the Organization in relation to this issue; and noting with appreciation the work done by the International Maritime Bureau of the International Chamber of Commerce in providing the industry with warnings in relation to incidents occurring in waters off the coast of Somalia and assistance in resolving cases where ships have been hijacked and the seafarers on board have been held hostage,

RESPECTING FULLY the sovereignty, sovereign rights, jurisdiction and territorial integrity of Somalia and the relevant provisions of international law, in particular UNCLOS,

HAVING CONSIDERED the actions taken, following the adoption of resolution A.979(24), by the Council, at its 98th regular and 24th extraordinary sessions, and by the secretary-general in the light of the prevailing situation in the waters off the coast of Somalia,

1. CONDEMNS AND DEPLORES all acts of piracy and armed robbery against ships irrespective of where such acts have occurred or may occur;
2. APPEALS to all parties which may be able to assist to take action, within the provisions of international law, to ensure that:
   .1 all acts or attempted acts of piracy and armed robbery against ships are terminated forthwith and any plans for committing such acts are abandoned; and

.2 any hijacked ships, seafarers serving in them, and any other persons on board are immediately and unconditionally released and that no harm is caused to them;

3. STRONGLY URGES governments to increase their efforts to prevent and suppress, within the provisions of international law, acts of piracy and armed robbery against ships irrespective of where such acts occur and, in particular, to cooperate with other governments and international organizations, in the interests of the rule of law, safety of life at sea, and environmental protection, in relation to acts occurring or likely to occur in the waters off the coast of Somalia;

4. ALSO STRONGLY URGES governments to promptly:
   .1 issue, to ships entitled to fly their flag, as necessary, specific advice and guidance on any appropriate additional precautionary measures ships may need to put in place when sailing in waters off the coast of Somalia to protect themselves from attack, which may include, inter alia, areas to be avoided;
   .2 issue, to ships entitled to fly their flag, as necessary, advice and guidance on any measures or actions they may need to take when they are under attack, or threat of attack, whilst sailing in waters off the coast of Somalia;
   .3 encourage ships entitled to fly their flag to ensure that information on attempted attacks or on acts of piracy or armed robbery committed whilst sailing in waters off the coast of Somalia is promptly conveyed to the nearby coastal states and to the nearest most appropriate Rescue Coordination Centre;
   .4 provide a point of contact through which ships entitled to fly their flag may request advice or assistance when sailing in waters off the coast of Somalia and to which such ships can report any security concerns about other ships, movements or communications in the area;
   .5 bring to the attention of the secretary-general information on attempted attacks or on acts of piracy or armed robbery committed against ships entitled to fly their flag whilst sailing in waters off the coast of Somalia for him to take appropriate action in the circumstances;
   .6 encourage ships entitled to fly their flag to implement expeditiously, for the ship's protection and for the protection of other ships in the vicinity, any measure or advice the nearby coastal states or any other state or competent authority may have provided;
   .7 establish, as necessary, plans and procedures to assist owners, managers and operators of ships entitled to fly their flag in the speedy resolution of hijacking cases occurring in the waters off the coast of Somalia;
   .8 investigate all acts or attempted acts of piracy and armed robbery against ships entitled to fly their flag occurring in the waters off the coast of Somalia and to report to the Organization any pertinent information;
   .9 take all necessary legislative, judicial and law enforcement action so as to be able, subject to national law, to receive and prosecute or extradite any pirates or suspected pirates and armed robbers arrested by warships or

military aircraft, or other ships or aircraft clearly marked and identifiable as being on government service; and

.10 with respect to ships entitled to fly their flag employed by the World Food Programme or the delivery of humanitarian aid to Somalia, where such ships are to be escorted by warships or military aircraft, or other ships or aircraft clearly marked and identifiable as being on government service, to conclude, taking into account operative paragraph 6.4, any necessary agreements with the state(s) concerned;

5. REQUESTS governments to instruct national Rescue Coordination Centres or other agencies involved, on receipt of a report of an attack, to promptly initiate the transmission of relevant advice and warnings, through the World-Wide Navigation Warning Service, the International SafetyNet Service or otherwise, to ships sailing in the waters off the coast of Somalia so as to warn shipping in the immediate area of the attack;

6. REQUESTS ALSO the Transitional Federal Government of Somalia to:

.1 take any action it deems necessary in the circumstances to prevent and suppress acts of piracy and armed robbery against ships originating from within Somalia and thus depriving them of the possibility of using its coastline as a safe haven from where to launch their operations;

.2 take appropriate action to ensure that all ships seized by pirates and armed robbers and brought into waters within its territory are released promptly and that ships sailing off the coast of Somalia do not henceforth become victims of acts of piracy or armed robbery;

.3 advise the Security Council that, in response to the pressing request of the Council of the International Maritime Organization, it consents to warships or military aircraft, or other ships or aircraft clearly marked and identifiable as being on government service, operating in the Indian Ocean, entering its territorial sea when engaging in operations against pirates or suspected pirates and armed robbers endangering the safety of life at sea, in particular the safety of crews on board ships carrying, under the World Food Programme, humanitarian aid to Somalia or leaving Somali ports after having discharged their cargo, together with any conditions attached to the consent given; and

.4 advise also the Security Council of its readiness to conclude, taking into account operative paragraph 4.10, any necessary agreements so as to enable warships or military aircraft, or other ships or aircraft clearly marked and identifiable as being on government service to escort ships employed by the World Food Programme for the delivery of humanitarian aid to Somalia or leaving Somali ports after having discharged their cargo;

7. CALLS UPON governments in the region to conclude, in cooperation with the Organization, and implement, as soon as possible, a regional agreement to prevent, deter, and suppress piracy and armed robbery against ships;

8. ALSO CALLS UPON all other governments, in cooperation with the Organization and as requested by those governments in the region, to assist these efforts;

9. REQUESTS FURTHER the Secretary-General to:
   .1 transmit a copy of the present resolution to the Secretary-General of the United Nations for consideration and any further action he may deem appropriate;
   .2 continue monitoring the situation in relation to threats to ships sailing in waters off the coast of Somalia and to report to the Council, as and when appropriate, on developments and any further actions which may be required;
   .3 establish and maintain cooperation with the Monitoring Group on Somalia; and
   .4 consult with interested governments and organizations in establishing the process and means by which technical assistance can be provided to Somalia and nearby coastal states to enhance the capacity of these states to give effect to the present resolution as appropriate;

10. REQUESTS the Maritime Safety Committee to review and update, as a matter of urgency, MSC/Circ.622/Rev.1, MSC/Circ.623/Rev.3 and resolution A.922(22), taking into account current trends and practices;

11. ALSO REQUESTS the Council to continue to monitor the situation in relation to threats to ships sailing in waters off the coast of Somalia and to initiate any actions which it may deem necessary to ensure the protection of seafarers and ships sailing in waters off the coast of Somalia;

12. REVOKES resolution A.979(24).

Notes

1. See J. Peter Pham, "U.S. National Interests and Africa's Strategic Significance," *American Foreign Policy Interests,* Volume 27, Issue 1 (2005): 19–29.

2. George W. Bush, interview by Jim Lehrer, NewsHour, PBS, February 16, 2000.

3. The White House, Office of the Press Secretary, "President Bush Creates a Department of Defense Unified Combatant Command for Africa" (February 6, 2007).

4. Princeton N. Lyman, "A Strategic Approach to Terrorism," in *Africa-U.S. Relations: Strategic Encounters,* ed. Donald Rothchild and Edmond J. Keller (Boulder, CO: Lynne Rienner Publishers, 2006), 49.

5. The White House, *National Security Strategy of the United States of America* (September 2002).

6. Ibid.

7. Abu Azzam al-Ansari, "Al-Qaeda tattajih nahwa Ifrikya" ("Al-Qaeda Is Moving to Africa"), Sada al-Jihad, no. 7 (June 2006): 27–30. For a full translation of the article along with analysis, see Reuven Paz and Moshe Terdman, "Africa: The Gold Mine of Al-Qaeda and Global Jihad," *PRISM Occasional Papers* 4, no. 2 (June 2006): 1–6.

8. See Elizabeth Spiro Clark, "Somaliland: A Democracy under Threat," *Foreign Service Journal* 83, no. 11 (November 2006): 30–38.

9. On the Islamic Courts Union takeover of Mogadishu and the ensuing crisis in the Horn of Africa, see J. Peter Pham, Testimony before the Subcommittee on Africa, Global Human Rights, and International Operations and the Subcommittee on International

Terrorism and Nonproliferation, U.S. House of Representatives Committee on International Relations (June 29, 2006).

10. See J. Peter Pham, "Mired in Mogadishu," *World Defense Review* (July 26, 2007).

11. U.S. Department of Defense, Office of the Assistant Secretary of Defense (Public Affairs), "Terror Suspect Transferred to Guantanamo" (June 6, 2007).

12. The video was posted to the http://www.alhesbah.org/ Web site on September 11, 2006.

13. See J. Peter Pham, "Al-Qaeda's Franchise in Africa," *World Defense Review* (June 21, 2007).

14. See J. Peter Pham, "The Growth of Militant Islamism in East Africa," World Defense Review (September 28, 2006).

15. See J. Peter Pham, Testimony before the Subcommittee on International Organizations, Human Rights and Oversight and the Subcommittee on Africa and Global Health, U.S. House of Representatives Committee on Foreign Affairs (May 10, 2007).

16. See Douglas Farah, *Blood from Stones: The Secret Financial Network of Terror* (New York: Broadway Books, 2004); also J. Peter Pham, *The Sierra Leonean Tragedy: History and Global Dimensions* (New York: Nova Science Publishers, 2005).

17. State of the Union Address by the President (January 31, 2006).

18. See Energy Information Administration, *U.S. Total Crude Oil and Products Imports* (May 27, 2007).

19. See J. Peter Pham, "Nigeria: Flailing State," World Defense Review (June 14, 2007).

20. See J. Peter Pham, "China's African Strategy and Its Implications for U.S. Interests," *American Foreign Policy Interests* 28, no. 3 (June 2006): 239-253.

21. See J. Peter Pham, "Hu's Selling Guns to Africa," *World Defense Review* (June 28, 2007).

22. See J. Peter Pham, "Securing the New Strategic Gulf," *World Defense Review* (June 7, 2007).

23. International Chamber of Commerce, "IMB Piracy Report Notes Decline in Piracy (April 25, 2007).

24. See Eric Pape, "West Africa: The New 'Drug Triangle,'" Newsweek (August 29, 2005): 25; also see J. Peter Pham, "The Security Challenge of West Africa's New Drug Depots," *World Defense Review* (July 10, 2007).

25. Marine Resources Assessment Group, *Review of Impacts of Illegal, Unreported and Unregulated Fishing on Developing Countries* (July 2005).

26. The White House, *The National Strategy for Maritime Security* (September 20, 2005).

27. The White House, *National Security Strategy of the United States of America* (March 16, 2006).

28. Combined Joint Task Force-Horn of Africa (CJTF-HOA), Fact Sheet (December 2006).

29. Jim Garamone, "Aircraft Attack Al Qaeda, Ike Moves off Somalia," *American Forces Press Service* (January 9, 2007).

30. See J. Peter Pham, "Violence, Islamism, and Terror in the Sahel," *World Defense Review* (February 22, 2007).

31. Gerry J. Gilmore, "U.S. Naval Forces Prepare for AFRICOM Stand Up," *American Forces Press Service* (June 1, 2007).

32. We defined the Caribbean Basin using the boundaries established in the U.S. trade programs known collectively as the Caribbean Basin Initiative (CBI). In 1983 the Caribbean Basin Economic Recovery Act (Pub. L. No. 98-67, 97 Stat. 369 (1983)), enacted the CBI into law. The CBI was substantially expanded in 2000 through the U.S.-Caribbean Basin Trade Partnership Act (Pub. L. No. 106-200, 114 Stat. 251 (2000)), and currently provides 24 beneficiary countries with duty-free access to U.S. markets. These countries are Antigua and Barbuda, Aruba, Bahamas, Belize, British Virgin Islands, Costa Rica, Dominica, Dominican Republic, El Salvador, Grenada, Guatemala, Guyana, Haiti, Honduras, Jamaica, Montserrat, Netherlands Antilles, Nicaragua, Panama, St. Kitts and Nevis, St. Lucia, St. Vincent and the Grenadines, and Trinidad and Tobago. For the purposes of this letter, however, five additional countries were included: Colombia, Cuba, Mexico, Suriname, and Venezuela.

33. Pub. L. No. 109–347, 120 Stat. 1884 (2006).

34. The International Ship and Port Facility Security Code was adopted under the auspices of the International Maritime Organization (IMO) by the Conference of Contracting Governments to the International Convention for the Safety of Life at Sea (SOLAS). In accordance with the SOLAS Convention as amended in 2002, the code establishes requirements for contracting governments of countries where ports are located, contracting governments of countries where ships are registered, operators of port facilities, and operators of vessels traveling on the high seas. Individual nations can set higher standards for facilities on their soil and for vessels registered in that country. As of November 30, 2006, there were 156 contracting governments to the SOLAS Convention.

35. Of the five countries we visited, the Coast Guard had issued final reports of its country visits to four of them, while one had just been visited.

36. See Report on the Consultation process—COM(2007) 574. See also: Green Paper on *A Future Maritime Policy for the Union: a European Vision of the Oceans and Seas*—COM(2006) 275.

37. See pages 8 and 77 of UNCTAD's *Review of Maritime Transport, 2006* (http://www.unctad.org/rmt2006) for data on global container port throughput and seaborne trade.

38. 2004 data on global container port throughput and seaborne trade have been used (see UNCTAD's *Review of Maritime Transport, 2006*). According to the IMO secretariat, as of October 2006, the total number of the declared ISPS port facilities amounted to 10,652.

39. See UNCTAD's Review of Maritime Transport, 2006 (http://www.unctad.org) for 2004 data on global freight costs. The 2004 data on international maritime freight costs have been estimated by the UNCTAD secretariat to amount to about 67 percent of global freight costs.

40. UNCTAD. United Nations Conference on Trade and Development. Rep. 14 Mar 2007. UNCTAD Secretariat. http://www.unctad.org/en/docs/sdtetlb20071_en.pdf.

41. The operator security officer functions may be assigned to the ship security officer on board the ship.

42. The operator security officer functions may be assigned to the ship security officer on board the ship.

43. Voyages include all segmented voyages.

44. "Piracy" is defined in article 101 of the United Nations Convention on the Law of the Sea as follows:

"Piracy consists of any of the following acts:

(a) any illegal acts of violence or detention, or any act of depredation, committed for private ends by the crew or the passengers of a private ship or a private aircraft, and directed:

(i) on the high seas, against another ship or aircraft, or against persons or property on board such ship or aircraft;

(ii) against a ship, aircraft, persons or property in a place outside the jurisdiction of any State;

(b) any act of voluntary participation in the operation of a ship or of an aircraft with knowledge of facts making it a pirate ship or aircraft;

(c) any act inciting or of intentionally facilitating an act described in sub-paragraph (a) or (b)."

45. "Armed robbery against ships" is defined in the Code of Practice for the Investigation of the Crimes of Piracy and Armed Robbery Against Ships (resolution A.922(22), annex, paragraph 2.2), as follows: "Armed robbery against ships means any unlawful act of violence or detention or any act of depredation, or threat thereof, other than an act of "piracy," directed against a ship or against persons or property on board such ship, within a State's jurisdiction over such offences."

46. The number of the resolution will be allocated after the end of the 25th regular session of the Assembly.

47. Established by the Security Council through resolution S/Res/1519(2003) and its mandate was renewed and expanded through resolutions S/Res/1558(2004), S/Res/1587(2005), S/Res/1630(2005), S/Res/1676(2006), S/Res/1724(2006) and S/Res/1766(2007).

48. See United Nations document S/2007/436, paragraphs 89 to 91 and 118 and 119; Report of the Monitoring Group on Somalia pursuant to Security Council resolution S/Res/1724(2006).

49. See United Nations document S/PRST/2006/11.

9

Private-Sector Perspectives:
Industry and Trade Organizations

INTERCARGO DIRECTION PAPER
International Association of Dry Cargo Shipowners
January 24, 2001*

I) THE REALITY

As our Association ponders on ways to change the attitude of our industry, we need to reflect on the realities that it faces. These include the following:

i) Shipping Is the Oldest of the Old World Economy

In a world shaken by the changes brought about by information technology and enthralled by the promises of the "New Economy," shipping continues to

*Courtesy of Intercargo, http://www.intercargo.org/pdf/direction_paper.pdf.

operate in a paradigm established in the beginning of the industrial age. As we witness the monumental changes in other sectors, we appear to resign ourselves to the belief that it is too difficult to reinvent ourselves to the new environment.

ii) The Growing Importance of Safety and Environmental Issues

Public awareness and concern on safety and environmental issues has been awoken, and this awareness and concern will only increase over time. As members of the global community, shipowners share this concern. Shipowners must work within ever tightening constraints brought about by increasing public expectations in these areas.

iii) "Bottom of the Food Chain"

With the growing sophistication of businesses regarding "supply chain management," pressures to reduce costs are put to bear on the entire supply chain. Unfortunately, shipping is at the bottom of this "food chain" and therefore has to bear the cumulative cost pressures of the various components. As an industry, we are subject to a vicious cycle of endless cost cutting. Take, for example, the way that cost pressure forces shipowners to press for lower shipbuilding prices. The shipyards respond by refining their safety margins by exerting pressure on classification societies. However, as owners compete, such cost savings eventually get passed on to the consumer. Over time, the liability for such corner cutting always hits the shipowning community, which ends up "carrying the baby."

iv) The Mindset

Because it is so difficult to achieve long-term profit sustainability, many owners resort to pure speculation in freight and/or assets. Such speculative behavior forces the industry to focus on perceptions rather than concentrating on providing real services to satisfy true client needs. Everyone is forced to take a short-term view, creating instability and irrationality in the marketplace. Initiatives that could upgrade the industry in the long term are made untenable due to the drastic swings in the market. The speculative mindset of some players causes deep underlying problems for the entire industry.

v) Substandard Ships

Cost pressures and inconsistent enforcement of standards give rise to substandard ships. Some owners resort to manipulating the rules, as they find it cheaper to pay the penalties of noncompliance than to operate within prescribed standards. The market is too focused on rates, and there is little price differentiation based on quality. When the market does not recognize quality, it is no wonder that there are pressures to minimize standards.

vi) Challenge to Provide a Worthwhile Career

The quality of the industry ultimately depends on the quality of the people in it. It is increasingly difficult to draw the right caliber of entrants into the industry, both for shipboard and shore jobs. We need to improve the condition and the image of the industry so that those who serve in it can have a safe, rewarding, and fulfilling career.

vii) Higher Demand on Quality

Concurrent with the pressures on costs is the rising expectation on performance. Quality demands on ship performance rises relentlessly even as our industry struggles with the perennial cycles of cost reduction.

II) THE INDUSTRY WE WANT

All those who are committed to our industry in the long term must surely agree on the characteristics of the industry that we want:

i) Safety

We want our industry to be a safe one for our crews, ships, cargo, and the environment in which we operate.

ii) Quality

We want our industry to be able to deliver a high standard of service to our clients, and we want this standard to be measured not only in freight rates but also in the way we can truly provide solutions to enhance their business.

iii) Stability

We want our industry to be stable. Stability enables us to think long term, and embark on upgrading and training programs. It reduces the financial risks, thereby ultimately reducing the costs to our client. Stability also removes the attraction of the industry to speculative activities.

iv) Equitability

Too often the risks borne by shipowners and the labor of their crews are invisible to the general public. The industry's role in supporting the world economy and maintaining the standard of living of its people is very much undervalued. We want our industry to be accorded the right level of appreciation and to attain an equitable position among world industries.

v) Careers

We want our industry to be able to provide a rewarding, safe and fulfilling career to those who are committed to it, so that over time it can attract its share of committed and talented new entrants.

vi) A Fair Return

Shipping requires huge commitment in capital and effort. We want an industry that can provide us with a fair return, so that it makes continual sense to allocate valuable resources to it.

III) WHAT CAN BE DONE?

To achieve the industry that we want, we need to embark on an agreed direction:

i) Mobilize for a More United Shipping Front

For shipowners to be more clearly heard, we must all speak with one voice. To do so, we should embark on a process of consolidation. This is achieved at two levels; the coordination and integration of shipping associations, as well as the rationalization of the industry. These are not pioneering moves, for we have seen such consolidation and rationalization in many industries in order to deal with new realities. Such consolidation reduces the duplication and wastage of resources and minimizes sectors of the industry pulling in different directions. It also enhances the clarity of the viewpoints that we want to put forward.

Consolidation also signifies our determination to act collectively to bring about change—for collective action is the only way to deal with the deep rooted and complex problems of the industry.

ii) Promotion of Quality

The following are the directions that we can take to promote quality in shipping:

a) Elimination of Substandard Ships

Substandard ships can be eliminated only if we have a clear differentiation in quality. To achieve this, our industry should adopt common standards and take on the responsibility of self-regulation.

b) Promotion of a "Chain of Responsibility"

The level of quality provided by shipowners (including areas of safety and the environment) ultimately depends on the requirement of cargo interests and the charterers. The current situation in which only the shipowner bears the onus of quality while the charterer and cargo owner make their decisions only on the basis of the freight rate, clearly leads to an inequitable division of responsibility. We need to promote an awareness of the "Chain of Responsibility," so that the effect of the decisions by charterers, cargo owners, insurers, and bankers on the level of quality provided is transparent to all. If an incident arises because a substandard vessel is employed on the basis of cost alone, the charterer and insurance must surely also be called to account.

c) Reengineering the Infrastructure

We need to "level the playing field" by reengineering the infrastructure through which the different important international bodies and agencies come together to identify and prioritize issues, establish activities, and initiate actions on industry matters. The global economy has for some time been undergoing major structural changes. The institutions and agencies that govern our industry must also similarly change to ensure that they continue to be relevant. We need to look at the existing processes and promote changes to take better account of the shipowners' viewpoint as well as the interdependencies that govern our industries and the wider economy beyond. We also need to promote consistency in the enforcement of international shipping regulation. For example, we should push for some sort of unification of port state standards and practices.

iii) Rationalize and Coordinate Industry Development

    a)   We need to be more aware of the effect on shipping by decisions and policies made within the maritime community. To do so, we need to set up a platform for discussion and consultation of all parties that can influence shipping: owners, charterers, cargo interests, insurers, bankers, class, port and flag states, shipyards, and international agencies.

    b)   We must promote a better flow of information and greater transparency on the effect on shipping and the general public due to decisions and actions made in other sectors.

iv) Creating Public Awareness

We need to educate the public on the importance of shipping to our daily life and to raise their awareness of the interdependencies that bind our industry and the greater economy. We should persuade the public that it is a very small price to pay to achieve quality in shipping.

v) Leadership

To persuade others to accommodate the vision of the industry that we want, we must first demonstrate that we have the determination and leadership to bring about these changes. We must also demonstrate that we can also change ourselves. We should therefore be prepared to take up the challenge of driving the self-regulation of the industry.

IV) COLLECTIVELY CHANGING THE CURRENT REALITY

If we are not satisfied with the current reality in shipping, we can change it. But this can only be done collectively because the issues are many and the problems are entrenched. Yet, they are not insurmountable. They only require collective determination and effort. If we take the first step, we should be able, in time, to realize the industry that we want.

By definition, making long-term changes is time-consuming, but the effort can be made easier if it is undertaken by many. Through a persistent and sustained effort, Intercargo believes that it is possible to have the industry that we all seek.

PREVENTION AND SUPPRESSION OF ACTS OF TERRORISM AGAINST
SHIPPING, PORT AND MARITIME SECURITY, GUIDANCE FOR THE
DEVELOPMENT OF SHIP AND PORT SECURITY PLANS

International Association of Ports and Harbors and International
Chamber of Shipping
Maritime Safety Committee
75th Session Agenda Item 17 International Maritime Organization
April 12, 2002*

1. INTRODUCTION

Ports and ships have long been potential targets for criminals, and now consideration also has to be given to the use of ships and their cargoes as potential terrorist weapons. There is consequently a need to reassess existing ship and port security plans to address potential terrorist activities.

Because both ships and ports differ widely in their characteristics, layout, and vulnerability, it is not practical to develop detailed and uniform standard comprehensive ship or port security plans. However, IAPH and ICS believe that it is possible to develop generic guidelines for ship operators and port facilities from which specific issues can be selected to address in respect of each port and ship, to a greater or lesser degree, threats applicable to them.

To be effective, it is very important that ship, port and port facility security plans can be dovetailed together to form a comprehensive set of security measures relevant to the specific location. This document provides guidance for the development of interrelated ship, port, and port facility security plans.

2. SECURITY POLICY

Shipowners, port authorities and others involved in the port industry need to consider their own responsibilities with regard to security. To accomplish this, various steps need to be taken, such as

- to appoint and empower suitably senior staff members with overall responsibility for security within the port facility, shipping company and individual ship;
- to assess the security risks and to minimize the implications of any incident;
- to cooperate with the responsible authorities and to act on advice from those authorities;
- to promote security awareness among all employees;

---

*Courtesy of the International Association of Ports and Harbors (IAPH).

- to give a commitment to provide appropriate security guidance and advice;
- to establish a reporting and recording system for incidents.

In all cases, the following issues need to be addressed:

- responsibility for handling different types of incidents
- promulgation of information to other parties involved;
- issuing guidance or instructions to employees;
- liaison with other authorities;
- methods of communication in different circumstances;
- plans for handling media interest;
- plans for informing and supporting the relatives/next of kin of persons involved.

The approach can be visualized as follows:

$$\text{Awareness} \rightarrow \text{Preplanning} \rightarrow \text{Preparation} \rightarrow \text{Prevention} \rightarrow \text{Resolution} \rightarrow \text{Follow-up}$$

3. INDIVIDUAL SHIP AND PORT SECURITY PLANS

Individual ship and port security plans should be developed in close cooperation with all the relevant industry stakeholders and authorities involved. Their main characteristics are that they should address either the ship or port as a whole as well as the individual components.

The security plan can be considered as

- defining appropriate scenarios;
- describing all measures that need to be taken to address those scenarios;
- describing the resources available to assist the application of those measures;
- describing the responsibilities of the different entities involved;
- providing contingency plans in the event of incidents occurring.

The plan should address all the elements of the security chain, from awareness initiatives to the actual organization of incident combating and subsequent policy review.

4. PORT SECURITY PLAN

It is essential that the overall coordination rests with a Port Security Committee in which all relevant authorities closely cooperate. Such authorities may differ from country to country, or even from port to port within a country, but they will almost always include the port authority, police and other law enforcement or security bodies, the justice department, customs authority, fire and other emergency services, and the environmental department. It is also imperative that the Port Security Committee works closely together with port users and others located within the port environment. Such cooperation is necessary for creating awareness and involvement and to mutually develop security toolkits.

5. THE PORT FACILITY SECURITY PLAN

The overall Port Security Plan requires the active involvement of the local port industry. Through that cooperation generic guidance should be developed for individual port facilities, terminals, industries, et cetera, so as to enable these to develop their own, custom-made Facility Security Plan. Such a plan should contain measures to increase the alertness of personnel, to counter criminal infiltration of the organization and to secure the company area and its installations. It should also pay attention to procedures in the event of incidents, information supply, communication and education and training of personnel.

6. THE SHIP/PORT INTERFACE

An essential element in overall security is the liaison between the visiting ship and the port and the respective persons responsible for security.
Between them, the following issues need to be addressed:

a)   The security of the immediate ship environs, quayside:
   • Mooring lines, linesmen, and their means of transportation
   • Gangway, access control of people boarding, lighting
   • Traffic alongside the quay
   • Overhead equipment: cranes, other loading/discharging equipment
   [. . .]
b)   The security of the immediate ship environs, waterside:
   • Ships alongside: bunkers, water, supplies, ship/ship cargo transfer
   • Ship service providers, tugs
   [. . .]

7. SHIP SECURITY PLANS

The development of ship security plans needs to be considered in respect of each individual vessel. The essential focus is the protection of the perimeter of the ship from unauthorized access and, within the vessel itself, the identification and protection of secure areas, vulnerable points, and essential services.

8. ESSENTIAL ELEMENTS OF A SECURITY PLAN

A number of essential elements should be addressed:

- Security awareness among all relevant partners, authorities, private enterprise, and employees
- Vulnerability assessment
- Knowledge, experience in security matters
- Cooperation
- Information management
- Communication

8.1. Awareness

In the introductory paragraphs it is accepted that both ports and ships are susceptible to criminal activities, including acts of terrorism. However, experience shows that in general, the possibility of serious criminal activity is seldom recognized as such by an individual ship operator or port. It is necessary, therefore, to develop programs aimed at creating awareness by identifying various potential threats and their impact, in both human and economic terms.

8.2. Vulnerability Assessment

Measures described in individual ship or port security plans should be directed at those areas where they are likely to have the maximum effect. For an effective security approach, it is therefore essential that risk analyses are conducted both at overall as well as an individual level. Weak spots, both in a physical sense and in an organizational sense, should be revealed through the analysis process. Vulnerability assessments should be carried out at regular intervals.

8.3. Knowledge and Experience

Knowledge and experience in security issues are essential elements for a successful approach. These elements are usually not available at individual company level. By establishing a network in which all relevant authorities participate, this deficiency can be addressed. Such a network may serve as a central platform for addressing complex security issues and could also facilitate education and training of port facility personnel. Care needs to be taken to secure the integrity of the information handled through the network.

8.4. Cooperation

Port and ship security is a complex issue which requires close and intensive cooperation between all the actors involved. This will range from local cooperation between the port industry, port users, and authorities to international cooperation between authorities and ports, port organizations, and the shipping industry.

Cooperation between the port users and service providers in the port is essential. Port users include visiting ships, passengers boarding and disembarking and cargo or stores deliverers and collectors. Service providers are often the first to personally contact the ship and its crew. Pilots, tug boat companies, linesmen and suppliers of other services such as stevedores, and those providing other services to ships such as drinking water and bunkers, should be aware of the potential threats and of ways of handling such situations.

8.5. Information Management

An effective security system requires high-quality information and information exchange. Accurate and timely information is crucial for the identification of potential threats and for taking the proper countermeasures. It is necessary to lay the prime responsibility for information collection, interpretation, and dissemination with an identified and experienced organization such as the police or other security organizations. This focal point should maintain close contact with relevant national authorities as well as local parties in the port area, both authorities and industry. In the case of ships, the flag state has responsibilities here.

8.6. Communication

Proper and unambiguous information to all relevant parties, including the population in areas adjacent to the port, and the personnel involved with the ship, is of importance in order to create a firm basis for the measures to be taken. A communication plan should therefore be part of the port, ship operator, or ship security plan. At regular intervals all relevant parties should be informed about security projects without endangering the integrity of these plans by disclosing sensitive details.

9. PREVENTIVE MEASURES

Preventive measures must be taken on the basis of local circumstances. They should be aimed at protection of the ship, the port and its industrial complex as well as persons on board (passengers and crew) and ashore (port personnel and others potentially affected). Issues to be considered include the following:

- Briefing the personnel involved
- Access control, personal identification, and authorization
- Liaison with port security
- Threat assessment in respect of stowaways, drug trafficking, terrorism, other unlawful activity, civil unrest
- The identification and protection of secure areas
- The identification and protection of vulnerable areas/facilities or essential services
- Lighting arrangements
- Alarm systems
- The provision and role of security personnel
- Contingency plans in the event of unauthorized boarding, bomb threat, suspicious packages
- Searching—for stowaway, drugs, explosive devices
- Notification to authorities and others
- Ship to shore communications
- Reporting procedures
- Reaction to incidents
- Training of personnel
- The provision of security equipment

10. ACTION TO BE TAKEN

The Committee is requested to note the views of IAPH and ICS on the concept of developing generic ship, port, and port facility security plans and to endorse this approach.

PORT AND MARITIME SECURITY

International Association of Ports and Harbors
IAPH Policy and Guidance Paper
April 23, 2002*

1. INTRODUCTION

The world in which we live and conduct our business is subject to rapid change. Globalization and liberalization of trade accelerate that process. Open frontiers lead to less involvement and control of regulatory authorities and

---

*Courtesy of the International Association of Ports and Harbors (IAPH).

all elements in the logistic chain can be potential targets for illegitimate organizations.

However, since the tragic events of September 11, 2001, consideration has also to be given to the use of ships and their cargoes as potential terrorist weapons. There is consequently a need to reassess existing ship and related port security plans to address potential terrorist activities. This is all the more important in view of the economic importance of most ports for their national economy.

Ship security is the responsibility of international organizations such as the International Chamber of Shipping (ICS), and proposals to that effect have been prepared by them. Port security is first and foremost a responsibility for the Port Authority and an issue that is dealt with in IAPH. Ports differ widely in their characteristics, layout, and vulnerability, and it is therefore not practical to develop detailed and uniform standard comprehensive port security plans. However, IAPH believes that it is possible to develop generic guidelines for port authorities from which specific issues can be selected to address in respect to each port, to a greater or lesser degree, threats applicable to them. This paper provides guidance on these issues.

To be effective, it is very important that ship and port security plans can be dovetailed together to form a comprehensive set of security measures relevant to the specific location. Guidance thereon is contained in the joint ICS/IAPH submission to IMO.

Port authorities are usually the main orchestrator of their port as a logistic nodal point and as such they can provide a valuable contribution to the establishment of an integral port and maritime security policy. Such a policy should address the source of the potential threats as well as minimization of the effects.

The approach can be visualized as follows:

$$\text{Sensitization} \rightarrow \text{Pro-action} \rightarrow \text{Prevention} \rightarrow \text{Preparation} \rightarrow \text{Repression} \rightarrow \text{Aftercare}$$

2. PORT SECURITY POLICY

The port's security policy should be developed in close cooperation of all the authorities involved. Its main characteristic is that it addresses two main elements: the port area as a whole and the individual companies operating in the port.

1. Multidisciplinary (Overall) Port Security Plan

The overall port security plan can be considered to be the scenario, describing all measures that need to be taken with regard to the security of the port as a whole. Apart from a description of the measurers and the facilities available for these measures, it should also contain a description of the division of responsibilities of the different actors.

The plan should address all the elements of the security chain, from sensitization initiatives (creating awareness) to the actual organization of incident combating and cyclic policy review. It is essential that the overall coordination rests with a port security committee in which all relevant authorities closely cooperate. These may differ from country (port) to port, but they will almost always include the port authority, police, justice department, customs, fire brigade, medical services, and the environmental department. It is also imperative that this port security committee works closely together with the local port industry. That cooperation is necessary for creating awareness and involvement and to mutually develop security toolkits.

2. Port Facility Security Plans

As said, the overall Port Security Plan requires the active involvement of the local port industry. Through that cooperation generic guidance should be developed for the individual port facilities, terminals, industries, and so on, so as to enable these to develop their own custom made Facility Security Plan. Such a plan should contain measures to increase the alertness of personnel, to counter criminal infiltration of the organization, secure the company area and its installations. It should also pay attention to procedures for calamities, information supply, communication and education and training of personnel.

3. Essential Conditions for a Successful Port Security Plan

The approach as described before requires a number of essential conditions in order to be successful.

- Awareness among all relevant partners, authorities, and private enterprise
- Vulnerability assessment
- Knowledge, experience in security matters
- Cooperation
- Information management
- Communication

4. Awareness

In the introductory paragraphs it is argued that ports are susceptible to criminal activities, including acts of terrorism. However, experience shows that in general, this is not experienced as such in the average port industrial community. As a result, there is no or insufficient basis for initiating activities, investing funds, and cooperating with other actors. For that reason it is necessary to develop a program aimed at creating awareness among the industry by explaining the various potential threats, in terms of calamities as well as economic damage.

5. Vulnerability Assessment

It will be clear that the measures described in the Port or Facility Security Plan should be directed at those areas where they are likely to have the maximum effect. For an effective security approach it is therefore essential that risk analyses are conducted both at overall port level as well as on individual port facility level. Weak spots, both in a physical sense and in an organizational sense, should be made visible through the analysis process. Vulnerability assessments should be carried out at regular intervals and be part of the management process of the port or the port facility.

6. Knowledge and Experience

Knowledge and experience in security issues are essential elements for a successful approach. These elements are usually not available at individual company level. By establishing a Knowledge Center in which all relevant authorities cooperate, and make their knowledge and experience available to the local port industries, this deficiency can be remedied. Such Knowledge Center may also serve as central platform for addressing complex security issues and could also facilitate education and training of port facility personnel. Obviously care should be taken at securing the integrity of the information handled through the Knowledge Center.

7. Cooperation

The nature of port security is very complex, and it therefore requires close and intensive cooperation between all actors involved. This will range from local cooperation between the port industry and authorities to international cooperation between authorities and ports and port organizations. In this context cooperation between the service providers in the port should be addressed. These service providers are often the first to personally contact the ship and its crew. Pilots, tugboat companies, linesmen, and suppliers of other services such as drinking water and bunkers should be trained in identifying potential danger and in ways to handle such situations.

8. Information Management

An effective security system requires high quality information and information exchange. Accurate and timely information is crucial for the identification of potential threats and for taking the proper countermeasures. It is
necessary to lay the responsibility for information collection, interpretation, and dissemination with an experienced organization such as the
police. This focal point should maintain close contact with relevant
national authorities as well as local parties in the port area, both authorities
and industry.

9. Communication

Proper and unambiguous information to the relevant parties, including the
population in areas adjacent to the port is of importance in order to create a
firm basis for the measures to be taken. A communication plan should therefore be part of the Port Security Plan. At regular intervals the population
should be informed about security projects without endangering the integrity
of these plans by disclosing sensitive details.

10. Preventive Measures

Preventive measures must be taken on the basis of local circumstances.
They are aimed at protection of the port and its industrial complex as well as
persons on board (passengers and crew) and ashore (port personnel and
inhabitants of nearby living quarters).

11. Cargo Inspections

Cargo inspections aimed at identifying weapons, drugs, explosives, and
other matters of a threatening nature. Rather than inspect cargo at random,
inspections should be targeted. Targets will be established on the basis of document checks in combination with a system of risk analysis. This will enhance
the probability that targeted cargo proves to be noncompliant with regulations or to contain contraband.

Because containers are considered to be most susceptible to criminal activities, special attention should be paid to containerized cargo. Suitable equipment
is x-ray machines, portable detection equipment, and sniffer dogs. In order not
to disturb the logistic process in an unacceptable manner, the number of physical checks should be carefully chosen. Percentages will differ from port to port,

but experience has shown that even a limited percentage, coupled with a targeted approach based on risk analysis, can provide an acceptable security level.

12. Identification Check of Passengers and Crews

In most cases the responsibility for checking the identification of both crews and passengers rests with the seaport police or the immigration authorities. For passengers this will involve a passport check. For crew members an identity card based on the provisions of ILO will serve as a suitable identity document.

13. Identification Check of Port Personnel

For personnel engaged in the port industry, this issue should be part of the facility or industry security plan.
For personnel engaged in security enforcement: To be developed.

14. Integration with Maritime Security

A Port Security Plan is not enough to guarantee security and reliability throughout the total logistic chain, including the hinterland of the port and the sea transport. To that end, similar measures, as described above, need to be developed for the individual links throughout the logistic chain.

15. Concluding Remarks

Regarding sea transport, including the immediate ship/shore interface, IMO is presently developing international regulations that should be endorsed at a diplomatic conference in November or December 2002. It will be essential that regulations relating to maritime security dovetail with port and port facility security plans. Close cooperation of all international actors is necessary to ensure the establishment of effective measures to ensure maritime security both at sea and in ports and their hinterland.

IAPH is dedicated to play an active role in this process. This document should provide the basis for generic guidance for ports to develop their own custom made security plans based on their particular characteristics.

BIMCO'S VISION AND OBJECTIVES
The Baltic and International Maritime Council
June 17, 2004*

BIMCO'S VISION

To be the leading interest group and membership organization offering practical and tangible services to shipowners, managers, brokers, agents, operators, associations, and other entities connected with the international shipping industry.

BIMCO'S OBJECTIVES

BIMCO's aim is that of free trade, access to markets, trade facilitation and harmonization, promotion of quality, and safety plus security.

BIMCO's focus is on the promotion of high shipping standards and support of existing measures to ensure quality shipping as well as the standardization of regulations and the implementation thereof on a worldwide basis.

BIMCO is to consolidate its position as the recognized leader in the production of standard documents for the maritime industry, thus providing a tangible contribution to trade facilitation and harmonization of the shipping industry.

BIMCO is to continue to provide core services such as intervention, charter party advice, IT products, and training courses as well as maritime, port-related, and company information.

BIMCO is to actively continue to urge firm and timely action against those engaged in the breach of ship and crew security, piracy and armed robbery, smuggling, refugee transportation, and, last but not least, terrorism.

BIMCO is to endeavor to retain its profile as a private, independent, non-political organization and be thus recognized by governments and intergovernmental and nongovernmental organizations. When relevant issues arise, BIMCO is to make a strong case on behalf of its members and the shipping industry thereby becoming part of the process, also through the media.

BIMCO is to ensure that the industry's position and pragmatic solutions are brought to the attention of the United States, the EU, and other global maritime authorities.

BIMCO is to continue to maintain contact with other maritime organizations, associations, and interest groups in order to seek, when necessary, mutual understanding and cooperation on industry matters.

BIMCO's resources are to be focused on the key areas, which provide the most benefits to members.

---

*Courtesy of Baltic and International Maritime Council (BIMCO)

AN INTRODUCTION TO THE IFSMA
International Federation of Shipmasters' Associations
October 2004*

IFSMA was formed in 1974 by eight European Shipmasters' Associations to unite the world's serving shipmasters into a single professional coordinated body. It is a non-profit-making apolitical organization dedicated solely to the interest of the serving shipmaster. The Federation is formed of over 8,000 shipmasters from about 60 countries either through their national associations or as individual members.

Established to uphold International Standards of Professional Competence for Seafarers, IFSMA is a Federation with a policy to ensure Safe Operational Practices, Preservation from Human Injury, Protection of the Marine Environment, and Safety of Life and Property at Sea.

The structure of IFSMA is explained in the statutes and bylaws of the Federation. The responsibility of the functioning of the Federation is vested in the Executive Council, which comprises a president, a deputy president, and five vice presidents, who are elected by the members. Further assistance is given by the secretariat, which at present comprises a secretary-general, a deputy secretary-general, and an administration officer.

With its Headquarters in London, IFSMA's secretariat is located close to the International Maritime Organisation (IMO). In 1975, IFSMA was granted consultative status as a nongovernmental organization at IMO, which enables the Federation to represent the views and protect the interests of the serving shipmasters unfettered and unfiltered by others. To enable IFSMA to function effectively at IMO, it is represented by the secretary-general and a team of active or former shipmasters who attend the four main committees, namely the Maritime Safety Committee, the Maritime Environmental Protection Committee, the Legal Committee, and the Facilitation Committee. This team is also active in the nine subcommittees of IMO and their working and drafting groups as well as attending the council meetings and the assemblies.

IFSMA has always tried to support IMO in practical ways and has provided consultants to assist in the Comprehensive Review and Revision of the 1978 STCW Convention, and actively participated in the Joint ICAO/IMO Group of Experts on the Harmonization of Aeronautical and Maritime Search and Rescue. IFSMA also sat on the Steering Committee on Ro-Ro Ferry Safety which supervised the work of the panel of experts and made recommendations to MSC 65.

IFSMA also provided two maritime specialists forming part of an IMO needs assessment and programming team within the framework of IMO's Integrated Technical Cooperation Programme (ITCP).

---

*Courtesy of the International Federation of Shipmasters' Associations.

IFSMA has a history of submitting relevant papers on various aspects to the committees and subcommittees of IMO, which often result in successful debates leading to MSC circulars and improvements in various instruments. IFSMA is a strong supporter of IMO in its quest for security, safer shipping, and cleaner oceans. It is the desire of the Federation to assist IMO in achieving a truly global implementation and rigorous enforcement of its international treaties so that there is no need for any country to resort to regulatory measures on either a national or a regional basis. IFSMA fully recognizes the need to establish a strong improved safety culture within the shipping industry and the early implementation of both the ISM Code and the 1995 amendments to the STW Convention. IFSMA members are provided with the facility to access the IMO documents Web site for research and information purposes.

IFSMA has long held the firm belief that shipowners and ship management companies should hold a Safety Management System (SMS) and Document of Compliance (DOC) issued by the Flag State Administration before being permitted to operate ships, that increased scrapping of antiquated and substandard ships should be speeded up, and that worldwide regional port state control is now a top priority. In particular there should be a total ban, effective worldwide, on the reregistration of ships for commercial trading once they have been sold for scrap and demolition.

IFSMA also participates in the deliberations at the International Labour Organization (ILO) where there is work at present with the merger of all previous conventions and recommendations regarding seafarers into a new Super International Maritime Labour Convention.

IFSMA is also asked by various bodies all over the world to participate in seminars and conferences and to produce training and educational courses.

Furthermore IFSMA is conscious of the needs for shipmasters in the future and has joined with the Nautical Institute, Trinity House, and the Honourable Company of Master Mariners in organizing a Command Seminar. This seminar is arranged every 2 years and visits a number of maritime centers around the world to seek the views of both mariners and the industry and how shipmasters should be prepared to meet the needs of the twenty-first century.

IFSMA defines shipmasters as those who are in possession of an internationally recognized Certificate of Competency, issued by the government of an established maritime nation who are serving, or have previously served, in command of seagoing ships whether or not engaged upon international or domestic trade.

Once a man has risen to the rank of shipmaster he is entitled to belong to IFSMA and there is no requirement in our statutes for the periodic revalidation of his Certificate of Competency. But if he were to lose his license due to negligence, incompetence, or misconduct, then he would no longer qualify for membership of the Federation. Trade unions, national associations, professional institutes, and learned societies are all (when representing shipmasters) equally welcome as organizations in affiliation with IFSMA, and there is no distinction made between them.

REMARKS OF CHRISTOPHER KOCH
President and CEO, World Shipping Council
Before the Maritime Security Expo 2006
New York City
September 19, 2006*

I appreciate the opportunity to address this fifth annual Maritime Security Expo and provide some comments on the state of maritime security initiatives and the international liner shipping industry.

The year 2006 has demonstrated that world trade volumes continue to grow at a rapid pace, that the transportation infrastructure handling these volumes is often operating at or close to capacity, that further efficiencies, speed and investment are needed to handle future trade volumes, and that the efforts and the need to enhance maritime and containerized cargo security are a continuing obligation and challenge. In the limited time available this morning, I would like to briefly touch on security policy developments in both the United States and the European Union.

I. U.S. DEVELOPMENTS

Maritime Security

The basic architecture of U.S. maritime security is well known and understandable. First, there is vessel and port security, overseen by the Coast Guard and guided in large measure by the International Ship and Port Facility Security Code (ISPS). Second, there is personnel security, overseen by various Department of Homeland Security agencies and the State Department. Third, is cargo security, which in regards to containerized cargo is addressed through the well-known "three legged stool" of Customs and Border Protection's 24-Hour Rule advance cargo screening initiative, C-TPAT, and the Container Security Initiative—all of which are reinforced and made more effective by the increased deployment of container inspection technology at U.S. and foreign ports.

The liner shipping industry's operations are consistent and repetitive—its vessel services and crews call at the same ports every week. So long as there is consistent and professional implementation of the security rules, which is a hallmark of the Coast Guard, liner shipping has found no problem in operating in the new vessel or port security environment.

We also appreciate the Coast Guard Commandant's admonition that the "concept of maritime security cannot be reduced to a single threat vector." There are numerous potential vectors for terrorists attack on the maritime

---

*http://www.worldshipping.org/maritime_expo_speech.pdf

environment that don't involve cargo containers. For example, merchant vessels are in fact defenseless against small boat attacks. We fully support the Coast Guard in its efforts to secure an enormous Maritime Domain against a variety of risks.

Personnel Security

Personnel security is one of the more active areas of DHS attention and development, for fairly obvious reasons. The most significant and difficult new undertaking in this regard is the Transport Worker Identification Credential (TWIC).

Before touching on that, I would like to briefly address the continued criticism from some quarters of the U.S. government's treatment of seafarers, its unwillingness to accept the recent ILO Convention's seafarer credential, and its insistence on an individual visa for seafarers who wish to enter the country.

The fair and humane treatment of seafarers is an important issue and deserves serious consideration by industry and government. However, it is no more correct to argue that the government is characterizing seafarers as "potential terrorists" than it is to say that the government is treating all 11 million nonimmigrant visitors to the United States from non-visa-waiver countries as "potential terrorists." All such persons, plus any foreign individual in the United States for work or educational reasons, are required to be in possession of individual visas that are issued after personal interviews and the collection of biometrics at U.S. diplomatic posts. The government, as directed by U.S. statutes, is requiring visitors to have proper government credentials for entry into the country, and is improving its monitoring of people entering and exiting the country though the U.S. VISIT program as strongly advocated by the 9/11 Commission Report and other security advisors, while at the same time trying to address the potential terrorist threat to shipping. In the last three years, nearly 700 persons have illegally entered the United States as seafarers illegally absconding or deserting their ship. While it is true that this number may be less than the number of people illegally crossing the Mexican border in a day, it is also true that the maritime industry has shown itself to be a potential vector of illegal immigration. Nations do have a legitimate interest in trying to devise effective ways to check who is crossing their borders. In that regard, a foreign seafarer is not different from a foreign airline pilot, businessman, student, or artist.

Seafarers have been clearly advised by the government to obtain visas in order to obtain shore leave. That requirement is unlikely to change. Those who do have valid visas are generally treated professionally and courteously and given shore privileges. For those who do not have visas, the U.S. government has made it clear that the proposed ILO seafarer credential cannot become a substitute for a visa. The government has made that determination because of the biometrics used in the credential, and the government's insistence that personal interviews are essential for screening out undesirable foreign visitors. Because liner shipping vessels operate on regular schedules, their crews know in advance if they are coming to the United States and whether they will need a visa. For those seafarers aboard vessels who do not know the vessel will call at the United States until after they sign on and do not have the necessary visa, one can and should sympathize with their desire to obtain shore leave when they arrive. As a way to try to address this concern, the State Department has stated that seafarers who don't know for certain but may be working on ships that will call at U.S. ports may apply for a visa. Improving the lot of these seafarers will require new ideas and a cooperative environment for the exchange of such ideas. The Council welcomes that the State Department has started an outreach to industry about these issues, and we are committed to offer our assistance wherever needed and relevant.

For U.S. shore-based maritime workers, the current initiative by the Coast Guard and the Transportation Security Administration (TSA) to devise and implement the TWIC system involves one of the more difficult and important maritime security challenges the industry has faced in recent years. Making sure that every port worker, every truck driver, and every other regular employee entering a secure port area has a proper TSA-approved security credential that can be efficiently and effectively read, under normal maritime operating conditions, with appropriate biometrics and matched against appropriate databases is an enormous task. To devise such a system that can work in all of the various maritime industry sectors, from offshore oil and gas, to inland waterways, to seasonal industries, to container terminals will require a close and cooperative partnership of industry and government.

The liner shipping industry and the marine terminal operators who service the liner shipping industry have all consistently supported the TWIC concept and its implementation. However, as the National Maritime Security Advisory Committee recently advised the Department of Homeland Security, this program must be implemented carefully and correctly the first time. Addressing the technology issues associated with the TWIC and the TWIC readers, increasing the clarity of who must obtain a TWIC, and addressing the various real world implementation issues that different sectors of the industry face will require a steady, careful implementation and dialogue with the industry.

Container Security

CBP's basic container security strategy—to perform cargo shipment security risk assessment before vessel loading, to cooperate with the governments of trading partners though agreements negotiated via the Container Security Initiative, to enhance security of supply chains via C-TPAT, and to scan all arriving containers for radiation and to inspect any other shipment considered potentially risky with nonintrusive technology—is fundamentally sound.

It also must mature and improve. How and in what way should that occur? Two improvements under development and review are entirely appropriate, needed, and important. One is the acquisition of better cargo shipment data for cargo screening and risk assessment. Another is the expanded piloting and use of radiation and density container inspection technology.

1. Improving Risk Assessment Data

The DHS strategy of using risk assessment and targeting techniques to review all containerized cargo shipments before vessel loading is logical from a security, an operational, and a practical perspective. The liner shipping industry fully supports it. But the Congress, DHS, and the industry all recognize that reliance on ocean carriers' cargo manifest data, while a fine start, has substantial shortcomings. The present system provides either no or unreliable data regarding the commercial parties involved in buying and selling the goods, where the goods are originating and who produced or supplied them, where the goods are ultimately going, and where and by whom the container was stuffed. The data submitted to the government's cargo risk assessment system should be enhanced. Cargo manifest data should be supplemented in order to provide better security risk assessment capabilities. Currently, there is no data that is required to be filed into the government's container shipment targeting system by the U.S. importer or the foreign exporter that can be used in the pre-vessel-loading security screening process. This occurs, even though these parties or their agents possess shipment data that government officials believe would have security risk assessment relevance that is not available in the carriers' manifest filings, and notwithstanding the fact that the law requires the cargo security screening and evaluation system to be conducted "prior to loading in a foreign port."

Accordingly, CBP has been working on an initiative to improve its targeting and risk assessment capabilities—called the "10 plus 2" initiative, because it would require 10 data elements to be submitted by importers or their agents 24 hours before vessel loading, and 2 additional data streams from carriers or their agents. Implementation of "10 plus 2" would not be simple or cost-free, but the security logic of the proposal is obvious. A system that bases the nation's container security screening strategy on the information in a carriers' bill of lading will continue to be the subject of legitimate criticism from Congress, the Inspector General, Government

Accountability Office, and anyone else performing a critical analysis of present security tools.

There are some challenging issues to make this plan a success, including the following:

- Developing clear definitions of the data to be provided (e.g., is it the "manufacturer" of the goods or the "supplier" of the goods?)
- Determining what Customs information system will be used for the transmission of the data to CBP
- Determining who will be authorized and trusted, and under what criteria, to submit the shipment data into Customs data systems

As CBP continues to develop the specifics of this proposed concept, it will be important for the various parts of the import business community to come together in a way that will help CBP make this program a success. Ocean carrier members of the Council have already begun pilot efforts with CBP on the "2" data streams of interest to CBP from the maritime sector.

A final point regarding this initiative is its relationship to trade continuity in the event of a transportation security incident involving containers. Although this initiative is needed to improve the government's ability to detect security questions and to prevent them from disrupting commerce or threatening populations, it could also be very important in the event the government had to manage the consequences of a major maritime security incident involving a container. The "10 plus 2" initiative would greatly enhance the government and industry's ability to analyze and respond to what may have happened, and to determine what trade may be allowed to continue—an issue the trade community insists is a priority concern. If the trade community wants the government to allow its imports to face little delay in such difficult circumstances, it should make a priority of determining how to provide the government with the additional data it will need to be confident of the security of the cargo shipments. Although "10 plus 2" will not solve all containerized cargo security concerns, there is no convincing reason for CBP's pre-vessel-loading container risk assessment system to continue relying on the limited information it has access to today.

2. Improved Container Inspection Capabilities

CBP and the Department of Energy's Megaports project deserve considerable credit for the effective improvement and expanded deployment of container inspection technology without substantially disrupting the flow of commerce. With respect to the priority risk—detecting radiological and nuclear materials—CBP's strategy is to perform radiation scanning on virtually all containers entering the United States. Presently, roughly 68 percent of inbound ocean containers are scanned for radiation, and CBP expects to get that close to 100 percent by the end of next year. In addition, DHS is working to improve the quality of the radiation detection equipment being used, with its July announcement of the award of Advanced Spectroscopic Portal (ASP) program contracts totaling $1.157 billion to enhance the detection of radiological and nuclear material.

In addition to the objective of scanning all containers for radiation, CBP performs a density image inspection of all containers that its container targeting system identifies as presenting any significant potential risk using non-intrusive inspective (NII) equipment.

Thus, the government is making substantial progress on its objective of inspecting every inbound container for radiation, and every container that its targeting system says may present a security risk with an NII or physical exam. The obvious limitation of these efforts is that the vast majority of these inspections are occurring after the vessel and cargo are in the United States at the port of discharge, whereas the ideal state would be for any such inspection to occur before the container is loaded aboard a vessel.

It is for that reason that the Department of Homeland Security, with the support of Congress, is moving ahead with increased pilot testing of its advanced overseas screening initiative, which will seek to undertake radiation and NII image capturing of all containers before vessel loading at select foreign marine terminals. This too is a laudable strategy and direction. The "pilot" done to date—which most observers know as the Integrated Container Inspection System or "ICIS" operated at two Hong Kong marine terminals—provided a public relations boost to the concept; however, it did not even try to address the difficult, real world operational issues that hopefully this next round of pilots will begin to address. ICIS captured images from Radiation Portal Monitors and NII equipment of the containers entering the terminal gate, but did nothing with them. No analysis of the images was performed. No actions were generated. No transshipped containers were scanned. No containers were delayed or had follow-up exams. No space in the marine terminal had to be set aside for secondary inspections. No demands on the foreign customs authorities to inspect containers were generated. No protocols with the host government were negotiated.

The promise of the advanced overseas screening initiative pilots is that they can analyze and try to address the realities that would arise from the concept's real world implementation, namely:

- Negotiating the necessary agreements and protocols with the host government customs authorities
- Agreeing how to efficiently address and resolve radiation readings or other questions about shipments prior to vessel loading—a common occurrence
- Addressing health and safety issues involved in the deployment of such technology
- Addressing terminal operator liability and cost acceptance, and

- Determining how to efficiently scan transshipped containers that don't enter the marine terminal via a gate, such as transshipped cargoes.

3. Why Are These Container Security Initiatives Important?

On any given day, on average, approximately 370,000 containers of cargo are loaded aboard vessels that are under way and en route to the United States. Those containers and the ships they are on utilize approximately one-third of all the vessel capacity serving U.S. international containerized commerce. If the government does not have confidence that the pre-vessel-loading security screening of containerized cargo under the "24-Hour Rule" is adequate, and the vessel capacity bound for the United States were to have significant restrictions placed on its operations because of security concerns about containers that have already been permitted to be loaded onto them, there would be substantial, adverse consequences to the import and export transportation network and global supply chains.

Furthermore, for every day the government cannot provide assured instruction regarding what can be reliably loaded onto and discharged from the remaining two-thirds of the industry's vessel capacity, the problem would grow.

It is for this reason that the World Shipping Council and the liner shipping industry continue to support development of a more robust and reliable pre-vessel-loading cargo screening capacity, including:

1. Customs' obtaining more complete shipment data from cargo interests before vessel loading to be used in the container security screening and targeting process. The carrier's bill of lading data provided to Customs under the 24-Hour Rule is an important component of effective targeting, but no critical examination finds it to be adequate by itself, and
2. Close examination of the feasibility and merits of implementing an advanced overseas container inspection system and strategy, which uses gamma ray nonintrusive inspection technology and radiation scanning technology on containers before vessel loading.

4. Container Seals and CSDs:

No proposed rulemaking has emerged from the Department of Homeland Security regarding container seal verification or "smart box" devices. Initially, both government officials and industry thought that a seal verification rule might be a valuable container security tool. After extensive analysis, however, this is an idea which sounds initially attractive, but in fact would probably provide marginal, if any, security protection in either the prevention or detection of a terrorist risk in a container. It would be difficult and expensive to implement, yet would not help answer the important and most relevant question: What is in the container?

Some of the reasons why DHS officials have expressed substantial reservations about the value or desirability of such a rulemaking include the following. First, a container seal verification requirement could not be realistically implemented without the deployment of technology on a global scale. In order to prepare for the possibility of a U.S. regulation on this issue, the Council and its member shipping lines have been working to help develop standards at the International Standards Organization for RFID container seal technology for over two years. We expect that a standard should be approved by the end of this year and will succeed in being a nonproprietary standard using two radio frequencies. However, the necessary reading infrastructure for RFID container technology requires a global infrastructure of thousands of readers placed at transportation choke points and ports in many different countries around the world. That would be a huge challenge for an infrastructure controlled by thousands of unrelated parties. The deployment of RFID container technology, dependent on fixed readers at thousands of locations around the world, faces real challenges.

Developers of satellite-based CSDs fully understand that point and hope to develop a product that can overcome these problems. That kind of container technology—in contrast to RFID, which is tied to the problem of fixed readers—may also be able to establish commercial supply chain management benefits with respect to container tracking and real-time event notification. Such technology, however, has not yet proven to be commercially available at an affordable price.

Second, even if one were to succeed in building such a global RFID container device reading infrastructure, what would it tell you? Somebody opened the container door. This happens thousands of times a year, usually by customs authorities, and every one of these anomalies would require the container shipment to be stopped while an investigation addressed the issue. This fact, plus the uncertain number of false alarms that such devices may generate, would cause many containers to be stopped for an undetermined time. That would probably be acceptable if the result were an assurance the container had nothing bad in it. But that would not likely be the result from such technology.

Although it is conceivable that al-Qaeda would decide to intercept a container shipment already in transit and insert what it intended to ship inside in the hope that it would not be detected, most security experts think that if terrorists were to use a container, they would be involved in the container stuffing origin of the shipment, and almost certainly affix appropriate container seals or devices to the container.

Third, contrary to many container device marketing efforts, such devices have not been shown to have significant supply chain management benefits to commercial shippers. Furthermore, a number of the technology vendors interested in such products apparently can only find a profit if they capture the devices' readings in a proprietary data network that they control and resell—a proposition that has clearly received little interest or support from container owners or from their customers. Any proposal for container seal verification or for application of container security devices warrants a much more detailed dialogue with carriers and shippers than has occurred to date, and a clear demonstration by the government that the effort is a security priority worth the effort.

Although the merits and shortcomings of container seals and CSDs can and will continue to be debated, there is no question that CBP's focus on the two ambitious strategies discussed earlier—better shipment data for better container targeting capability, and more complete inspection and scanning of containers—is a prudent and well-considered ordering of priorities, which have a far better chance of providing antiterrorist protection than devices attached to boxes that can't tell you "what's in the box."

II. EUROPEAN DEVELOPMENTS

The European Council of Ministers last year approved a regulation for the Community-wide application of advance ocean container security screening and of Authorized Economic Operator (AEO) programs for both security and trade facilitation purposes. These programs would be analogous, but not identical, to the "24-Hour Rule" and C-TPAT programs in the United States. Since then, the European Commission has been working to develop regulations that the 25 EU member states would be required to implement regarding these matters.

The most recent draft of the implementing regulation (Commission Regulation 1250), which has been the subject of extensive discussion with the EU member states and with industry, would become effective on July 1, 2009. The AEO program would become effective in all EU Member States on July 1, 2007.

The European Union's basic strategy appears to be properly focused on building advance containerized cargo screening or risk assessment capabilities that can be applied 24 hours before vessel loading, and on improving importers' supply chain security through voluntary AEO programs.

It is unfortunate, therefore, that the European Commission's most recent draft of these regulations has chosen an approach for the implementation of that strategy that contains a fundamental flaw and will not meet the stated objective of effectively enhancing the EU's cargo risk assessment capabilities.

The most significant problem with the pending draft of Regulation 1250 is that it includes a conscious decision to not require freight forwarders (NVOCCs under U.S. regulations)[1] to file advance summary declarations (or manifest information) for the shipments they control under their own bills of lading.

Only ocean carriers would be required to file pre-vessel-loading summary declarations to European national Customs administrations for containerized cargo risk assessment purposes under this 24-Hour Rule. The EU governments' cargo risk assessment system would thus have no meaningful visibility into forwarder-controlled shipments, making the entire container security screening effort and the associated costs for ocean carriers and national Customs administrations an empty exercise from a security perspective.

Under the present draft, European customs authorities would get the appropriate advance manifest information from ocean carriers for their shipments, but they would have no insight into those containers controlled by freight forwarders. Advance risk assessment for those forwarder-controlled shipments—which can constitute the majority of the shipments on some voyages—would thus be based only on knowing, from the ocean carrier's information filings, that a particular freight forwarder was controlling the carriage of various goods from Port A to Port B for undisclosed parties to undisclosed parties. There would be no insight into who the underlying shippers or consignees of the goods really are, or the origins or destinations of the goods.

In taking this approach in the current draft regulations, the Commission has to date rejected the industry proposals that the WSC submitted, jointly with the European Community Shipowners Association (ECSA), the European Shippers Council (ESC), the European freight forwarders (FFI), the international aviation industry (IATA) and the international road transport industry (IRU).

The industry's recommendation has been that freight forwarders should be obligated to file advance pre-vessel-loading summary declarations for the shipments they control, just as ocean carriers are obligated to do. This would be in conformance with international practice and with the guidelines approved—with the European Commission's support—by the World Customs Organization (WCO), and consistent with advance cargo security screening logic. This approach has been implemented and demonstrated to work satisfactorily under the U.S. and the Canadian 24-Hour Rules.

The Commission has not provided any security-based reasons for rejecting the joint industry filing proposals, other than forwarder filing would make things more complicated and involve more data. This, however, is not very convincing. Customs authorities are responsible for reviewing and processing customs entry of thousands of shipments on every arriving vessel. It hardly seems plausible that these same authorities could not establish an automated system that could accommodate the filing of freight forwarders' summary declarations.

While, as discussed earlier, it is debatable how effective a cargo risk assessment system that solely relies on bill of lading information can be, it is unarguable that a system that excludes bill of lading information for shipments controlled by freights forwarder/NVOCCs would be wholly inadequate and ineffective as a security risk assessment tool.

Without a filing obligation by freight forwarder/NVOCCs, any shipper could easily avoid advance screening of its shipment (e.g., the underlying shipper and consignee, and the origin and destination of the shipment) by simply contracting for transportation services with a forwarder instead of an ocean carrier. The resulting illogic is particularly pronounced in European containerized trades that historically have had a significant share of freight forwarder–controlled shipments. Without forwarder/NVOCC shipment information, Customs administrations would, for their cargo risk assessments, only be able to review the ocean carrier's bill of lading information. This is likely to show the freight forwarder as both the shipper and consignee, show the foreign load port as the origin and the Community port of unloading as the destination, and oftentimes will only include a general cargo description. This would be insufficient and misleading for cargo risk assessment purposes.

It is too soon to know if the Commission's current draft regulation will be adopted. There is still the hope that the Commission will take the logical step that other nations' 24-Hour Rule regulations have taken, and require freight forwarders to file their shipment data.

Although ocean carriers could physically comply with a regulatory requirement that doesn't include forwarder filings, it is apparent that all commercial parties, as well as the various European Customs authorities, would be better off by not implementing a system that has such a significant security flaw.

If governments want to build meaningful pre-vessel-loading security screening systems, that is an objective that the liner shipping industry can support. But all appropriate parties should play a proper role in such a system.

III. SOME CONCLUDING THOUGHTS

Whether we like it or not, we live in a world where vigilance against terrorist risks requires the development and implementation of prudent security measures, and the continuing enhancement of such measures as the risks change and take new forms. The international trading system is too valuable and important to be left unattended. And, as very recent developments have demonstrated, there is no reason to believe that the threat is going away soon.

The industry fully understands this and has cooperated with national governments and international organizations trying to construct meaningful security regimes. Industry will always be concerned that these measures not unduly delay or restrict commerce or impose costs that produce little added security; however, it will support measures that are well designed and provide real security value with as little impact as possible on legitimate trade.

This is clearly difficult work. It is not well suited to simplistic formulations or vague "slogan" solutions that aren't supported by clear and specific means to achieve them.

One must also guard against "security fatigue," which can result from trying to digest the mountains of security product promotions, security speeches and presentations, and the array of proposals that emerge from so many different sources. There are clearly some success stories. The International Maritime Organization's development of the International Ship and Port Facility Security (ISPS) Code, the Proliferation Security Initiative, the Container Security Initiative, the "24-Hour Rule" strategy, the C-TPAT/AEO concept—all have enhanced supply chain and maritime security. The government's expanded use of container inspection technologies is another example of sound strategy and implementation.

The World Customs Organization has developed international supply chain security standards; however, for various reasons, these are very high-level, voluntary guidelines that will need to be complemented by individual requirements by those nations that decide to undertake their own supply chain security programs. As a result, widespread mutual recognition of AEO programs is unlikely.

The IMO is considering following up on the WCO efforts by trying to determine how the WCO Framework might relate to possible amendment of various IMO conventions. As of now, however, no clear or coherent set of proposals has emerged for how or why WCO Guidelines could or should be converted into IMO convention amendments.

If we are to avoid drifting unproductively in addressing these issues, and if we are to make true progress in enhancing maritime and supply chain security, progress is far more likely to occur if:

1. There is a clear and specific definition and agreement on what should be done to improve security.
2. There is a clear and thoughtful prioritization of initiatives.
3. There is sufficient certainty and clarity in purpose to do it right. In the absence of that, time and resources are poorly used and the efforts are less likely to improve security.

At the same time, industry has a responsibility to support well-designed security enhancements.

Global containerized shipping is, in much of the public's mind, dominated by very large importers who generate little public sympathy, and by foreign business enterprises, which can be the subject of political fearmongering, as the Dubai World Ports debacle so vividly demonstrated. The industry's vulnerability is exacerbated by the fact that, as with most business-to-business enterprises that don't directly touch consumers, most people have no appreciation of the role, importance, or magnitude of international trade to their lives and their livelihoods.

The best defense against such risks is to help and support the creation and improvement of a well-conceived, effective, and workable security regime. The current efforts of CBP and DHS with respect to maritime and supply chain security improvement are certainly worth the industry's support. All sectors of the industry have a reason to work closely and cooperatively with them as they try to define the best way to implement their proposed security strategy improvements.

Note

1. In the United States, a freight forwarder that issues a bill of lading for the carriage of goods is defined as a "non-vessel operating common carrier" or NVOCC, whereas in Europe they are simply called freight forwarders regardless of whether they undertake the carrier obligations arising from their issuing a bill of lading.

Selected Bibliography

TERRORISM: GENERAL

Adeniran, Tunde and Yonah Alexander, eds. *International Violence*. New York: Praeger, 1983.

Alexander, Yonah, ed. *International Terrorism: National, Regional, and Global Perspectives*. New York: Praeger, 1976.

Alexander, Yonah, ed. *Combating Terrorism: Strategies of Ten Countries*. Ann Arbor, MI: University of Michigan Press, 2002.

Alexander, Yonah and Donald Musch, eds. *Terrorism: Documents of Local and International Control—U.S. Perspectives*, Vol. 35. Dobbs Ferry, New York: Oceana Publications, 2002.

Alexander, Yonah and David C. Rapoport, eds. *The Morality of Terrorism: Religious and Secular Justifications*. New York: Pergamon Press, 1982.

Buzan, Barry. *People, States, and Fear: The National Security Problem in International Relations*. Chapel Hill: University of North Carolina Press, 1983.

Chadwick, Elizabeth. *Self-determination, Terrorism, and the International Humanitarian Law of Armed Conflict*. Boston, MA: M. Nijhoff, 1996.

Cline, Ray S. and Yonah Alexander. *Terrorism as State-Sponsored Covert Warfare*. Fairfax, VA: HERO Books, 1986.

Combs, Cindy. Terrorism in the Twenty-First Century (2nd Edition). Upper Saddle River, NJ: Prentice Hall, 1997.

Cordesman, Anthony H. *Terrorism, Asymmetric Warfare, and Weapons of Mass Destruction: Defending the U.S. Homeland*. Westport, CT: Praeger, 2002.

Corbin, Jane. *The Base: In Search of Al Qaeda, the Terror Network That Shook the World*. London: Simon and Schuster, 2002

Crenshaw, Martha, ed. *Terrorism, Legitimacy and Power: The Consequences of Political Violence*. Middletown, CT: Wesleyan University Press, 1984.

Dobson, Christopher. *The Terrorists: Their Weapons, Leaders, and Tactics*. New York: Facts on File, 1982.

Harmon, Christopher C. *Terrorism Today*. Portland, OR: Frank Cass, 2000.

Higgins, Rosalyn, and Maurice Flory, eds. *Terrorism and International Law*. London and New York: Routledge, 1997.

Hippchen, Leonard Joseph. *Terrorism, International Crime, and Arms Control*. Springfield, IL: Thomas, 1982.

Hoffman, Bruce. *Inside Terrorism*. New York: Columbia University Press, 1999.

Hoge, James and Gideon Rose, ed. *How Did This Happen? Terrorism and the New War*. New York: Council on Foreign Relations, 2001.

Laqueur, Walter. *No End to War: Terrorism in the 21st Century*. New York: Continuum International Publishing Group, 2003.

Laqueur, Walter. *A History of Terrorism*. New Brunswick, NJ: Transaction, 2001.

Laqueur, Walter. *Terrorism: A Study of National and International Political Violence*. Boston: Little Brown & Co., Inc., 1977.

Leventhal, Paul and Yonah Alexander, eds. *Preventing Nuclear Terrorism: The Report and Papers of the International Task Force on Prevention of Nuclear Terrorism*. Lexington, MA: Lexington Books, 1987.

Livingstone, Neil C. *The War against Terrorism*. Lexington, MA.: Lexington Books, 1982.

Maniscalco, Paul M., and Hank T. Christen. *Understanding Terrorism and Managing the Consequences*. Upper Saddle River, NJ: Prentice-Hall, 2002.

Martin, Gus. *Understanding Terrorism: Challenges, Perspectives, and Issues*. Thousand Oaks, CA: Sage Publications, 2003.

Noone, Michael F. and Yonah Alexander. *Cases and Materials on Terrorism: Three Nations' Response*. The Hague: Kluwer Law International, 1997.

O'Niel, Bard E. *Insurgency and Terrorism: Inside Revolutionary Warfare*. Washington DC: Brassey's, 1990.

Piller, Paul. *Terrorism and U.S. Foreign Policy*. Washington DC: Brookings Institution Press, 2001.

Rapoport, David C. *Inside Terrorist Organizations*. 2nd ed. London: Frank Cass, 2001.

Simon, Jeffrey D. *The Terrorist Trap: America's Experience with Terrorism*. 2nd ed. Bloomington: Indiana University Press, 2001.

Simonsen, Clifford E., and Jeremy R. Spindlove. *Terrorism Today: The Past, the Players, the Future*. Upper Saddle River, NJ: Prentice Hall, 1999.

Stern, Jessica. *The Ultimate Terrorists*. Cambridge, MA: Harvard University Press, 2001.

Tanter, Raymond. *Rogue Regimes: Terrorism and Proliferation*. New York: St. Martin's, 1999.

Timmerman, Kenneth R. *Preachers of Hate: Islam and the War on America*. New York: Crown Forum, 2003

Waugh, William. *International Terrorism: How Nations Respond to Terrorists*. Salisbury, NC, Documentary Publications, 1982.

Wolfgang, Marvin E., ed. *International Terrorism*. Beverly Hills, CA: Sage Publications, 1982.

Monographs, Articles, Conferences, & Government Documents

Allan, Richard. *Terrorism: Pragmatic International Deterrence and Cooperation*. New York: Institute for East-West Security Studies; Boulder, CO: Distributed by Westview Press, 1990.

Flynn, Stephen. "America the Vulnerable," *Foreign Affairs*, January/February 2002.

Flynn, Stephen. "Beyond Border Control," *Foreign Affairs*, November/December 2000.

Freedman, Lawrence A. "Why Does Terrorism Terrorize?" *Terrorism: An International Journal* 6 (1983).

Green, L. C. "Terrorism and Its Responses." *Terrorism: An International Journal* 8, no. 1 (1985).

Holton, Gerald. "Reflections on Modern Terrorism." *Terrorism: An International Journal* 1, nos. 3/ 4 (1978).

Kupperman, Robert M. "Terrorism and National Security." *Terrorism: An International Journal* 8, 3 (1985).

United States. Congress. Senate. *Current and Projected National Security Threats to the United States and Its Interests Abroad.* Hearing before the Select Committee on Intelligence of the United States Senate, 104th Congress, 2nd session, Thursday, February 22, 1996.

United States. Congress. Senate. Subcommittee on Security and Terrorism. *The Origins, Direction and Support of Terrorism.* Hearings before a Subcommittee of the Senate Committee on the Judiciary. J-97-17. 97th Congress, 1st sess., April 24, 1981.

United States. Congress. Senate. Subcommittee on Security and Terrorism. *The Historical Antecedents of Soviet Terrorism.* Hearings before a Subcommittee of the Senate Committee on the Judiciary. J-97-40. 97th Cong., 1st sess., June 11 and 12, 1981.

Woolsey, J. "Global Organized Crime: Threats to U.S. and International Security," *Global Organized Crime: The New Evil Empire.* Conference proceedings, Center for Strategic and International Studies (September 26, 1994).

Wright, Jeffrey W. "Terrorism: A Mode of Warfare." *Military Review.* Ft. Leavenworth, KS: U.S. Army Command and General Staff College (October, 1984).

TERRORISM & BUSINESS

Alexander, Dean C. and Yonah Alexander. *Terrorism and Business: The Impact of September 11, 2001.* Ardsley, NY: Transnational Publications, 2002.

Alexander, Yonah and Robert A. Kilmarx, eds. *Political Terrorism and Business: The Threat and Response.* New York: Praeger, 1979.

MARITIME SECURITY & TERRORISM

Baer, George. *One Hundred Years of Sea Power: The United States Navy, 1890–1990.* Palo Alto, CA: Stanford University Press, 1994.

Burnett, John S. *Dangerous Waters: Modern Piracy and Terror on the High Seas.* California: EP Dutton, 2002.

Gottschalk Jack A. and Brian P. Flanagan. *Jolly Roger with an Uzi: The Rise and Threat of Modern Piracy.* Annapolis, MD: Naval Institute Press, 2000.

Guidelines on Co-Operation between customs administrations and port aimed at the prevention of drug smuggling, Customs Co-Operation Council, prepared for the International Association of Ports and Harbors; November 1989.

Parritt, Brian A. H., ed. *Violence at Sea: A Review of Terrorism, Acts of War, and Piracy, and Countermeasures to Prevent Terrorism.* Paris: ICC Publications, 1986.

Tangredi, Sam J. *Globalization and Maritime Power.* Washington DC: National Defense University Press, 2002.

Monographs, Articles, Conferences, & Government Documents

Farley, Mark C. *International and Regional Trends in Maritime Piracy, 1989–1993.* M.S. dissertation; Naval Postgraduate School, 1993.

Galdorisi, George. "It's Time to Sign On." *U.S. Naval Institute Proceedings*, vol. 124, January 1998: 511–513.

Herberger, Albert J. "Maritime Security Act: Fulfilling a Strategic Maritime Imperative." *Defense Transportation Journal* 53 (1997): 8, 10–11.

International Symposium on Maritime Security & Terrorism. *International Symposium on Maritime Security & Terrorism.* Arlington, VA, 1981.

Maritime Security: Progress Made in Implementing Maritime Transportation Security Act, but Concerns Remain. GAO-03-1155T September 9, 2003.

Menefee, Samuel Pyeatt. *Trends in Maritime Violence: A Special Report from Jane's Intelligence Review.* Alexandria, VA, 1996.

Ong, Graham Gerard. "Pre-empting Maritime Terrorism is Southeast Asia" *Institute of South East Asian Studies* (ISEAS) November 29, 2002.

"Plans to thwart terror creating a storm in any port." *The Age*, May 13, 2003.

Seper, Jerry. "Advance data required for cargo on U.S.-bound ships." *The Washington Times* (January 16, 2003): A8.

United Nations. *Maritime Security: The Building of Confidence.* United Nations Publications, New York, 1992.

United States. Congress. House. Committee on Foreign Affairs. *Overview of international maritime security: hearing before the Committee on Foreign Affairs*, House of Representatives, 99th Congress, 1st session, October 23, 1985. Washington DC, 1986.

United States. Congress. House. Committee on government Operations. Legislation and National Security Subcommittee. *Management of Ready Reserve Force ships: hearing before a subcommittee of the Committee on government Operations*, House of Representatives, 100th Congress, 1st session, November 17, 1987.

United States. Congress. House. Committee on Foreign Affairs. *Overview of international maritime security*: 99th Congress, 1st session, October 23, 1985, Washington DC.

United States. Congress. House. Committee on Transportation and Infrastructure. Subcommittee on Coast Guard and Maritime Transportation. *Port Security: Hearings before the Subcommittee on Coast Guard and Maritime Transportation of the Committee on Transportation and Infrastructure*, House of Representatives, 107th Congress, 2nd session, December 6, 2001, February 13, March 13, and March 14, 2002.

United States. Congress. Senate. Governmental Affairs Committee. Stephen E. Flynn, Ph.D., Commander, U.S. Coast Guard (ret.); Jeane J. Kirkpatrick, Senior Fellow in National Security Studies and Director, Council on Foreign Relations Independent Task Force on Homeland Security Imperatives, March 20, 2003.

United States. Congress. Senate. Subcommittee on Technology, Terrorism, and Government Information and the U.S. Senate Judiciary Subcommittee on Border Security, Citizenship, and Immigration. Stephen E. Flynn, Ph.D., Commander, U.S. Coast Guard (ret.); Jeane J. Kirkpatrick, Senior Fellow in National Security Studies and Director, Council on Foreign Relations Independent Task Force on Homeland Security Imperatives, March 12, 2003.

United States. Congress. House. Department of Homeland Security, United States Coast Guard. *Statement of Admiral Thomas H. Collins on the Coast Guard & Maritime Transportation Act of 2003* Before the Subcommittee on Coast Guard and Maritime Transportation Committee on Transportation and Infrastructure, May 22, 2003.

United States. Department of Transportation. Maritime Administration. *Maritime Trade & Transportation 99*. Washington DC: U.S. Department of Transportation, [1999], 128p. Internet: http://www.bts.gov/programs/btsprod/maritime/maritime.pdf.

MARITIME AND INTERNATIONAL LAW

Alexander, Yonah and Edgar H. Brenner, eds. *Legal Aspects of Terrorism in the United States*. Vols. 1–4. Dobbs Ferry, NY: Oceana, 2000.

Alexander, Yonah and Edgar H. Brenner, eds. *Terrorism and the Law*. Ardsley, NY: Transnational Publications, 2001.

Alexander, Yonah and Edgar H. Brenner, eds. *U.S. Federal Legal Responses to Terrorism*. Ardsley, NY: Transnational Publications, 2002.

Alexander, Yonah and Edgar H. Brenner, eds. *The United Kingdom's Legal Response to Terrorism*. Ardsley, NY: Transnational Publications, 2003.

Bassiouni, M. Cherif, ed. *Legal Responses to International Terrorism: U.S. Procedural Aspects*. Dordrecht; Boston: M. Nijhoff; Norwell, MA: Kluwer Academic Publishers, 1988.

Cassese, Antonio. *Terrorism, Politics, and Law: The* Achille Lauro *Affair*. Cambridge, England: Polity, 1989.

Chadwick, Elizabeth. *Self-determination, Terrorism, and the International Humanitarian Law of Armed Conflict*. Boston, MA: M. Nijhoff, 1996

Galdorisi, George V. and Kevin R. Vienna. *Beyond the Law of the Sea: New Directions for U.S. Oceans Policy*. Westport, CT: Praeger, 1997.

Lambert, Joseph J. *Terrorism and Hostages in International Law: A Commentary on the Hostages Convention 1979*. Cambridge: Grotius Publications, 1990. Including the International Convention Against the Taking of Hostages (1979).

Larson, David L. *Security Issues and the Law of the Sea*. Lanham, MD: University Press of America, 1994.

Leach, Edmund Ronald. *Custom, Law, and Terrorist Violence*. Edinburgh: University Press, 1977.

Li, K. X. *Maritime Law and Policy in China*. Hong Kong Polytechnic University and Colin WM Ingram, 2002.

Malanczuk, Peter. *Akehurst's Modern Introduction to International Law*. New York: Routledge, 1997.

Ronzitti, Natalino. *Maritime Terrorism and International Law*. Dordrecht, The Netherlands: Martinus Nijoff, 1990.

Schoenbaum, Thomas J. and Ronald H. Rosenberg. *Admiralty and Maritime Law*. West Group, 2000.

Sterba, James P. *Terrorism and International Justice*. Oxford: Oxford University Press, 2003.

Stoessinger, John G. *Why Nations Go to War*. 4th ed. New York: Marcel Dekker Inc., 1979.

Monographs, Articles, Conferences, & Government Documents

Astley, John and Michael N. Schmitt. "The Law of the Sea and Naval Operations." *Air Force Law Review*, 42, (1997): 119–155.

Bassiouni, M. Cherif, ed. *Legal Responses to International Terrorism: U.S. Procedural Aspects*. Dordrecht, The Netherlands: Kluwer Academic Publishers, 1988.

Brandon, John. "Terrorism on the High Seas." *International Herald Tribune* (June 5, 2003).

Charney, Jonathan I. "Entry into Force of the 1982 Convention on the Law of the Sea." *Virginia Journal of International Law*, 35, Winter 1995: 381–404.

Joyner, Christopher C, ed. "The New Law of the Sea." *Ocean Development and International Law*, 27, January–June 1996: 1–179 [Special double issue].

Larson, David L., Michael W. Roth, and Todd I. Selig. "An Analysis of the Ratification of the UN Convention on the Law of the Sea." *Ocean Development and International Law*, 26, 1995: 287–303.

Law of the Sea: Report of the Secretary-General, United Nations General Assembly 50th Session, November 1, 1995, agenda item 39 (A/50/713); report on developments pertaining to the implementation of the UN Convention on the Law of the Sea.

Leitner, Peter M. "A Bad Treaty Returns: The Case of the Law of the Sea Treaty." *World Affairs*, 160, Winter 1998: 134–150.

"The Marine Environment and the 1982 United Nations Convention on the Law of the Sea." *The International Lawyer*, v. 28, Winter 1994: 879–901.

Office of Naval Intelligence & U.S. Coast Guard Intelligence Coordination Center. *Threats and Challenges to Maritime Security 2020*. Washington DC, 1999.

Oliver, John T. *Freedom of Navigation, Rights of Passage, International Security, and the Law of the Sea*. (Hein's legal theses and dissertations, 1993).

Oxman, Bernard H. "Law of the Sea Forum: The 1994 Agreement on Implementation of the Seabed Provisions of the Convention on the Law of the Sea." *American Journal of International Law*, 88, October 1994: 687–714.

Pomper, Miles A. "Administration Revives Efforts to Get Law of Sea Treaty Underway in Senate." *CQ Weekly*, 56, August 15, 1998: 2248–2249.

Stephens, Dale G. "The Impact of the 1982 Law of the Sea Convention on the Conduct of Peacetime Naval/Military Operations." *California Western International Law Journal*, 29 1999: 283–311.

Stevenson, John R. and Bernard H. Oxman. "The Future of the United Nations Convention on the Law of the Sea." *American Journal of International Law*, 88, July 1994: 488–498.

United States. Congress. Senate. Committee on Foreign Relations. Maritime counterterrorism convention, with related protocol: report (to accompany Treaty Doc. 101-1), Senate, 101st Congress, 1st session, Washington DC, 1989.

MISCELLANEOUS

Alexander, Yonah and Charles K. Ebinger, eds. *Political Terrorism and Energy: The Threat and Response*. New York: Praeger Publishers, 1982.

Alexander, Yonah and Richard Latter, eds. *Terrorism and the Media: Dilemmas for Government, Journalists and the Public.* Washington DC: Brassey's (U.S.), 1990.

Alexander, Yonah and Eugene Sochor, eds. *Aerial Piracy and Aviation Security.* Dordrecht, The Netherlands: Martinus Nijhoff, 1990.

Alexander, Yonah and Michael S. Swetnam, eds. *Cyber Terrorism and Information Warfare: Threats and Responses.* Ardsley, NY: Transnational Publications, 2001.

Index

About the Authors

YONAH ALEXANDER is a professor emeritus at State University of New York (SUNY) and currently director of the Inter-University Center for Terrorism Studies, a consortium of academic institutions in some 35 countries. He is also a senior fellow at the Potomac Institute for Policy Studies and director of its International Center for Terrorism Studies, and co-director of the Inter-University Center for Legal Studies (at the International Law Institute). Among his many books are Combating Terrorism: Strategies of Ten Countries; Usama bin Laden's al-Qaida: Profile of a Terrorist Network; and The New Iranian Leadership: Ahmadinejad, Nuclear Ambition and the Middle East.

TYLER B. RICHARDSON has served as the director of research for the Inter-University Center for Terrorism Studies and as defense fellow for the Long-Term Strategy Project, both in Washington, D.C. His work on maritime terrorism and port security issues has been published by the Washington Times, United Press International, the Jerusalem Post, and the Lexington Institute. Mr. Richardson holds a BA in English from Georgetown University and an MBA from the University of North Carolina at Chapel Hill. He currently works as a senior analyst in North Carolina.